Eliminating Exclusionary Zoning:
Reconciling Workplace and Residence in Suburban Areas

Eliminating Exclusionary Zoning:

Reconciling Workplace and Residence
in Suburban Areas

Edward M. Bergman
Department of City and Regional Planning
University of North Carolina
Chapel Hill, N.C. 27514

Ballinger Publishing Company ● **Cambridge, Mass.**
A Subsidiary of J.B. Lippincott Company

711.5
B 49e

International Standard Book Number: 0-88410-450-8

Library of Congress Catalog Card Number: 73-18252

Printed in the United States of America

Library of Congress Cataloging in Publication Data

Bergman, Edward M
        Eliminating exclusionary zoning.
           1. Zoning—United States. 2. Zoning law—United States.
I. Title.
HT167.B47   352'.961   73-18252
ISBN 0-88410-450-8

Contents

List of Tables   ix

Acknowledgments   xiii

PART I. Zoning and Exclusion   1

Chapter One
Exclusionary Effects of Zoning   3

Chapter Two
Getting the Exclusion Out of Zoning   15

Chapter Three
A Performance Standard for Zoning   33

PART II. Analyzing Exclusionary Zoning Ordinances   51

Chapter Four
Looking At Suburban Zoning Ordinances   53

Chapter Five
Zoning Ordinances and Housing Prices in Suburban Townships   59

Chapter Six
Zoning Ordinances and Worker Household Incomes in
Suburban Townships   85

v

PART III. Nonexclusionary Zoning: Performance and Policy   147

Chapter Seven
Measuring Exclusion in Suburban Townships   149

Chapter Eight
Rezoning to Eliminate Exclusion   165

Chapter Nine
Policy Implications of Applying the Zoning Standard   181

Appendixes   195

A.   Township Selection Criteria and Townships Selected   197

B.   Apartments in Commercial Zoning Districts   201

C.   Estimating Rents for Multi-Family Structures from First Count Census Rent Distributions in Enumeration Districts, 1970   205

D.   Converting Economic Activities Allowed by Zoning Ordinances into Equivalent SICs   213

E.   Deriving Floor Area Ratios from Township Zoning Ordinances   219

F.   Estimating Values for A and B from Township Zoning Ordinances   223

G.   Procedures Used in Calculating Township Parking Standards   225

H.   Parking Space Requirements for Customers, by District   227

I.   The Calculation of j Values and Their Relationship to k Values in the Floor Area Ratio Algorithm   229

J.   Converting Central Administrative Office and Auxiliary Employment to Equivalent SIC Employment   231

K.   Deriving Mean Number of Floors, by SIC Three-Digit Industries   235

L.   Ratio of Main Shift to Total Workers, and Mean Number of Floors, by SIC Three-Digit Industries   237

M.   Employment Algorithm Coefficients in Coding Sheet Form   241

N.   Reference Area and Employment Statistics   251

O.   Computer Program for Employment Algorithm and Sample Estimate of Employment for District 62   253

P.   Corrected Computer Program and Resultant Figures   259

Q. Program for Weighting Two Sets (Male-Female) of Earnings
    Distributions   265

R. Occupational Coefficients by Three-Digit SIC; U.S., 1975   267

S. Effect on Mean Income Estimates of Substituting 1975 U.S.
    Occupational Coefficients for Adjusted 1975 Philadelphia
    Occupational Coefficients   277

T. Percentage Distribution of All Worker Earnings by Industry and
    Occupational Group, U.S., 1969   281

U. Housing Demand Algorithm, Computer Program, and Data Inputs   287

    Bibliography   293

    Index   303

    About the Author   309

List of Tables

4-1   Major Uses of Township Zoning Ordinances   55
5-1   Summary of Residential Zoning Provisions for Six Developing
      Townships, 1971   63
5-2   Minimum Lot Size Categories by Gross Land Area, Number of
      Housing Units, and Township, 1971   64
5-3   Tenure and Structure Type of Existing Housing Units in the
      Six Developing Townships, Delaware County, Pennsylvania, 1970   65
5-4   Housing Units in Delaware County, Pennsylvania Township
      Residential Districts by Minimum Lot Size and Tenure, 1971   66
5-5   Minimum Prices of New Housing in Delaware County by Density
      and Type of Housing, 1971   69
5-6   Value Distribution of Owner-Occupied Houses by Minimum
      Lot Area, Delaware County, Pennsylvania, 1970   73
5-7   Value Distribution of Owner-Occupied Houses Located in ED
      Sample and Delaware County, Pennsylvania, 1970   74
5-8   Minimum Lot Sizes by Media and Interdecile House Values of
      Housing in Developing Townships, Delaware County, Penn-
      sylvania, 1970   75
5-9   Percent Houses by Value Interval and Density Class in Delaware
      County, Pennsylvania, 1970   76
5-10 Value of Owner-Occupied Houses by Gross Residential Density
      and Township, 1970   77
5-11 Equivalent Rents and Values for Single-Family Houses by
      Gross Residential Density, 1970   78
5-12 Percent of Housing Unit Rents in Developing Townships, Dela-
      ware County, Pennsylvania, by Density and Structure Type, 1970   80
5-13 Rents of Units by Structure and Township, 1970   80
6-1   Employment Districts: Type, Size Identification, and Town-
      ship, 1971   89

6-2   Values for A and B and Their Determination   94
6-3   Parking Standards for Industrial Zoning Districts   95
6-4 k Values of Parking Requirements   96
6-5 k Values for Combined Customer and Employee Parking in
       Business Districts   97
6-6   Floor Area per Worker by Type of Enterprise, FAC j Value and
       Zoning District   98
6-7   Height Restriction in Floors and Feet, by District and FAC 99
6-8   Summary of Township Residential Zoning Districts by Potential
       Dwelling Units and Population   101
6-9   Summary of Potential Households and Population, by Town-
       ship, 1971   102
6-10   Summary of Algorithm for Deriving Employment by SIC: An
       Illustration   106
6-11   State Employees by County and Source of Data   110
6-12   Federal Civilian Employment by County, 1969   110
6-13   Estimates of Floor Area per Worker for Selected SICs   111
6-14   Derivation of Single Job Holding Rate for SICs and Industries,
       1969   113
6-15   Employment and Unemployment Rates of Industries and SICs,
       1969   115
6-16   Ratio of Local Government Employment to Population, 1967   116
6-17   Postal Employees per 100,000 Population   117
6-18   Agricultural Workers by Township, 1969   119
6-19   Land Area, Floor Area, and Floor to Land Area Ratio, Main
       Shift Jobs, Total Jobs, Total Workers and Labor Force of
       Districts   121
6-20   Representation of all Three-Digit SICs in Districts   122
6-21   Potential Labor Force by Township and District, and Housing
       Units by Township, as per Zoning Ordinance   123
6-22   Agricultural, Local Government, Postal, and Private Household
       Worker Labor Force, by Township   123
6-23   Total Township Labor Force by Type of District   124
6-24   Illustrative Calculation of SIC Earnings Distribution   130
6-25   Illustrative Calculation of Household Income Distribution for
       SIC xxx   131
6-26   Earnings of All Workers, Durable Goods Industries, U.S., 1969   134
6-27   Mean Incomes of Households Whose Head Works in Selected
       SICs, Using Adjusted and Unadjusted 1975 National Occupational
       Coefficients   135
6-28   Ratio of Households to Workers in Dollar Earnings/Income Inter-
       vals by Industry, U.S., 1969   136

6-29   Illustrative Earnings to Income Calculation: Distribution of Earnings and Income for SIC 7390, Business and Repair Service Industry and All Industries for Concord Township   138

6-30   Estimated Worker Household Income Distribution by Township   140

6-31   Number of Households and Worker Household Income Distributions for Concord Township, Based Upon Alternative Assumptions   142

6-32   Median Worker Household Incomes and Percentage of Total Potential Employment in Industrial Districts, by Township   143

6-33   Income Distribution and Medians for Households, by Six-Township, Four-County, and U.S. SMSA Fringe Areas   144

7-1   Adjusted Value and Rent Distributions of Housing by Income Level, New Haven, Connecticut, 1967   152

7-2   Revised Tenure Split by Household Income Level, New Haven, Connecticut, 1967   154

7-3   Potential Housing Demand of Aston Township Households in $8,000–$9,999 Income Class   157

7-4   Potential Requirements for and Stock of Housing Units in Township Zoning Ordinances, by Tenure, Rent, Price, Surplus, Shortfall, and Median Household Income, Delaware County, Pennsylvania, 1971   158

7-5   Measures of Exclusion for Township Zoning Ordinances   160

7-6   Exclusion of Households by Median Household Income and Township   163

8-1   Potential Housing Units in Concord Township's Zoning Ordinance by Tenure, Rent, Price, Shortfall, Surplus, and Median Household Income, 1971   169

8-2   Requirements for Housing Units and Land in Concord Township's Residential Zoning Districts   171

8-3   Households Requiring Housing Assistance by Income and Tenure   173

8-4   Zoning Strategy Map for Residential and Economic Districts in Concord Township   175

9-1   Zoning Strategy Map for Rezoning Economic and Residential Districts   184

9-2   Potential Ratios of Worker Households to Housing Units for Six Hypothetical Townships   185

9-3   Mix of Worker Housing Units and Worker Households Yielded Under Various Illustrative Zoning Patterns for Six Hypothetical Townships   187

A-1   Classification Data for Developing Townships   198

B-1   Ratio of Apartments to Total Use District Areas   202

C-1   Distribution of Rents of Mixed Multi- and Single-Family Units, for Block Groups, by Percent of Cash Rental Units to Nonowned Single-Family Units in Delaware County Census Tracts and Enumeration Districts, 1970   207

D-1   Light Industry SICs by Township   214

D-2   SIC Equivalents of CAO and A Establishments   216

J-1   U.S. Percentage Distribution of *CAO* and *A* Employment by Major Industry Group, 1967   231

J-2   County Employment in Types of *CAO* and *A,* 1969   232

J-3   *CAO* and *A* Employment in "Equivalent" SICs, 1969   233

N-1   Township Main Shift Jobs, Total Jobs, Total Workers, and Total Labor Force, Based on Two Reference Areas   252

Acknowledgments

This volume represents the final stage of an inquiry into exclusionary zoning which first began with a research project and evolved midway in the form of a Ph.D. dissertation. Accordingly, I wish to acknowledge the accumulated contributions of many people whose support and assistance made this sustained investigation possible.

The bulk of the research upon which this volume is based was originally supported by the Fels Center of Government, University of Pennsylvania through a grant from the U.S. Department of Housing and Urban Development during 1971 and 1972. Although I benefited from innumerable discussions with many of the Fels' staff during the course of my work there, the contributions of Janet R. Pack, Kent Eklund, Arnold Goldstein, Faye Griesemer, and Morton Lustig must be singled out as particularly beneficial.

Financial support necessary to pursue further dissertation research and writing was generously provided by the Department of City Planning, University of Pennsylvania. Special thanks are due to members of my dissertation committee who provided the valuable advice and criticism which writers of dissertations so typically require: Morton Lustig for his continued and seasoned counsel spanning both research project and dissertation writing; Ann R. Miller for her expert assistance on employment and labor force matters; and William G. Grigsby for his valuable advice on housing and residential development.

The Department of City and Regional Planning, University of North Carolina at Chapel Hill, with funds made available by the National Institute of Mental Health, provided the support necessary for revising earlier drafts during the summer of 1973. The patient efforts of Joan Clark, Miriam Dunham, Jeanie Hanna, and Shirley Ritter in typing these revisions are gratefully acknowledged. Laurent V. Hodes, Edward J. Kaiser and David J. Brower read various chapters during the process of revising my earlier drafts and offered many timely suggestions which enhanced both the readability and relevance of the final draft. Daniel R. Mandelker of the School of Law, Washington University and John P. Prior of the National Committee Against Discrimination in Housing each read the final manuscript and made a number of valuable observations and comments.

Finally, the editorial assistance rendered by Elizabeth Fink, Sally Rogers and Robin Ratliff of the Institute for Research in Social Science, University of North Carolina at Chapel Hill eased considerably the onerous burden of preparing index and bibliographic entries for the final manuscript.

On the assumption that all the participants mentioned above accept my acknowledgements as stated, I can do no less than to record here my gratitude for the sum of their contributions and to accept full responsibility for the product of that mutual effort.

Part I

Zoning and Exclusion

Chapter One

Exclusionary Effects of Zoning

> The plain truth is that the true object of the ordinance in question
> is to place all property in an undeveloped area of 16 square miles
> in a straightjacket. The purpose to be accomplished is really to
> regulate the mode of living of persons who may hereafter inhabit
> it. In the last analysis, the result to be accomplished is to classify
> the population and segregate them according to their income or
> situation in life.

> Justice David C. Westerhaver, trial judge in
> *Village of Euclid* v. *Ambler Realty Co.*

Municipal zoning has long been accepted as a legitimate and proper tool for
local communities to control land development within their political boundaries
in the public interest.[1] The power to zone was constitutionally established
by the landmark *Euclid* v. *Ambler Realty Co.* case in 1926 and has undergone
evolutionary change and refinement in legislatures and courts since that
time.[2] Currently, strong pressures are forming to place limits on the exercise of zoning because it has become abundantly evident that its effects are
a mixed blessing. Individual communities have often mistakenly zoned against
their own best interests either out of ignorance or incompetent administration,[3] but even more frequently suburban communities have zoned in such
a manner that much of the population in the metropolitan area has been
adversely affected. In his book, *Zoned American*, Seymour Toll traces the
pre-Euclidean concern of Bruno Lasker, Lewis Mumford, and Ernest Freund
that zoning would eventually be used to partition the population.[4] These
men, and doubtless others as well, voiced early reservations about the potential
for misuse of zoning.

      In the opinion given to amplify his *Village of Euclid* v. *Ambler
Realty Co.* trial decision, District Judge Westerhaver anticipated with astonishing

3

accuracy the present state into which zoning has fallen. Some thirty years later, but still far in advance of general public recognition (and even of the scholarly interest among his colleagues), Norman Williams, Jr. provided the seminal analysis of how zoning effectively stratifies the population along age, income, racial and class lines.[5] The contemporary practices of zoning which segregate and stratify the population have since become known as exclusionary zoning.

The Exclusionary Use of Zoning

Scholarly journals and the popular press alike have pointed to the growing tendency of municipalities to engage in exclusionary zoning and, more particularly, the practice of zoning residential districts heavily or entirely for expensive, large-lot development.[6] Exclusionary zoning has come to be recognized as that form of zoning which municipalities [7] employ to exclude lower-income groups by erecting a barrier of prohibitively high housing prices.

Despite the fact that exclusionary zoning has come to be widely known in terms of its effects, there is still some confusion about the legitimate purpose of exclusion in *separating* uses within a municipality and the exclussionary purpose of *banning* uses from the municipality. This confusion is exemplified in the following passage:

> Exclusionary zoning is actually a redundancy. All zoning is exclusionary, and is expected to be exclusionary; that is its purpose and intent. The provisions governing almost every zoning district operate to exclude certain uses of property from certain portions of the land, and thereby in the case of housing, the people who would [otherwise] occupy the housing [are] excluded.[8]

Unquestionably, zoning seeks to "exclude" some uses from certain zoning districts. There is a substantial body of case law starting with *Euclid* which documents the exclusion of noxious or nuisance-creating uses from residential districts [9] and residential uses from commercial and industrial zones.[10] But such "exclusion" is merely the sorting out and separation of incompatible uses as between districts within a municipality.

The term exclusion is more properly applied to the uses which were historically banned by zoning from an entire municipality. Abattoirs, gutta percha manufacture and similarly unpleasant activities with archaically pleasant names have long been excluded by zoning ordinances, only to be joined more recently by such commonly known activities as the manufacture of building supplies and their storage.[11] All these earlier cases of use exclusion from municipalities were justified, however shakily, by the public interest argument for avoiding a community-wide nuisance. During the time span in which the realm of excluded, nuisance-type uses underwent expansion, pressures instrumental to the practice of zoning were also developing. Emphasis was shifting from a primary concern with interdistrict exclusion to intercommunity exclusion. Daniel R. Mandelker identifies the shift of emphasis in these terms:

> . . . . planning and zoning took on an entirely different character
> when it dropped the unit of legal ownership—the lot—as the basis
> of planning and zoning control, and moved to the community
> level as the area of concern within which the exercise of planning
> and zoning powers was to be justified.[12]

As the community level became the area of concern, communities began to exhibit a "country club" approach to decisions about the nature and pace of their membership expansion.[13] When pressures to join increased, communities dramatically upgraded their membership requirements by rezoning residential uses to larger and larger lot sizes.[14] The term exclusionary zoning was gradually appropriated to describe this process and the concomitant excluding or banning of certain residential uses from entire municipalities. Prohibition of mobile homes, apartments, row houses, and small-lot single-family houses effectively exclude a large spectrum of residential structures, densities and environments, but bear no necessary relationship to nuisance avoidance. Instead, it reflects the public interest of "Local Government as the Representative of Those Who Got There First."[15]

A number of factors can be cited to account for this form of municipal behavior. Evidence of exclusionary zoning is most prevalent in towns which have recently experienced heavy growth or which are likely to do so in the immediate future. Rapid growth is often unsettling in its effects upon municipal capital and operating budgets, and upon the quality and supply of urban services. Consequently, municipalities are tempted to use large-lot zoning and restrictions on nonsingle-family residential structures to stem growth or to channel it toward development which generates high taxes and low municipal service costs.

As demands for urban services escalate, while local tax yields are legally or otherwise constrained, fiscal zoning strategies may appear to be an easy route to relief.[16] The elements of such a strategy are by now obvious: ". . . attract 'good ratables,' primarily nonresidential development, and discourage 'bad ratables,' primarily low- and moderate-cost housing."[17] Fiscal strategies combine with other non-economic motivations into convenient rules of thumb about zoning residential areas paying their own way.[18]

The reasons which municipalities offer in support of large-lot zoning are varied. Some developing towns proclaim a strong interest in maintaining a low density, rural atmosphere and have zoned accordingly. A few justify large-lot zoning on ecological grounds, basing their actions on concern for the environment. Others try to stem the tide of urbanization, using large-lot zoning as a holding action. Finally, many towns openly engage in large-lot zoning simply because it effectively filters or screens potential residents by income, and indirectly by race or other unwanted income-related attributes, thereby assuring a homogenous population. Any or all of these motivations might account for large-lot zoning in a given municipality, but whatever the motivations may be, exclusionary zoning is the result.

Large-Lot Zoning and Housing

The most important element of exclusionary zoning in effectively screening moderate- to middle-income families from residing in municipalities is large-lot single-family zoning. Large-lot zoning carried on by municipalities for their own well-being—zoning which is demonstrably in *their* public interest—has incidental effects which spill over and impinge upon the interests of others. Widespread zoning of large lots in suburban, developing areas distorts the land and housing market throughout a metropolitan area.[19] Even though the exclusionary zoning practice of a single municipality would have negligible effect on the entire metropolitan area, substantial effects are felt when many or most such municipalities act in concert, according to the best interests of each. To do otherwise would be an irrational act, i.e., "For any one locality to act in the total social . . . interest is for it to put itself in a position to be beggared by others who do not accept similar responsibility voluntarily."[20] Two direct effects of extensive large-lot zoning on housing are immediately obvious. First, the price of new housing built upon large lots is substantially higher than it might otherwise be. Second, due to the characteristically low-density residential patterns and to the typically high price of housing on large lots, the bulk of reasonably located, developable housing sites and the potential volume of new housing construction in the metropolitan area are both limited in size and available only to higher-income households.[21]

The first direct effect has great impact on all metropolitan citizens, because the prices of all newly constructed housing are intimately tied up with the area-wide schedule of prices for new residential construction on large lots. The price of new residential construction built on large lots is higher due to three important and distinct factors. Large-lot zoning encourages and often permits only the erection of certain structures whose size and type are characteristically more expensive than other forms of residential development.[22] By definition, large-lot zoning necessarily forces consumption of an unduly large amount of land which, of course, raises the price of housing.[23] Finally, large-lot zoning indirectly affects housing prices by fueling, if not launching, the skyrocketing cost of land. Widespread large-lot zoning effectively reduces the potential number of building lots and houses on a given supply of close-in, developable land; this reduction, in turn, results in "bidding up" prices on remaining portions of land zoned for small- or moderate-sized lots. According to the President's Committee on Urban Housing, land costs rose from 12 percent of total house price in 1950 to 20 percent by 1967,[24] and large-lot zoning is at least partially responsible for that increase.[25]

The second direct effect of large-lot zoning is a reduced volume of new residential construction. The total volume of new construction is inevitably lower because only a fraction of the households which can afford new construction of any kind are able to afford the price of houses built on large lots. The households who prefer, and can afford, the price of new suburban housing on large lots enjoy a large selection of sites from an overabundant supply of potential housing opportunities, plus the fruits of whatever price competition might logically ensue in that situation.[26] Conversely, since new housing construction which the remaining population might otherwise afford is not possible on large lots which are restricted to single-family structures, these households are all but confined to the existing stock of more modestly priced residences. Those households at the very bottom of the income gradient will find that filtering chains leading to better housing opportunities are few and fragmentary, given that households higher up the income ladder cannot afford new construction and thereby vacate their currently occupied houses.

Large-lot single-family zoning even affects the potential volume of subsidized housing in developing portions of metropolitan areas. Rent supplement programs which could place families in low-cost new structures are compromised by the added costs associated with large-lot one-family residential development. Moreover, public housing authorities and nonprofit sponsors of low- to moderate-income housing units cannot erect structures of the type and residential density which are economically feasible in the presence of large-lot residential zoning. While it is true that the provision of housing for the lowest-income households in developing suburban areas is seriously hampered by many barriers other than large-lot zoning alone, such zoning practices frustrate the building of ". . . a large share of the new housing, included subsidized housing, developed in the coming decade [which] will have to be located outside of the central cities."[27]

Fiscal Imbalances and Exclusionary Zoning

The price of new single-family construction alone, unfettered by large-lot zoning, acts as a natural economic barrier to low-income households. When large-lot zoning is added, moderate- to middle-income households are also screened out. The net result is that both groups must occupy and compete unevenly for the only housing they can afford—the older single-family and multi-family units which are predominantly in the central cities and in older, close-in suburbs.

The tendency toward undue concentration of low- to moderate-income households in cities is further reinforced by the fiscal dimension of exclusionary zoning. Since low- to moderate-income housing is simply unavailable on the developing metropolitan fringe, suburbs are able to maintain a high residential tax base for households having modest urban service requirements. Meanwhile, central cities and older developed suburbs must minister to increasing proportions of low-income households which have high urban service requirements but which occupy a housing stock of stable or declining tax yield. The divergence of residential tax base and household service costs, as between central and suburban minor civil divisions, is accentuated by still other metropolitan forces.

With property and commerce taxation of business and industry, central cities were once able to afford public facilities for the benefit of residents and nonresidents alike. But, due to loss of mercantile, property and employee income tax revenues, the city budget which previously supported these regional facilities must be applied increasingly to the residents' immediate and growing needs. Loss of taxation revenues from enterprises can be traced, in part, to the well-recognized and secular trend in plant, office and retail location in suburban areas.[28] Production, distribution, marketing and personnel considerations are instrumental in many such moves,[29] but so, too, are the increasing property and mercantile tax rates of financially desperate cities as compared with lower, occasionally equal, suburban rates.[30] Suburban municipalities are attuned to this secular trend and vie with each other by zoning generously for commercial and industrial uses to capture or attract the tax largess. Successful municipalities face the comfortable prospect of taxing newly locating commercial and industrial employers without, at present, having to accommodate those employees who cannot afford housing in the suburban municipality. Norton E. Long observes that these forces ". . . have produced a set of municipal real estate corporations controlled and motivated by the logic of the property tax rather than any theory of responsible government."[31]

Housing market imbalances due to large-lot single-family residential zoning and trends in suburbanizing employment tend to be twin, mutually reinforcing phenomena which precipitate from and further catalyze current exclusionary zoning patterns. That is, the potential attraction of commercial or industrial tax base offers added incentive for current suburban residents to zone out lower-income families whose residential property taxes would be so low that the average level of public service would have to be depressed at a given tax rate or else the tax rate would have to rise to meet the higher public service costs.

The majority of households, including the bulk of working households which are unable to afford the cost of new housing in suburban townships, face a housing market in which there is restricted locational choice. This locational disparity contributes to longer commute patterns for many workers whose employment is situated where housing opportunities are lacking, particularly for workers from low-income households. Households which can find few housing opportunities where jobs are growing, often those families and individuals with the greatest need for public urban goods and services, are increasingly confined to cities that are losing tax base and revenue yields. Conversely, residential and nonresidential tax bases, underlying both income and property taxation, are being accumulated at a faster rate in developing suburban areas than in the cities where basic needs are greater and growing.

Other Effects of Exclusionary Zoning

In addition to the housing market distortions which affect many households in the region, there is a class of related metropolitan-wide effects which impinge upon everyone. Large-lot zoning has often been justified in the past by the need for the extensive filtering beds of septic tanks. Unfortunately, experience has shown that septic tanks often saturate the natural filtering medium and eventually pollute fresh water reserves. One observer warns: "Contamination of shallow wells by suburban septic tanks is a well-known danger, but the danger of widespread contamination through aquifers is a much more sophisticated problem."[32]

More recently, large-lot zoning has sought justification on the basis of environmental considerations, yet, low-density residential development necessarily alters and converts natural habitats into expensive residential areas (whose ecological consequences are unknown) for a handful at the absolute loss of natural surroundings to the many.[33] A recent study has noted "While large-lot zoning may be environmentally sound in particularly fragile environments, it has the disadvantages of resulting in the inefficient use of land through scattered development and it is also under fire as a form of exclusionary zoning in the name of environmental protection."[34]

This pattern of residential scatteration and extensive development has other metropolitan-wide implications. First, the increased travel burden placed on individual households due to disjointed patterns of workplace and residence necessitates very complicated and costly transportation systems to service unduly long commutes. Such extensive transportation systems are more costly both to build initially and to maintain over time, compared with transportation systems designed for higher density development patterns. Since they also exact greater time loss and out-of-pocket expense from the commuting public, the substantially higher total costs of low-density development are spread over the entire metropolitan area. Apart from the waste of scarce public funds and household budgets to overcome the frictions of excessive residential separation by means of transportation systems, air pollution from the energy input to transport has, of late, become a very serious problem in many large metropolitan areas.[35]

The causes of these larger metropolitan problems cannot be placed exclusively at the doorstep of unfettered suburban zoning, but all the problems are in greater or lesser degree traceable to such zoning in one or more direct ways and must be considered in the argument against exclusionary zoning.

NOTES

1. An absorbing account of the social forces and personalities which underlay zoning in America may be found in Seymour I. Toll, *Zoned American* (New York: Grossman, 1969).
2. Numerous publications and articles have explored zoning's evolution over time; two eminently useful source books are Charles M. Haar, *Land Use Planning: A Casebook on the Use, Misuse, and Re-Use of Urban Land* (Boston: Little, Brown and Co., 2nd ed., 1971) and Norman Williams, Jr., *The Structure of Urban Zoning* (New York: Buttenheim, 1966).
3. Consult American Society of Planning Officials, "Failure to Produce the Intended Results," *Problems of Zoning and Land Use Regulation* (Washington: National Commission on Urban Problems, 1968), pp. 24–27.
4. Toll, *Zoned American,* pp. 258–268.
5. Norman Williams, Jr., "Planning Law and Democratic Living," *Law and Contemporary Problems,* vol. 20, no. 2, Spring 1955, pp. 317–350; also reprinted in *The Structure of Urban Zoning,* pp. 76–107.
6. A fairly recent review of both scholarly and popular articles on exclusionary zoning in suburbs may be found in Ambrose Klain, *Zoning in Suburbia: Keep it, Reject it, or Replace it?; Exchange Bibliography 180* (Monticello, Ill.: Council of Planning Librarians, 1971).
7. At this point it is pertinent to mention that several interchangeable terms, such as jurisdiction, town, community, minor civil division, locality, etc., will be used as synonyms. All are taken to mean local bodies of government which (a) control zoning within their boundaries, and (b) have fiscal powers of property taxation and expenditure.
8. Bernard H. Siegan, *Land Use Without Zoning* (Lexington, Mass.: Lexington Books, 1972), p. 88.
9. Williams, *Structure of Urban Zoning,* pp. 192–199.
10. Ibid., pp. 225–227.
11. Ibid., pp. 221–225.
12. Daniel R. Mandelker, *The Zoning Dilemma* (New York: Bobbs–Merrill, 1971), p. 41.
13. Country Club analogy adapted from "A Fable of Exclusionary Incentives" in Task Force on Land Use and Urban Growth, *The Use of Land: A Citizens' Policy Guide to Urban Growth,* A Task Force Report Sponsored by the Rockefeller Brothers Fund (New York: Thomas A. Crowell, 1973), prepublication copy, pp. 224–225.
14. A fairly typical case description may be found in Ellen Szita, "Exclusionary Zoning in the Suburbs: The Case of New Canaan, Connecticut," *Civil Rights Digest,* Vol. 5, No. 4, Spring 1973, pp. 2–14.
15. Title and subject of subsection from Chapter VI, "Creating What We Want: Incentives and Opportunities" in *The Use of Land,* pp. 225–226. For additional references on the political use of zoning, see Irving

Schiffman, *The Politics of Land Use Planning and Zoning: An Annotated Bibliography,* (Davis, Cal.: Institute of Governmental Affairs, University of California, 1970).

16. For a fairly typical research piece which advocates explicit attraction of industry to supplement the tax base and which contains a very succinct discussion of local revenue sources and their limitations, see Bureau of Business and Economic Research, *Industry as a Local Tax Base,* Studies in Business and Economics, Vol. 14, No. 1 (College Park: University of Maryland, 1960).

17. Norman Williams, Jr. and Thomas Norman, "Exclusionary Land-Use Controls: The Case of Northeastern New Jersey," *Land Use Controls Quarterly,* Vol. 4, No. 4 (Chicago: American Society of Planning Officials, 1970), p. 3.

18. In commenting on the perversive relation between municipal fiscal policy and zoning, Morton Lustig notes "It goes without saying that the real property tax, especially for school purposes, is a distorting factor in all land-use control. We need, first, changes in the tax system, and, second, a massive attack on the pseudocost-benefit planning analysis that shows what kind of development 'pays its own way' and what doesn't." Quoted in American Society of Planning Officials, *Problems of Zoning and Land Use Regulation.* Accommodating consultants have been only too eager to engage in "psuedo cost-benefit planning" analyses for community clients who sought fiscal rationalizations to buttress purely selfish or bigoted intentions. For a far more responsible analytic approach, see Ruth R. Mace and Warren J. Wicker, *Do Single Family Homes Pay their Own Way?* (Washington: Urban Land Institute, 1968).

19. For a fuller discussion of the effects which zoning has on the development of metropolitan areas, see National Commission on Urban Problems, *Building the American City* (Washington: Government Printing Office, 1968), pt. III, chap. 1, "Land Use Controls: Zoning and Subdivision Regulations," pp. 199–234.

20. Advisory Committee to the Department of Housing and Urban Development, National Academy of Sciences–National Academy of Engineering, *Freedom of Choice in Housing: Opportunities and Constraints* (Washington: National Academy of Science, 1972), p. 31.

21. For a discussion of related points, see Siegan, *Land Use Without Zoning,* pp. 87–99.

22. Largely in accordance with market preferences, builders and lenders employ established rules of thumb for house value to lot size or lot value, thereby assuring high housing structure costs. Building coverage or minimum floor areas are often part of zoning codes to force consumption of a minimum structure size and cost. See Norman Williams, Jr. and Thomas Norman, "Exclusionary Land Use Controls."

23. Fully 20 percent of the price increase of new FHA-insured housing in the

San Francisco Bay area between 1950 and 1962 has been directly
traced to larger lot sizes. President's Committee on Urban Housing,
A Decent Home (Washington: Government Printing Office, 1968),
p. 140.

24. Ibid.

25. A detailed examination of statistical evidence gathered for the "Kaiser
Commission" reveals a 56 percent increase in costs for housing
sites of median value between 1960 and 1966 and a 42 percent
increase in the cost of housing sites at the third quartile. Such
evidence is entirely in keeping with an enlarged supply of larger,
more expensive sites and a reduced supply of smaller, less expensive
sites. Calculated from the President's Committee on Urban Housing,
Technical Studies (Washington, Government Printing Office, 1968),
Vol. II, Table 56, p. 359.

26. Data on the change in site costs cited in footnote 25 offer evidence that
price increases of more expensive sites were substantially lower than
the price increases in smaller, less expensive sites.

27. *A Decent Home,* p. 140.

28. The Philadelphia SMSA is a case in point. In 1959 the four suburban
Pennsylvania counties' (Bucks, Chester, Delaware, and Montgomery)
combined household population was a little less than three-quarters
that of Philadelphia, and the market value of their taxable property
was 110 percent that of Philadelphia. Thus, the four-county area
had about $14,000 of property value per household in 1959—at
that time significantly higher than the $9,400 property value per
household for Philadelphia. The gap between the four suburban
counties and the city widened between 1959 and 1969 to $16,100
and $10,200 respectively; in percentage terms, the four-county
area's "lead" of 52 percent in taxable property per household over
Philadelphia in 1959 increased to 57 percent by 1969. A sizable
portion of this gap is due to the value of more costly housing, but
commercial and industrial development was also significantly on
the rise during the same 10-year period in the four suburban
counties. This can be appreciated by noting the relative change
in quarterly taxable payrolls per household as reported in *County
Business Patterns.* In 1959, the four-county area averaged about
$832 per household, nearly 64 percent of the $1,300 per household
in Philadelphia where the bulk of jobs were historically located. By
1969, the $1,520 per household in the four-county area amounted
to over 77 percent of the city's $1,980 per household, a relative gain
of over 13 percentage points in 10 years. On balance, then, the total
taxable property per household of the four suburban counties
increased their large lead over Philadelphia by an additional five
percentage points between 1959 and 1969, at the same time that
the lead in wages per household held by the city over the suburban
counties was cut by 13 percentage points. Calculated from figures
in the *1971 Pennsylvania Statistical Abstract* (Harrisburg, Pa.:

Bureau of Statistics, Department of Commerce, Commonwealth
of Pennsylvania, 1971) and *Pennsylvania County Business Patterns*
(Washington: Department of Commerce, Government Printing
Office, 1959 and 1969).

29. For references to further reading on the movement of business to the
suburbs, consult G.L. Berlin and J.R. Lancaster, *Industrial Suburbanization: Exchange Bibliography 223* (Monticello, Ill.: Council
of Planning Librarians, 1971).

30. ". . . in the suburb of West Milwaukee, where taxes were 72 percent of the
average of all suburbs and 59 percent of Milwaukee's, there was
a high concentration of industry . . . 'the appealing tax island'
feature of the village plus the fact that nearly two-thirds of the
village is zoned for industrial use appears to account for the concentration of industry." Thomas F. Stinson, *The Effects of Taxes
and Public Financing Programs on Local Industrial Development—A
Survey of the Literature,* Agricultural Economic Report No. 133
(Washington: U.S. Department of Agriculture, Economic Research
Source, 1968).

31. Norton E. Long, "Creative Politics and Urban Citizenship," *The Urban-
Industrial Frontier,* David Popenoc, ed. (New Brunswick: Rutgers
University Press, 1969), pp. 86–87.

32. Eric C. Freund, "Zoning Ordinances and Pollution Control," in *Change: The
Recurring Zoning Issue,* Clyde W. Forest, ed. (Urbana-Champaign:
Bureau of Urban and Regional Planning Research, University of
Illinois, 1970), p. 22.

33. See Urban Land Institute, "Rural Appearance Will Not Necessarily Follow
Large-Lot Zoning," *The Effects of Large Lot Size on Residential
Development,* Technical Bulletin No. 32 (Washington: Urban Land
Institute, 1958) p. 10.

34. Edward J. Kaiser, Karl Elfers, Sidney Cohn, Peggy A. Reichert, Maynard M.
Hufschmidt, and Raymond E. Stanland, *Promoting Environmental
Quality Through Urban Planning and Controls* (Washington: Office
of Research and Development, U.S. Environmental Protection
Agency, 1973), p. 141. For a somewhat more acerbic view of
"environmental exclusion," see Richard F. Babcock and David L.
Callies, "Ecology and Housing: Virtues in Conflict," in *Modernizing
Urban Land Policy,* Marion Clawson, ed. (Baltimore: Johns Hopkins,
1972), pp. 205–220.

35. For an excellent overview of the relationship between transportation and air
pollution, see *The Relationship of Land Use and Trasnportation
Planning to Air Quality Management,* George Hagevik, ed. (New
Brunswick: Center for Urban Policy Research, Rutgers University,
1972).

Chapter Two

Getting the Exclusion Out of Zoning

> The nature of zoning is such that it is difficult to disentangle its control over physical development per se, its influence over the economic status of prospective residents, and its use to discriminate against specific ethnic or racial groups.[1]

As pressures mount for relief from exclusionary zoning practices which are now distorting the delicate social and economic fabric of metropolitan areas legislatures, administrations and the judiciary find they are asked to take active measures to reduce or at least stabilize an urban crisis of growing proportions.[2] There are, very generally, three possible ways of dealing with exclusionary zoning: reduce the institutional incentives to zone in an exclusionary manner; repeal the enabling legislation, thereby eliminating all forms of zoning; and, curb the exclusionary abuses of zoning through a variety of sanctions. All of these approaches are now being seriously considered and we shall review each of them briefly on their merits.

Reduce the Institutional Incentives
In examining the relationship between the suburbanizing metropolitan economy, fiscal imbalances and large-lot single-family zoning in Chapter 1, we sought to show that exclusionary zoning is not merely a capricious exercise of local prerogatives. The multiplicity of local governments within a metropolitan area, each with fiscal and police powers, are each engaged in a "zero sum" game whereby the tax base gains while avoidance of urban service costs for one municipality comes at the expense of some other municipality.[3] The institutional incentives are such that exclusionary zoning happens to be one of the most useful tactics to employ in "beggaring thy neighbor" at the metropolitan level. In recommending the federal institution of more effective incentive systems, Daniel P. Moynihan summarizes the dilemma with customary felicity:

. . . For better than half a century now, city governments with the encouragement of state and federal authorities have been seeking to direct urban investment and development in accordance with principles embodied in zoning codes, and not infrequently in accord with precise city plans. However, during this same time the tax laws have provided the utmost incentive to pursue just the opposite objectives of those incorporated in the codes and plans. Government has, in fact, established two sets of purposes, and provided vastly greater inducements to pursue the implicit rather than the avowed ones. Until public authorities, and the public itself, learn to be much more alert to these situations, and far more open in discussing and managing them, we must expect the present pattern of self-defeating contradictions to continue.[4]

Although the general public may still be somewhat less than fully informed, public authorities at virtually all levels of government have come to recognize the self-defeating contradictions of contemporary metropolitan governance. The rash of studies, reports and recommendations on metropolitan governance which emerged during the 1960s emphasized local governments' need to generate additional revenues to finance the crushing costs of urbanization, but an equally recurring theme stressed the need for revenue redistribution via metropolitan-wide finance.[5] While the proposed structure of various governance schemes varied somewhat, presumably because of the predilections of the proposer, nearly all would eliminate or substantially reduce the fiscal incentives for exclusionary zoning.

Since metropolitan-wide governance implies a de facto leveling of tax equalization and a redistribution of public resources (albeit a potentially larger sum) which would invariably improve the lot of some communities but not others, one could expect considerable local opposition to metropolitan reorganization. Lowden Wingo warns,

> However convincing the logic of governmental reform, the reformers must ultimately confront the fact that radical changes in the institutions and processes of society imply extensive redistribution of societal goods—wealth, power, security, honor—and it is hardly surprising that those asked to surrender what they consider to be disproportionate shares will resist such demands and develop a counter logic to sanctify their existence.[6]

Still, Karl Deutsch and Richard Meier have seen in the growth of Councils of Governments (COGs), from about 12 in 1965 to 100 in 1968, a harbinger of metropolitan government and have elaborated a series of cooperative principles which appear to be leading us toward "A New Government Synthesis."[7] Melvin Mogulof, however, notes that the growth in the number of

COGs to over 300 by 1971 is instead directly related to federal grant programs which established regional clearinghouse functions, principally Section 704 of the Demonstration Cities and Metropolitan Act of 1966 and Title IV of the Intergovernmental Cooperation Act of 1968, which established the A-95 review process.[8] Barring the enactment of far more explicit federal-regional-local linkages, Mogulof concludes "We are convinced . . . that there are tasks requiring a capacity for metropolitan governance, and we are equally convinced that the COG does not and cannot have this capacity."[9] Extending Mogulof's argument somewhat, one could in fact expect a *lessening* of COG's regional importance once federal-to-local special revenue sharing begins to replace the categorical grants that now require A-95 regional review.[10] Finally, to the degree that general revenue sharing has eased the financial crunch of local government finance and redistributed public revenues somewhat, the thirst for metropolitan reorganization which crested during the late 1960s is likely to slacken.

It would thus appear that metropolitan reorganization, while highly desirable in many regards, is not likely to be realized soon. Were, however, reorganization of metropolitan fiscal resources and expenditures to occur in the near future, only the purely fiscal incentives for exclusionary zoning would diminish. In the absence of metropolitan-wide governance and zoning, localities could well continue their exclusionary zoning practices out of confirmed prejudices or an interest in preserving the layers of social strata embedded in existing residential patterns and municipal boundaries.

Eliminate the Tool

Another suggestion for dealing with exclusionary zoning which recurs from time to time is the suspension of all forms of zoning. Eliminating zoning would certainly appear to solve the immediate problems associated with the exclusionary abuses which often accompany its use. The arguments offered for the elimination of zoning stem from two quite different and incompatible propositions: the first claims the legal basis for zoning is inherently inadequate to the task of controlling and organizing rational uses of land and should therefore be replaced with more appropriate means; the second argument claims that zoning controls are unnecessary and interfere with free market forces which would otherwise maximize the public welfare.

In enumerating a series of questions and propositions about the practice of zoning in the mid-60s, John W. Reps finds the legal framework for zoning and sound land use control woefully lacking.[11] Although one might read into Reps' recommendations a concern that zoning could be used for exclusionary purposes,[12] it is quite safe to conclude that he was most concerned with suspending present enabling legislation for zoning and replacing it with more broadly based legislation. Such legislation would integrate the

advice, control, inducements and development activities surrounding urbanization into a comprehensive "guidance system." As Reps makes clear, he is
interested in more efficient control of land uses; exclusion could well increase
under such a comprehensive system.

Where Reps sought to remove and replace zoning due to its inade-
quacies, Bernard H. Siegan seeks the absolute suspension of zoning on grounds
of its inherent inappropriateness.[13] Basing his argument almost entirely on
the Houston, Texas, experience with nonzoning and the Chicago School's economic theory, Siegan systematically associates zoning with residential exclusion,
curtailed urban development, reduced competition and loss of marketplace
freedoms. His most telling argument against zoning concentrates on the exclusionary uses to which zoning is put; in purely numerical terms, Siegan devotes
about one and a half times (in pages) as much analysis of zoning's effect on
housing and residential exclusion as on the combined other three consequences
of zoning.[14] Portions of the argument against exclusionary zoning in Chapters
1 and 3 of this volume parallel a number of similar arguments made by Siegan,
but the implications drawn from roughly comparable analyses are quite diver-
gent.

Siegan seems to equate zoning functionally with exclusionary (and
other) consequences: he concludes that by abolishing zoning and relying upon
private market operations and municipally enforced restrictive covenants, as
Houston now does, the worst consequences are avoidable and appropriate levels
of control are retained. However, restrictive covenants are fully capable of
maintaining or even increasing the exclusionary potential of current zoning. As
Siegan notes in quite another context:

> Frequently, covenants contain controls not normally found in
> zoning ordinances. *Provisions governing architectural requirements,
> cost of construction, aesthetics, and maintenance of the lot and
> exterior of the house found in covenants are rarely found in zoning
> or other city ordinances and might be illegal if they were.* Zoning
> does not, however, preclude property owners from imposing such
> restrictions if they desire. Nor does the adoption of a zoning
> ordinance nullify existing restrictive covenants (Italics added.).[15]

Where zoning becomes exclusionary through an indirect influence on the price
of housing via lot size, restrictive covenants have a more direct effect upon
several cost factors over which zoning has only limited or no control. There can
be little question about the potential for exclusionary practices within a system
of restrictive covenants, particularly when they are broadly enforced by the
same local body of government that now regulates zoning.

Abolishing zoning would be tantamount to turning over to private
interests the form and relationship of land uses in communities. The argument

given is that governments should not act to create values in land uses that are incompatible with market processes. However, taxation and expenditure patterns within localities create use values in land as surely as zoning does. As a recently released Task Force Report sponsored by the Rockefeller Brothers Fund argues:

> Development potential, on any land and in any community, results largely from the actions of society (especially the construction of public facilities). Other free societies, notably Great Britain, have abandoned the old assumption in their legal systems and now treat development rights as created and allocated to the land by society.[16]

The question then is, why should local bodies of government allow private interests to reap the positive benefits of such public actions or to develop the land in such a manner that undue public costs are incurred? It is well established that piecemeal, fragmented development costs the public far more for provision of basic urban infrastructure and services than does orderly, staged development. The fact that zoning is already too responsive to private interests contributed, in part, to the argument presented above by Reps for abolishing zoning and replacing it with a more efficacious land use guidance system. Whether Reps' guidance system would be more impervious to the pressures of private interests remains an open question we need not pursue here. It is clear, however, that abolishing zoning would result in a development pattern the dimensions and location of which would be exceedingly difficult to predict, thereby complicating the provision of public infrastructure.[17] The very real possibility that no discernible pattern would emerge from uncontrolled market actions could also cause a skyrocketing of costs for the infrastructure to service diffuse development patterns. These are dilemmas which urban planners have faced for over a half century and which have formed the bulk of their arguments in favor of such land use controls as zoning and subdivision regulations.

Finally, the loss of zoning would remove the only effective preventive measure local governments now have over negative externalities or spillovers. Following Daniel R. Mandelker,

> ... when we inspect the underlying purpose of the original zoning legislation, we find ... that its dominant rationale was the separation of incompatibilities in land use in order to limit and prevent the visitation of externalities arising out of land use interdependencies in an urban setting.[18]

Examples of incompatibilities abound: the smoke, fumes, noise, glare and traffic which often accompany certain industrial and commercial enterprises are quite detrimental to residential districts, an incompatibility zoning ordinances have long sought to eliminate by separating uses into zoned districts. Avoidance of negative externalities, as an argument for zoning, is quite distinct from support for zoning on the grounds of orderly and efficient development of land. Recalling the example cited above, the separation of industrial from residential uses through zoning is justified in the first case because of environmental externalities visited by one use upon the other, and in the second case because each use requires differing scales and mixes of public infrastructure, the cost and provision of which necessitates orderly development.

One need not worry, it is claimed, about industries locating near residential districts because considerations of corporate self-interest dictate other, noninjurious, locations. Thus, Siegan asserts:

> Most industrial users would prefer avoiding homes they might possibly offend with noise, odor, smoke, heavy traffic or perhaps even with late or early working hours. Industry has found complaining owners or tenants to be costly and time-consuming, and productive of a bad image with resulting injury to sales. In many conversations with officers of manufacturing companies, I have come to the conclusion that heavy industry may now be equally as anxious to avoid homeowners as homeowners are to avoid industry.[19]

Siegan's assessment of the situation appears to overlook one of the important, early precedents for zoning. An important factor in the legal acceptance of zoning was the inability of nuisance law to deal with industrially generated externalities, and this inability occurred at a point in economic history when firms were far more susceptible to ineffectual market censure than are the integrated plants of present-day firms and concentrated industries.[20] It would appear that expectations of self-policing on the part of land users to minimize or prevent negative externalities is not realistic. Nor has nuisance law developed beyond its inherent limitations in dealing with externalities. For example: nuisance law can not prevent externalities; nuisance damages for wronged parties are often restricted by compensible limits to less than the value of the externality; nuisance damages are frequently restricted to physical externalities of persons most directly affected; and, nuisance law is least effective in developing areas in which the nature of predominate uses determines its applicability.[21]

Summing up, abolishing zoning to eliminate exclusion is not without its perils. First, there is no assurance that exclusion would, in fact, cease. Reps' recommendations would appear to increase exclusionary potential in a more efficient and rational set of land use controls. Exclusion could also continue under the municipally enforced system of restrictive covenants (and subdivision regulations) which Siegan proposes. Second, the complete abolishment of zoning poses a distinct "baby-bath water" dilemma—assuming for the moment that the exclusionary bath water can be thrown out with zoning, are we also willing to practice infanticide on public zoning control over the staging of urban development and prevention of negative externalities?

Reform the Tool

Discussion in earlier sections of this chapter explored the potential for eliminating exclusion in zoning by reducing the institutional incentives for its practice or by its outright elimination. Neither approach was without limitations: metropolitan reorganization might not prevent all forms of exclusionary zoning, but, more to the point, its appearance is quite unlikely in the foreseeable future; abolishing zoning is not a clear-cut guarantee against the practice of exclusion in other forms, and it entails a considerable loss of public control over land uses without demonstrable, compensating gains.

Reform of zoning practice is a third approach to the task of eliminating the exclusionary abuses found to be so damaging. Reforms in zoning have a long history; the most recent one which has met with a measure of some success is improvement in zoning as an integrated component in a system of land use controls.[22] This reform had not yet run its course by the time pressures began to build for reforming what has widely become known as exclusionary zoning.[23]

Where the exclusionary potential of zoning had been identified much earlier by, among others, Justice Westerhaver and Norman Williams, Jr., there can be little question that since the late 1960s Paul Davidoff and the Suburban Action Institute, which he and Neil Gold co-founded, have been most instrumental in arousing widespread interest in and action against exclusionary zoning.[24]

Reforms are a particularly viable option because they often draw together incumbent administrators and politicians who prefer more evolutionary changes and such activists as Davidoff and Gold who push at every margin to enlarge the realm of social equity. Both recognize that reforms are a stopgap measure, but the former group assumes that reform will stifle or at least moderate pressures for structural changes of considerable magnitude, whereas the latter sees reform as providing a transitional vehicle for structural alterations. On the purely pragmatic level, many planning professionals doubtless prefer and would support zoning reform because they require the technically useful function zoning provides in the rational organization and ordering of urban development.[25]

Reform of zoning was officially legitimated in 1968 with the simultaneous release of two major presidential commissions on urban housing and urban problems.[26] Each proposed a series of recommendations to reform exclusionary zoning and other land use controls [27] which were held to be instrumental in widening the economic and racial separation diagnosed that same year by the National Advisory Commission on Civil Disorders.[28] The courts had also moved, belatedly but rapidly, between the late 1960s and into the early 1970s by striking down or severely limiting exclusionary practices of municipalities, particularly in the state courts in New Jersey and Pennsylvania.[29] As layers of precedent are thereby established, reforms automatically receive legal sanction.

Concern at the national level over some of the problems occasioned by exclusionary zoning has prompted actions on the part of the executive branch and the Congress. The bulk of recent executive branch activity was concentrated during the month of June, 1971, and it involved a presidential policy statement and actions by the Department of Housing and Urban Development, the Department of Justice, and the General Services Administration.[30] The White House released a statement on equal housing opportunity, pledging full enforcement of antidiscrimination statutes.[31] However, the President cautioned: "We will not seek to impose economic integration upon our existing local jurisdiction; at the same time, we will not countenance any use of economic measures as a subterfuge for racial discrimination." [32] This can be construed as a hands-off policy toward exclusionary devices which rely upon economic screening.[33] Immediately following this statement, the U.S. Attorney began legal action against Black Jack, Missouri, a suburb of St. Louis, on charges of racial discrimination in violation of civil rights laws, and the constitution, for the deliberate enactment of a zoning ordinance which barred a racially mixed housing development.

During the same period of time, the Department of Housing and Urban Development (HUD) and the General Services Administration (GSA) concluded an agreement whereby HUD will screen communities which might receive federal installations to assure that such communities offer low- and moderate-income housing on a nondiscriminatory basis.[34] Withholding federal employment installations by GSA from towns without such housing creates a modest incentive for them to rezone in a less exclusionary manner or to bear the loss of economic development which accompanies government spending. A somewhat more effective incentive to reduce exclusionary zoning was instituted by the Department of Housing and Urban Development, also in June 1971. This incentive took the form of awarding basic sewer and water grants on the basis of a preferential "point system": those communities wherein projects would benefit households of low- and moderate-income or project areas which have sizable proportions of low- and moderate-income housing received higher point scores.[35] Whether incentives of this sort are likely to be effective or not, HUD can act decisively in either of these, or similar, cases only when it is able to ascertain the present or potential availability of low- and moderate-income housing.

Administrative reforms at the national level are viable only as long as federal policymaking officials actively pursue them. Therefore, one must look to Congress for legislative relief and reform over the long term. Congress,

however, has of late been most concerned with establishing an overall envelope
for national land use policy as a backdrop for state and local actions. [36]
This concern has been sharpened by the current need for an organized response
to the ecological crisis—a crisis whose dimensions are so compelling to some
that the social fragmentation which also accompanies the profligate waste and
misuse of land has taken second billing. [37] Yet, Congress does continue to
consider exclusionary land use reform from the perspective of urban housing
needs, if not in terms of national land use policy. Consistent with, and building
upon, similar recommendations from both the Kaiser and Douglas reports,
Congress has been asked to consider granting authorization for ". . . federal
preemption of local zoning where such action is necessary to provide sites for
federally subsidized housing." [38] There is also encouraging evidence that
Congress will adopt incentives in legislation by attaching housing-related preconditions to the disbursement of federal urban development funds. [39] For
example, one piece of housing and urban development legislation placed before
the 92d Congress required evidence of an adequate supply of low- and moderate-
cost housing, particularly for individuals and families who are employed in the
community, as a precondition that the community must meet before receiving
federal assistance for housing, community development or technical planning
assistance. [40] As in the case of administrative reforms, legislative remedies are
effective only to the degree that housing needs can be reliably estimated and
the necessary rezoning determined to meet those needs.

Reform of zoning is probably most effective at the state level due
primarily to the fact that states are able to modify or restrict zoning practices by
changing the enabling legislation which delegates zoning powers to local bodies
of government. Recognizing the need for better state control over local zoning,
the American Law Institute (ALI) has developed and published *A Model Land
Development Code* [41] which is intended to replace the model zoning and
planning enabling acts issued by the Department of Commerce in the 1920s. [42]
Although early versions of the ALI model code did not include provisions
which would guard against exclusionary zoning, [43] changes in the model code
have been suggested to encompass such restrictions on local zoning. [44]

In the meantime, a number of states have taken other steps toward
the reorganization of land use control. [45] The most notable of these efforts
which deal directly with cases of exclusionary zoning are the Massachusetts
Zoning Appeals Law and the New York Urban Development Corporation. The
Massachusetts law provides for the state to overrule local zoning boards which
deny development permits for low- and moderate-income housing when the need
for such housing has been duly established according to the act's provisions. [46]
The law has proven to be both successful [47] and constitutional. [48] The
New York Urban Development Corporation (UDC) experience is less encouraging. Originally endowed with powers both to override local zoning and to
actually build low- and moderate-income housing, the track record of unex-

pectedly impressive results and future plans to implement a "fair share" housing plan in suburban Westchester County has allegedly resulted in the New York State Legislature's narrow passage of a law which both removes UDC's power to override local zoning and subjects UDC to a local veto over proposed development that does meet existing local ordinances.[49]

In legislation of this sort, care must be exercised to specify unambiguously the precise situations or conditions in which local zoning may be overruled. Although the Massachusetts law has successfully weathered a constitutional challenge,[50] the ambiguities in its provisions suggest the need for administrative clarification, even if secure from further challenges in the courts.[51] On the other hand, it is entirely possible that had the original legislation which created the New York Development Corporation specified more completely the circumstances and events which justify UDC's overruling local zoning, the New York State Legislature might not have restricted UDC's powers so precipitously. One could tentatively conclude that zoning reform laws which restrict local exclusionary practices require a rather explicit rendering of the allowable conditions which call for such restrictions and the manner in which these conditions are to be ascertained.

Moving to the regional and local levels, there has been much less active interest in zoning reform, due primarily to the lack of effective regional controls and sanctions and, quite obviously, to the self-interest of local communities which now engage in exclusionary zoning. Considerable local and regional interest has been generated over what have come to be known as fair share housing plans. These plans are generally drawn up by regional bodies which establish quotas of low- and moderate-income households for all municipalities in the region. First devised for the Dayton, Ohio region in 1970,[52] similar plans are now at various stages of development in several areas, including the Philadelphia, St. Louis, Atlanta, Washington, D.C., Denver and Minneapolis–St. Paul metropolitan areas, and in the California counties of San Bernardino and San Diego.[53] Most plans allocate housing responsibility to the local areas which then decide how to meet such quotas. Indirectly, at least, this would seem to imply that localities must rezone in a less exclusionary manner. The fact that since most fair share plans are based heavily upon voluntary compliance and that some establish quotas only for subsidized housing, over which the Nixon Administration has temporarily established a moratorium, inclines one against consideration of such fair share plans as a basis for substantial reform of exclusionary zoning.[54]

The only local or subregional body known to have voluntarily enacted direct reform of their development controls is Fairfax County, Virginia. Fairfax enacted an ordinance which required all new residential housing developments of 50 or more units, excluding single-family housing and high-rise apartments, to reserve at least 15 percent of the total units for low- and moderate-income housing and at least six of the 15 percent for low-income families.[55] Developers who provided more than these minimum requirements

were also given a density bonus of one additional housing unit for every two
low- and moderate-income housing units. Since the requirements were contin-
gent upon the availability of federal subsidies for low- and moderate-income
housing, federal authorizations for funding of subsidy programs which fall far
short of need severely compromise the effectiveness of this kind of ordinance.
Moreover, the conditional nature of the requirement was interpreted by the
circuit court of Fairfax County as an unlawful delegation of zoning authority
and statutory power to HUD, and the ordinance was nullified in late 1971.[56]
It was generally agreed by members of the local bar that the ordinance ". . . is
useful in creating a climate to stimulate developers to work on the problem, but
that the ordinance itself is bad and unworkable. No Fairfax lawyer could be
obtained to defend the ordinance when it was challenged . . ."[57] The reservations of local lawyers were apparently reflected by the court, which found the
ordinance unauthorized by Virginia's enabling act and concluded that the
ordinance was arbitrary and capricious, even if authorized by a suitable enabling
act.[58]

  Zoning reforms at the regional and local level are, then, as dependent
upon unambiguous, logical provisions which restrict unreasonable exclusionary
practices as are reforms at the state and federal levels. It is unclear to us at this
time where, in the hierarchy of governmental levels, reform should be focused or
which type of reform is the most probable candidate; nor do we care to speculate on the relative merits of each or the political acceptability of one as against
the others. Rather, we choose to concentrate on creating the conditions necessary to assure that any one approach might be maximally effective against
exclusion.

  The quotation used at the beginning of this chapter suggests the
essential task to be undertaken: how to disentangle the proper uses of zoning
from exclusionary uses. The complex web of real world relationships implicit in
an abstract zoning document requires more than a casual sorting if reforms are
to succeed in "getting the exclusion out" of zoning. For such reforms to be
effective, exclusion must be rigorously defined and its presence or absence in
particular zoning ordinances must be identified unambiguously.

  A performance standard for zoning would provide both definition
and identification of exclusion in particular ordinances. Chapter 3 develops
the conceptual basis for a performance standard for zoning which separates the
exclusionary provisions from the legitimate local functions of ordering and
controlling land uses.

NOTES

1. Advisory Committee to the Department of Housing and Urban Development, National Academy of Sciences–National Academy of
   Engineering, *Freedom of Choice in Housing: Opportunities and*

Constraints (Washington: National Academy of Science, 1972), p. 31.

2. Three presidential commissions, the President's Commission on Urban Housing (Kaiser Committee: 1968), the National Commission on Urban Problems (Douglas Commission: 1968), and the National Advisory Commission on Civil Disorders (Kerner Commission: 1968), have identified suburban development and zoning patterns as instrumental in producing the economic and social cleavages so visible in urban areas. A common thread running through all the commissions is the need to reorganize or reform the system of local development controls in metropolitan areas. For additional discussion of these and other similar findings, see Paul and Linda Davidoff and Neil Newton Gold, "Suburban Action: Advocate Planning for an Open Society," *Journal of the American Institute of Planners,* XXXVI, No. 1, 1970, pp. 12–21.

3. "As a former local governmental official subjected to these [fiscal] pressures, I know that they are difficult to resist. I have been involved in a situation where a company's industrial location personnel, in negotiating the location of a new plant, let it be known that they are considering several alternative sites for a new plant, some of them in neighboring jurisdictions. They suggest they prefer 'your town' but that a rezoning is necessary. . . . The city now rationalizes that the 'tax plum' will be built on one side of the street or the other and the only difference will be whether the city gets the property or sales tax or whether it doesn't." Eugene G. Moody, "Regional Implications of Local Land Use Changes," *Change: The Recurring Zoning Issue,* Proceedings of Institute on Zoning, C.W. Forest, ed. (Urbana-Champaign: Bureau of Urban and Regional Planning Research, University of Illinois, 1970), p. 3.

4. Daniel P. Moynihan, *Toward A National Urban Policy* (New York: Basic Books, 1970), p. 21.

5. Without question, the Advisory Committee on Intergovernmental Relations has been most responsible for continuous and detailed study of metropolitan governance. For a complete listing of ACIR studies, consult the bibliography of any recent ACIR Annual Report. A useful overview of ACIR recommendations may be found in *Unshackling Local Government: A Survey of Proposals By the Advisory Commission on Intergovernmental Relations,* (Washington: Government Printing Office, 1968). A sampling of other studies and recommendations from important or influential sources are: *Building The American City,* Pt. IV, "Government Structure, Finance and Taxation," pp. 323–416; Committee for Economic Development, *Reshaping Government in Metropolitan Areas,* (New York: CED, 1970); U.S. Chamber of Commerce, *Modernizing Local Government* (Washington: Chamber of Commerce of the U.S., 1967).

6. Lowden Wingo, "Logic and Ideology in Metropolitan Reform," in *Reform*

of Metropolitan Governments, Lowden Wingo, ed., (Baltimore: Resources for the Future, 1972), p. 1.

7. Karl W. Deutsch and Richard L. Meier, *The Confederation of Urban Governments: How Self-Controls for the American Megalopolis Can Evolve,* working paper, No. 77 (Berkeley: Institute of Urban and Regional Development, University of California, 1968).

8. Melvin B. Mogulof, *Governing Urban Areas* (Washington: Urban Institute, 1971).

9. Ibid., pp. 5–6.

10. For additional analyses of linking federal-local governance, consult The Urban Institute, "Reconstituting Urban Area Governing Capacity: Balancing Overall Needs and Local Self Rule," *Search,* Vol. 3, No. 4, July-August 1973, pp. 3–5, and Subcommittee On the Planning Process and Urban Development of the Advisory Committee to the Department of Housing and Urban Development, *Shifting the Locus of Responsibility For Domestic Problem Solving: Revenue Sharing and the Planning Process,* (Washington: National Academy of Sciences-National Academy of Engineering, 1973).

11. John W. Reps, "Requiem for Zoning," *Planning 1964* (Chicago: American Society of Planning Officials, 1964), pp. 56–67.

12. "Standards required in any single metropolitan area may vary enormously depending on the whims of local legislators. . . . Would it not be desirable to deny zoning powers to the smaller units of government and place this responsibility at the county level, or as a duty of some metropolitan government or agency, or as a function of the state government?" Ibid., p. 59.

13. The most fully elaborated argument is to be found in Bernard H. Siegan, *Land Use Without Zoning.* (Lexington, Mass.: Lexington Books, 1972). See also Robert J. Hartsfield, "The Houston Non-Zoning Experience," *Change: The Recurring Zoning Issue,* pp. 47–55.

14. Siegan, *Land Use Without Zoning,* Pt. IV, "The Effects of Zoning," pp. 85–146.

15. Siegan, *Land Use Without Zoning,* p. 34.

16. Task Force on Land Use and Urban Growth, *The Use of Land: A Citizens' Policy Guide to Urban Growth,* A Task Force Report Sponsored by the Rockefeller Brothers Fund (New York: Thomas Y. Crowell, 1973), prepublication copy, p. 143.

17. In his *Land Use Without Zoning,* Siegan offers assurances ". . . that the real estate market does not operate chaotically or haphazardly; it is quite rational and orderly. Economic forces are highly effective in causing uses to locate separately. The land use maps of medium-sized Texas cities that are not zoned provide dramatic evidence for this proposition. These maps disclose exceptions to the general pattern, but probably little or no more than might occur under zoning in these cities.", p. 73.

"The substantial increases in population [approximately threefold] since the adoption of zoning [in three medium-sized Texas cities] indicate that it has influenced land use patterns in these cities. Because land use maps of significant size [scale] are not available or are difficult to interpret, I have not been able to conclude that these cities are representative. At the very least, they do create doubt as to whether zoning is more protective than non-zoning against the proliferation of industry." Ibid., pp. 73–74. "To this observer the most noticeable physical distinction between Los Angeles and Houston lies in the residential area. In Los Angeles, serious about its detached, single-family areas, the medium-priced, single-family residential subdivision has managed to maintain its residential purity far better than its counterpart in Houston. This is precisely what zoning can do best." Richard F. Babcock, *The Zoning Game* (Madison: University of Wisconsin Press, 1966), p. 28.

The ambivalence inherent in such contrasting statements as "dramatic evidence for this proposition" and "At the very least, they do create doubt" suggests also that even Siegan, a strong advocate of nonzoning, is less than certain that use separation will prevail in an open market as it does under zoning. Nor does he contend that it is possible to anticipate and provide for whatever use separation which might occur in the absence of zoning.

18. Daniel R. Mandelker, *The Zoning Dilemma*, (New York: Bobs-Merrill, 1971, p. 23.
19. Siegan, *Land Use Without Zoning*, p. 62.
20. Mandelker, *The Zoning Dilemma*, p. 23.
21. Ibid., p. 23–31, 38, 40.
22. For a useful overview, see Seymour I. Toll, *Zoned American* (New York: Grossman, 1969), pp. 301–307. See also Norman Marcus and Marlyn W. Groves, *The New Zoning: Legal, Administrative, and Economic Concepts and Techniques* (New York: Praeger, 1970).
23. The Douglas Commission's report, *Building the American City,* issued in 1968, serves as an official referent for identifying the conjuncture of several reforms. The interest in metropolitan reorganization is represented in Pt. IV, reform of codes and standards to assure both orderly development and reduction of exclusion can be found in Pt. III, and improvement of the environment is discussed in Pt. VI.
24. Most of the work by Paul Davidoff and the Suburban Action Institute may be found in the following: Linda Davidoff, Paul Davidoff, Neil N. Gold, "Suburban Action: Advocate Planning for an Open Society," *Journal of the American Institute of Planners,* Vol. XXXVI, No. 1, 1970, pp. 12–21; William H. Brown III, Samuel C. Jackson, John H. Powell, Jr., *Open or Closed Suburbs: Corporate Location and the Urban Crisis* (Tarrytown, N.Y.: Suburban Action Institute, 1970); Paul Davidoff and Neil N. Gold, "Exclusionary Zoning," *Yale Review of Law and Social Action,* Vol. 1, Nos. 2 and 3, Winter 1970; Chris Kristensen, John Levy, Tamar Savir, *The Suburban Lockout Effect* (Tarrytown, N.Y.: Suburban Action Institute,

1971); Linda Davidoff, Paul Davidoff, Neil N. Gold, "The Suburbs Have to Open Their Gates," *New York Times Magazine,* November 7, 1971. The National Committee Against Discrimination in Housing has also been active in legal and political efforts to dislodge exclusionary zoning, an effort which grew out of its earlier concern for assuring nondiscriminatory treatment of minorities in the housing market.

25. Jack Noble argues "Naturally, there is still a lot of disagreement about which type of radical reform is best, and we must await a lot of experimentation before the best solutions can be chosen. Still, there is very widespread sentiment that zoning has limitations. Most of the reforms start from a recognition that those limitations exist. In this chapter, we are not concerned with far-out reforms. Instead, we are concerned with how to do the best possible job with the tools at hand—to operate within the system and make it work as well as possible," in "Zoning Limitations," *Regulatory Devices* (Chicago: American Society of Planning Officials, 1969), p. 12.

26. For an appraisal of the reports issued by the Kaiser Committee and the Douglas Commission, see review articles by Michael A. Stegman, "Kaiser, Douglas, and Kerner on Low Income Housing Policy," *American Institute of Planners,* Vol. XXXV, No. 6, November 1969,

27. President's Committee on Urban Housing, *A Decent Home* (Washington: Government Printing Office, 1968), pp. 25, 143–145; *Building the American City,* pp. 235–252, 478.

28. *Report of the National Advisory Commission on Civil Disorders* (New York: Bantam Books, 1968), pp. 389–409.

29. Although Norman Williams, Jr. and Thomas Norman provide a useful summary of exclusionary zoning case law as of late 1970, they warn that "The Law on exclusionary land use control is evolving so rapidly that a summary of the situation at any given point in time may be obsolete before it is in print. . . ." (pp. 20–23) in "Exclusionary Land Use Controls: The Case of Northeastern New Jersey," *Land Use Controls Quarterly,* Vol. 4, No. 4 (Chicago: American Society of Planning Officials, 1970); an up-to-date review may be found in Jerome G. Rose, "The Courts and the Balanced Community: Recent Trends in New Jersey Zoning Law," *Journal of the American Institute of Planners,* Vol. 39, No. 3, July 1973, pp. 265–276. Contributions to the legal literature are growing even more rapidly than relevant court decisions, a situation which calls forth monitoring efforts by such informed observers as Paul Davidoff at the Suburban Action Institute (Tarrytown, N.Y.) and Herbert Franklin at the Metropolitan Clearinghouse, Potomac Institute (Washington, D.C.) to sort out contributions upon which to base actionable reforms.

30. For a rather comprehensive review of executive branch activities in the general area of land use policy, see "The Executive Branch and Land Use Policy: Federal programs and Federal organization as they

relate to Land Use Policy," *National Land Use Policy*, background papers on past and pending legislation and the roles of the executive branch, Congress and the states in land use policy and planning, compiled at request of Henry M. Jackson, Chairman, Committee on Interior and Insular Affairs, U.S. Senate (Washington: Government Printing Office, 1972), pp. 79–94.

31. President Richard M. Nixon, *Statement by the President on Federal Policies Relative to Equal Housing Opportunity*, Office of the White House Press Secretary, released June 11, 1971.

32. *Statement by the President,* p. 10.

33. "He [the President] thus pledges presidential protection for the suburbs (a word he did not use) in continuing the exclusionary zoning and other practices which have created and maintained metropolitan apartheid." Comment titled "Suburban Snobbery," *The New Republic,* Vol. 164, No. 26, June 26, 1971, p. 7.

34. "Memorandum of Understanding Between the Department of Housing and Urban Development and the General Services Administration Concerning Low- and Moderate-Income Housing," Signature Agreement dated June 11, 1971 and June 12, 1971, pp. 2–3.

35. "Rules and Regulations, Title 44–Public Property and Works, Chapter VII– Department of Housing and Urban Development (Community Facilities), Pt. 707a–Evaluation of Preliminary Applications for Basic Water and Sewer Facilities Grants," *Federal Record,* June 29, 1971, p. 12219.

36. See "I. Introduction: The Land Use Crisis from a National Perspective," *National Land Use Policy,* pp. 3–11.

37. There is no provision in either Senator Jackson's bill (S.632) or the Administration's bill (S.992) for the curbing or reform of local exclusionary zoning practices. See "Table 1–Comparison of National Land Use Policy Bills," *National Land Use Policy,* pp. 18–20.

38. Sylvan Kamm, "Land Availability for Housing and Urban Growth, "Committee on Banking and Currency, U.S., House of Representatives, 92d Cong., in *Papers Submitted to Subcommittee on Housing Panels,* Pt. 1 (Washington: Government Printing Office, 1971), p. 278.

39. One of several similarly worded preconditions states these requirements as: ". . . (1) providing housing opportunities for all, particularly to low- and moderate-income individuals and families, (2) providing greater access to places of employment, and (3) providing housing in conjunction with improved community facilities." Committee on Banking and Currency, U.S., House of Representatives, *House and the Urban Environment,* Report and Recommendations of Three Study Panels of the Subcommittee on Housing, June 17, 1971, (Washington: Government Printing Office, 1971), p. 60.

40. Hon. Wright Patman, HR9688, Committee on Banking and Currency, U.S., House of Representatives, 92d Cong., July 8, 1971, (Washington: Government Printing Office, 1971).

41. First released in 1968, the American Law Institute's model code was, by late 1971, in its third, tentative draft stage and, while still undergoing further refinement, the final draft is expected sometime in 1974. Available in its latest form from the American Law Institute, 101 N. 33d St., Philadelphia, Pa., 19104. For a comparison of the ALI Model Code and selected pieces of recent land use legislation placed before Congress, see "Comparative Analysis: ALI Model Code and National Bills," *State Planning Issues, 1972* (Lexington, Ky.: The Council of State Planning Agencies and the Council of State Governments, 1972), pp. 115–119.

42. The Standard State Zoning Enabling Act (U.S., Department of Commerce, 1926) and the Standard City Planning Enabling Act (U.S., Department of Commerce, 1928). Both are reprinted in *A Model Land Development Code.*

43. David Heeter notes "All of the reports [examined], except for the ALI Model Code, are concerned to some extent with lowering the cost of and providing a wider choice of housing," in *Toward a More Effective Land Use Guidance System: A Summary and Analysis of Five Major Reports,* p. 88.

44. See panel discussion of American Law Institute Model Land Development Code in report of *Eighth Conference on Exclusionary Land Use Problems,* Herbert M. Franklin and Lois Craig, eds. (Washington: Exclusionary Land Use Clearinghouse [now the Metropolitan Housing Project], The Potomac Institute, 1971), pp. 15–25.

45. For useful reviews of recent state land use control policies, see "The States and Land Use Policy: Recent Developments," *National Land Use Policy,* pp. 95–101; see also Fred Bosselman and David Callies, "The Quiet Revolution in Land Use Control—Summary Report," and "Staff Report by Washington State Land Planning Commission," *State Planning Issues, 1972,* pp. 74–88, 104–112.

46. For a summary description of this act and its early impact, see Leon Charkardian, "Innovations Affecting State Planning: Massachusetts Antisnob Zoning Law," *State Planning Issues, 1972.*

47. MacDonald Barr, *The Massachusetts Zoning Appeals Law: Lessons of the First Three Years,* (Boston: Massachusetts Department of Community Affairs, n.d.).

48. Herbert M. Franklin, "Massachusetts Decision Upholds Zoning Appeals Law," *Metropolitan Clearinghouse Memorandum 73-5* (Washington: Metropolitan Housing Program, Potomac Institute, 1973), pp. 3–6.

49. Herbert M. Franklin, "Recent Developments: New York Legislature Severely Curbs UDC Power in Suburbs," *Metropolitan Clearinghouse Memorandum 73-6* (Washington: Metropolitan Housing Program, Potomac Institute, 1973), pp. 1–3.

50. Herbert M. Franklin, "Massachusetts Decision Upholds Zoning Appeals Law."

51. Before the courts upheld the Massachusetts Law, Leon Charkardian noted "In terms of the statute itself, there are a number of problems

relating to the language of the act which, unless amended, may open the statute to serious challenge in the courts. Terms such as 'reasonable' and 'consistent with local needs' require further clarification," in "Innovations Affecting State Planning: Massachusetts Antisnob Zoning Law," p. 57.

52. Miami [Ohio] Regional Valley Planning Commission, *A Housing Plan for The Miami Valley Region—A Reprint* (Philadelphia: Housing Association of Delaware Valley, 1971).

53. See Edward L. Holmgren and Ernest Erber, "Fair Share Formulas," *HUD Challenge,* April 1973, pp. 22–25. See also post-1972 issues of *NARC Housing Reporter* (Washington: National Association of Regional Councils) for current information on the status of fair share planning.

54. Herbert M. Franklin, "Expounding on Impounding," *Metropolitan Clearinghouse Memorandum 73–2* (Washington: Metropolitan Housing Program, Potomac Institute, 1973), p. 1.

55. Franklin and Craig, *Eighth Conference on Exclusionary Land Use Problems,* pp. 1–14.

56. Ibid, p. 2.

57. Ibid, p. 4.

58. Ibid, p. 2.

Chapter Three

A Performance Standard for Zoning

> The Commission recommends that the Congress amend the Housing Act to assert, as a matter of national policy, the desirability of providing for housing of employees of all income levels in areas reasonably close to places of employment. . . .[1]

Whatever combination of legislative, judicial or administrative remedies is eventually selected to reduce the unwanted effects of exclusionary zoning practices, each of these remedies requires some kind of standard by which particular ordinances may be evaluated. There is a large body of raw evidence which identifies the problem of exclusionary zoning in general terms, but specific instances are difficult to establish in the absence of a measurable yardstick or standard.[2] The task at hand is development of a measurable standard which can determine whether specific zoning ordinances are exclusionary or not. More specifically, the standard should: (1) detect individual cases of exclusionary zoning; and, (2) result in the reduction of some or all of the problems or undesirable effects which stem from exclusionary zoning once the standard is met.

PERFORMANCE STANDARD BASED ON
EFFECTS OF EXCLUSIONARY ZONING

Given that the standard should reduce the undesirable effects stemming from exclusionary zoning, one might attempt the design of a standard which is directed precisely at those effects. There is an emerging literature which deals with similar issues pertaining to urban development policy, principally the literature on test cases of zoning,[3] fair share housing plans, state delegation of zoning powers and land use guidance policy, that one might draw upon in devising such a standard.[4] However, simply by reviewing the classes of harmful effects to be avoided, one can readily assess the possibility of basing a performance standard on them. To facilitate such a review, four classes or

categories of harmful effects which allegedly stem from exclusionary zoning
are arbitrarily defined here as: (1) restricted housing choice; (2) effective loss
of consumer and citizen sovereignty; (3) lengthy, burdensome work journeys;
and (4) inequitable distribution of fiscal resources. Others might draw up somewhat different lists, but this list does contain the principal problems associated
with exclusionary zoning.

Restricted Housing Choice

The effects which exclusionary zoning has on the housing market
have been discussed at length in the professional and scholarly literature, and
were summarized in the introduction. While this discussion makes clear that
exclusionary zoning per se does not directly restrict newly constructed housing
and residential opportunity for low- to moderate-income families, zoning could
be altered in such a way that the prices and rents of residential construction
correspond more closely to household incomes in the metropolitan area. One
might expect substantial agreement that, at the metropolitan level, prices and
rents of new and existing housing should bear a reasonable relationship to household incomes for housing choice to exist, but far less agreement about how
particular municipalities should share in the total distribution of housing costs
and household incomes.

The simplest sharing formula is for each municipality to zone for a
metropolitan cross section of related housing costs and household incomes,
but this seemingly simple approach is fraught with complexities. To begin, a
perfect cross section is very unlikely, due to economic forces generated by the
use and users of urban land. Economic forces result in a general gradient of
economic site-intensity usage for land in the metropolitan area, where inner
locations are better suited to dense development and locations farther out are
usually less densely developed. Urban land market forces also determine, in
part, the structure and tenure characteristics of the residential stock and its array
of prices and rents. Closely related to the locational specialization of housing is
the uneven distribution of employment opportunities over the metropolitan
area. That is, if somehow all areas were to overcome locational specialization of
housing and provide a metropolitan cross section, there is good reason to believe
that employment might not be available for all workers near their "cross section" of residential opportunities. These two facts alone strongly suggest that
since some municipalities are, by virtue of their unique locations, better suited
to certain types and mixes of residential and economic development than to
others, requiring each municipality to adopt a cross section of metropolitan
housing opportunities is not the best course to follow. Finally, there is ample
evidence that a completely arbitrary metropolitan-wide mix of income classes in
each municipality would not be politically accepted. While it is true that some
middle- and upper-income families might welcome the opportunity for social
interaction with low- and moderate-income families, current zoning practices of

wealthy communities indicate that most would not, despite the benefits alleged to accrue to heterogenous communities.[5] On the other hand, ethnic and racial communities which comprise much of the low-income household population are less and less interested in becoming culturally integrated into the American mainstream, a view which is frequently advanced by spokesmen for the black community.[6]

In the absence of compelling evidence that each municipality should accept a cross section of metropolitan housing, there is no obvious way of designing a standard for exclusionary zoning which could divide the housing stock among municipalities so that expanded choice is guaranteed.

Effective Loss of Consumer and Citizen Sovereignty

The indirect effects of a locality engaging in exclusionary zoning may entail a loss of consumer and citizen sovereignty in the surrounding region. Consumer sovereignty is a concept associated with free market operations. If the market operated efficiently, the preferences of individuals and households for various types, costs and densities of housing "packages" are accurately communicated to producers and elicit a corresponding supply response so that preferences are satisfied to the maximum degree possible. Antitrust laws and powerful critiques of the tendency of producers to mold preferences, rather than respond to them, are evidence that consumer sovereignty in certain markets is often compromised. Strong parallels with supplier or producer manipulation of markets can be found in the restricted supply and choice of housing inherent in exclusionary zoning. If, as one qualified observer notes, the housing market approximates rather closely the characteristics of a free market,[7] then exclusionary zoning may be subject to the same reasoning upon which antitrust laws are based.[8] Restraint of free trade compromises consumer sovereignty for everyone if the entire market is distorted or if it reduces housing opportunities for low- and moderate-income families in particular. However, the only positive way of ensuring consumer sovereignty is to allow the land- and housing-market mechanisms to allocate land for residential and other use. One would again run the risks of negative externalities inherent in most private market operations; it was precisely this situation which stimulated the first arguments in favor of zoning. The concept of consumer sovereignty requires a free-market solution which, as discussed earlier in Chapter 2, is necessarily fraught with negative externalities and loss of public control over development. This line of reasoning does not, of course, yield a basis for the design of a performance standard to reform exclusionary zoning and reduce its deleterious effects; it is the now familiar argument for eliminating all zoning.

Citizen sovereignty is a term rigorously defined by Kenneth Arrow to designate certain situations in which the will of the majority determines public decisions.[9] Lack of citizen sovereignty is felt by nonresidents of an

area who are substantially affected by the area's zoning and who are unable
to influence the zoning decisions which affect them. As one observer has put
it:

> Suburbs alone regulate the use and development of most vacant
> land in metropolitan areas, yet this regulation has a pervasive effect
> upon the lives of people outside the borders of suburbs. State
> delegation of control over vacant land use to suburbanites . . . is
> serious . . . because identifiable groups are likely to be permanently
> excluded from participation. Restrictive land use policies purposely
> exclude those who, if they had access to the ballot box, would
> vote to change current policies.[10]

Once it has been established that some nonresidents are substantially
affected by local zoning decisions which they should have some hand in making,
by what rationale does one selectively identify and allow certain nonresidents
to somehow participate in zoning decisions? The simplest way to solve the
problem is to establish a metropolitan government in which all citizens are
represented and to vest it with all zoning powers. However, this solution differs
markedly from the reality of current local governance and does not represent
an effort to reform zoning within present institutional arrangements which,
from the discussion in Chapter 2, appear to be fixed over the short term.

The problem at hand is to identify certain groups whose non-
residence is a demonstrable hardship beyond that suffered by all nonresidents
who are similarly affected, say, in their choice of housing, so that something
less than the entire metropolitan electorate is involved. Two discrete populations can be cited. The first population is comprised of public servants whose
incomes are frequently inadequate in relation to the structure of housing prices
produced by the zoning in the communities for which they work. The net result
of housing market exclusion for these employees is the loss of workplace
franchise, the exercise of which bears directly on the manner in which their
livelihood is derived. Through their purchasing and voting powers, employees
in private concerns and resident public servants are at least assured of a voice
in the conduct of employer affairs which affects their livelihood, however small
or distorted. Municipal employees are systematically denied this voice so long
as a locality zones for high cost housing and pays them less than what is required
to afford housing in the municipality for which they work. A standard based
upon citizen sovereignty would relate the number and income of households
headed by public employees to a stock of housing which these households could
afford, so that the opportunity for residence is made available.

There is a second group which is also compromised by the housing
price structure characteristic of exclusionary zoning. Many workers in private
companies do not earn enough to live in the communities where they work.

Unlike the argument supporting residential rights to local franchise for municipal workers, citizen sovereignty through residential access for private workers is justified because they are being taxed indirectly through the property or other municipal tax payments by their employers in the taxing jurisdiction without representation or without receiving any benefits from that taxation.[11] If employers paid no tax, then employees would, assuming some measure of tax savings are passed on to workers, receive higher wages and salaries; or, if employers paid an equivalent amount of tax to a larger jurisdiction, then more workers would participate in decisions as to how the tax revenues should be spent and would enjoy the benefits of that tax revenue. Again, enhancing citizen sovereignty for employees of private companies produces a standard relating the number and income of households headed by employees of taxpaying companies to a stock of housing with prices they can afford.

Both of these sub-criteria establish precise linkages between distinct, identifiable groups of people who are adversely affected by exclusionary zoning. But a question remains as to whether the adversity they experience is so pronounced that citizen sovereignty constitutes a sufficiently sturdy base upon which a performance standard for the reform of exclusionary zoning justifiably might be constructed.

Lengthy, Burdensome Work Journeys

The argument for reducing metropolitan transportation is at least twofold, entailing elements of both efficiency and equality. Efficiency in the provision of highway and mas transport is a goal often cited by planners and public officials. To the degree that residences and workplaces are unnecessarily separated by zoning ordinances, trip lengths increase and loss of efficiency results. This situation could occur because of outright zoning prohibitions, insufficient provision of low-cost residential areas or a distortion of metropolitan land markets which tends to force industries (and employment) out of cities to the urban fringe. Maintaining an unnecessarily expensive transportation system drains regional resources to such an extent that either tax costs for current service levels are higher than necessary, or higher quality service could be made to result from the same tax burden. A related efficiency argument stressing environmental or ecological factors can rightly point to automobiles as the primary source of oxidant pollution in the regional "airshed." If, it is argued, some measure of pollution could be avoided by enabling workers to live closer to their place of work, thereby shortening or even eliminating some automobile work trips, then additional weight is added to the argument for reduction of transport for reasons of efficiency.

It may well be that workers might choose to live only slightly or no closer to their workplace, but this objection should not rule out the opportunity for workers to choose whatever proximity to work they might prefer. Reduction of transportation costs as the basis for a performance standard is vulnerable to criticism because it is not measurable. Large scale modeling of land uses and transport networks in metropolitan areas is still at such a primitive level that the locational behavior of households in the absence of zoning restrictions cannot be assessed readily. Nor can such models reliably estimate transport costs for a variety of workplace and residence configurations in a metropolitan area. In the absence of this kind of information, efficiency considerations in work journeys are inadequate to the task of designing a standard for zoning.

The efficiency argument stressed minimization of aggregate transport costs, independent of commute times or distances for certain individuals and classes of individual. However, a standard might also concern itself with unequal treatment if particular racial or economic classes are systematically forced to travel relatively long and costly distances to centers of employment. A good measure of whether there is unequal treatment is the amount of housing opportunities, by type and cost, within a reasonable commute (i.e., at affordable cost and time burdens) to employment centers.

Putting the concept into practice requires an estimate of what actually constitutes a nonburdensome, reasonable commute, and what proportion of workers should be able to find affordable housing within that commute. The need to establish a reasonable commute within which equal proportions of wage and salary earners can find housing is twofold. First, as distances become longer they are relatively more burdensome to low-wage earners, because travel costs rise more quickly relative to earnings and because travel times increase more precipitously due to a greater likelihood of time-consuming transfers between public transit lines and modes. Second, the distance or time for a reasonable commute must be known in order to calculate what proportion of all workers in a given employment center currently live within that radius. The overall percentage so derived can then be applied to workers of each earning level, to determine the availability of housing, by price or rent level which they can afford within that radius.

The problem of deciding what commute is reasonable is complicated, because as the number of workers in a given employment center becomes larger, either travel times or the housing density must also increase, with the cost of affordable housing being a function of the latter. In short, a formula for deriving a commute of varying lengths is not determinate, which, of course, complicates its calculation. Recourse to observed travel times in order to estimate statistically the length (e.g., the mean or median travel time) of a reasonable commute, or the proportion of workers who found housing within that commute, necessarily involves the use of current work and residence patterns which are already seriously distorted by past exclusionary zoning practice. However, a standard of equalized commutes, based upon observed commuter relationships, will provide minimal relief to the degree that low-density development and unnecessarily long commutes now observed are less severe than those likely to emerge from current exclusionary zoning. Potential cases of exclusionary or improper zoning would be judged as such by a commute distance standard only insofar as it produces worker commuting burdens greater than those observed and used to derive the standard. A commute standard based on observed relationships is, then, very conservative and it necessarily risks perpetuating a less than desirable status quo in those cases where a particular zoning ordinance produces commuting patterns that impose absolute hardships only somewhat less burdensome and more reasonable than the "standard" commute, which is nothing more than a statistical composite of observed commutes having both reasonable and plainly unreasonable lengths.

Closely related to the problem of quantitatively estimating a commute standard from currently distorted workplace and residence patterns is the difficulty of deciding which statistic is the appropriate one. Assuming that one knows the frequency distribution of journey-to-work commutes in a mythical metropolis wherein all households are located on the landscape in accordance with their individual preferences, does one then use the median or average trip length or the trip length at some higher or lower percentile to estimate the reasonable commute radius? The thorny methodological problems inherent in this standard can only be overcome by arbitrary decision rules.[12]

Even if a commute distance were estimated which most people would consider as reasonable, the pattern of residence and workplace which would satisfy this standard might leave other deleterious effects untouched. If, for example, the proportion of workers who must find affordable housing within the commute radius is based upon the observed average or median commute, then municipalities would only have to provide a fraction of the housing required on a regional basis. Moreover, if the standard were, instead, based upon a longer commute radius so as to encompass a larger proportion of worker families, the commute might become burdensome. It would also very likely span differing communities, allowing some municipalities with large employment centers and strong tax bases to avoid a portion or all of their responsibility for zoning low-cost housing simply because neighboring communities within the "standard" length commute had stocks of appropriately priced housing. These inherent weaknesses take on added importance when one considers that equalizing journeys to work eliminates what many observers consider to be one of the least serious of the deleterious effects allegedly caused by exclusionary zoning.

Inequitable Distribution of Fiscal Resources

Exclusionary zoning, combined with deliberate fiscal strategies, tends to concentrate both high-value residential and high-yielding nonresidential property in relatively few municipalities. Citizens living in municipalities which have been successful in acquiring a strong tax base enjoy a high level of public services at low tax cost; or, depending upon their preferences, they might pay a very small tax price for only average levels of public service. Families who cannot afford the housing prices and rents in these "tax colonies" pay a proportionately higher tax price for equivalent levels of service in less well-endowed communities, even though, on average, their need for such services may be many times greater.

The disparity in fiscal resources between communities has been studied in the past to devise tax equalization formulas and its continued presence has been well documented.[13] Most such formulas do not equalize fiscal resources much beyond the revenues expected if all communities exerted equal efforts to tap their tax bases, which, of course, all but avoids the issue of relative tax base size between municipalities. Since zoning patterns are instrumental in determining the distribution of tax base relative to the population, a standard which seeks to share the metropolitan area's fiscal resources with a larger number of families is a very attractive candidate.

A standard based upon greater sharing of the tax base could be developed in two separate ways: the distribution of fiscal resources between municipalities could be altered through controls on zoning for commerce and industry, or a larger number of families could share present and potential concentrations of fiscal resources through residential rezoning. Redistributing fiscal resources more evenly between municipalities through the use of zoning is likely to be frustrated by the same locational calculus of business and industry which all but prevents an even distribution of housing types and values across municipalities. There is theoretically a set of unique locational combinations of transport, resources and markets which various industries rationally select in metropolitan areas to minimize their costs and maximize their profits.[14] Since these combinations are relatively few in number, and because certain threshold levels of industrial concentration, per se, attract other industries, the metropolitan area well might suffer loss of potential employment and tax base if industrial development in communities with superior locations were limited through zoning in order to force distribution of industrial development between other fiscally deficient but less well-located communities. Although some actual redistribution might occur if zoning were to limit tax base development in each municipality by a formula share, the risk of losing some measure of potential aggregate economic development is sufficiently great to all but eliminate this strict interpretation of resource sharing from further consideration.

Increased sharing of fiscal resources also can be based upon allowing more families to reside in communities which have superior locational advantages and, consequently, higher levels of fiscal resources derived from a larger present or potential tax base. Although the citizens of a given local government seldom share all its public goods or services equally, the average citizen living in a locality with higher per capita public revenues and expenditures is demonstrably better off than one who lives in a less prosperous locality. Since one must reside legally in localities to enjoy the benefits of fiscal resources, the inability to rent or purchase housing—a prerequisite of residence—acts as an effective barrier to access. Differences in levels of fiscal resources are reduced to some extent by state and federal grants, but wealthy communities are still able to provide proportionately higher levels of public goods and services through self-taxation. While the maximum level of certain public goods in a few cities may equal, or even exceed, the actual level of these same goods in some wealthier municipalities, the overall potential level in prosperous communities is higher than maximum levels in poorer cities and older, close-in suburbs.

Communities in sound fiscal condition, at present, might easily be thought of as shirking their responsibility to provide public services for a reasonable share of the populace. This interpretation lays stress upon a metropolitan-wide responsibility for assuming a proportionate burden of public expenditure for low- and moderate-income families commensurate with those localities' "ability to pay"—a concept derived from theories of individual taxation.[15] A variant of this reasoning was used, in combination with several other criteria, to devise the Miami Valley Regional Planning Commission's regional housing plan, which allocated low- and moderate-cost housing units to each municipality.[16]

Raising the allowed residential densities would simultaneously increase the potential number of housing units, particularly rental units, which cost less to own and rent. The question is, with how many housing units of what price and rental, and with how many households of each income class should any particular community be required to share its tax base? Do "tax rich" communities have an obligation to accommodate all the families who want to live there, or may these communities be allowed to limit the number of families so as not to become "tax poor" due to heavy demand for public services? In the absence of firm knowledge about the number of families which could find housing in tax rich communities, or the propensity of these families to move there were zoning to be changed, it is extremely difficult to devise reasonable allocation procedures for this standard.

Other drawbacks from the performance standard itself bear mentioning. First, if allocation procedures were devised somehow, certain tax rich communities which prefer low levels of public services would be sharing only a low household tax rate, even though the newly allocated households might need a higher level of public services more than they would need tax relief. However, there doubtless are households whose public service demands are modest and for whom a sharing of tax relief might be a great boon—in particular, older individuals or childless couples. A hypothetical allocation of households to communities, based solely upon fiscal resources, also might create residential opportunities and fiscal resource sharing in communities which are deficient on other grounds. Access to public transportation systems, to metropolitan recreation or cultural facilities, to convenient shopping or to one's old neighborhood need not bear any necessary relationship to patterns of fiscal health. Another important discontinuity which may occasionally result is that between workplace and residence. A few communities may be fiscally healthy due to expensive residential developments or to industrial development with a narrow range of skill requirements—a fact which could result in some household heads who posses different skills to find employment elsewhere and to travel long distances to work.

Second, there exists a very small but definite chance that communities which currently offer high levels of public goods and services might cut them back to a significant degree were the communities compelled, in accordance with a fiscal sharing performance standard, to allow additional families to live there. If, for example, so many low tax-paying, high service-consuming families were added that heavy tax burdens resulted, a lessening of per capita expenditures for locally provided public goods and services might ensue. On the other hand, communities which have high fiscal capacity and low or moderate levels of public goods might elect to deliberately maintain "unattractive" levels indefinitely, merely to discourage lower-income families from coming into the community. Those communities in developing areas which typically provide low public service levels until they reach certain thresholds of population size or residential density would be hard pressed to maintain such a strategy for long, because internal pressures for additional services are generally sufficient to bring these services into being. Even mature, wealthy communities must at least establish public school systems. Those fiscally healthy communities which managed to cut back or maintain little more than elementary and secondary schools in the way of public goods and services generally offer education of such high quality that a sizable number of families with school-age children would still prefer to live there.

Finally, there is a troublesome problem which deserves recognition. The problem involves the possibility that families may be partially deprived of public goods and services, even if they live in a municipality with high average levels. This can occur because municipalities may deliberately try to create residential patterns for low- and moderate-income families which do not coincide with the spatial distribution or service areas of certain public goods and services. Municipal officials can rightly point to functional relationships such as residential density, transportation networks, open space, etc., which could, conceivably, justify the geographic separation of high- and low-density residential areas within municipalities. Therefore, it would be virtually impossible to specify, on an *ex ante* basis, the internal relationships between residential neighborhoods which zoning must produce to assure access to public resources, particularly when effective denial of access can be determined only after one knows the pattern of distribution of public resources. In jurisdictions of very large areas, the separation may be sufficiently great to effectively deny access of low- and moderate-income families to some measure of public wealth. The problem is, of course, most acute in developing metropolitan areas such as Washington, D.C. and Baltimore, Md., where potential separation within large counties—the smallest unit of local government—is much greater than in the many small towns or townships typical of the majority of metropolitan areas. In large communities, or wherever else spatial separation and effective denial of access can occur, the denial of internal access would require litigation and pressure similar to that brought by the NAACP Legal Defense Fund in the "municipal equalization" suits entered in southern towns and cities on behalf of black citizens. However, even if these tactics were necessary, new resident families would at least have the legal and moral standing which they now lack (due to their present nonresident status) to legitimately claim fair sharing of resources.

In short, the case for greater sharing of fiscal resources is compelling, but it is difficult to determine how the shares of family income levels should be allocated to individual communities and whether merely sharing a measure of public wealth sufficiently satisfies the widely varying needs of these households.

Summary

Designing a performance standard to control exclusionary zoning which is based upon the reduction of deleterious effects traceable to such zoning is an exercise fraught with difficulties. In basing the standard on any *one* of these effects, there is little or no assurance that improvement in that area would also mean improvement in others. Expanding housing choice, increasing consumer and citizen sovereignty, reducing journeys to work, or sharing fiscal resources would all be pursued in a relatively narrow, independent manner. Nor is there an obvious way of tying them together as a basis for a single comprehensive performance standard. At least part of the difficulty encountered in trying to derive an effects-related standard for exclusionary zoning can be traced to the fact that these effects are partially caused by other institutional structures and social forces. The two prime requisites of a standard to reform exclusionary zoning are securing relief from deleterious effects and the detection and measurability of exclusionary zoning. An effects-related standard is deficient on both counts: there is no certain way to reduce all the effects and the effects also reflect the presence and magnitude of other societal factors. Rather than basing a performance standard on the tenuous chain of consequences that ensue from exclusionary zoning, one might, instead, investigate the design of a standard based upon the phenomenon of exclusion per se.

PERFORMANCE STANDARD BASED ON EXCLUSION PRINCIPLE

In devising a standard which reduces or eliminates exclusionary zoning, it will pay to examine the nature of such zoning and to recall the reasons why, in fact, it is termed "exclusionary." All zoning necessarily restricts land areas to certain classes of use and could therefore be thought of as exclusionary in the broadest terms. However, the term exclusionary zoning is usually reserved to describe the purposeful design of zoning ordinances which do not permit the construction of inexpensive housing and therefore substantially or entirely exclude low- and moderate-income occupants from the municipality. Since it is this basic principle which results in what are widely known as exclusionary zoning patterns, and in the chain of deleterious effects which allegedly accompany such patterns, the principle of exclusion constitutes a more logical basis for the design of a performance standard. More simply, by reducing in zoning ordinances what is generally deemed exclusion, one necessarily mitigates the effects alleged to accompany exclusionary practices without the need to systematically prove the presence or subsequent reduction of these effects.

Therefore, the task at hand involves the determination of what the income spectrum of families should be in each municipality to eliminate or reduce exclusion. The total number of families allowed is a decision which should rightfully be left to each municipality, since the amount and character of developable, residentially suited land varies widely within each. However, the income mix of families and the mix of affordable housing is closely bound up with exclusionary elements in zoning. Quite obviously, then, the spectrum of household incomes, housing rents and housing prices should be enlarged, but by how much? If the income distribution of the SMSA population were adopted and arbitrarily applied to each municipality, many of the distortions noted earlier in the discussion of restricted housing choice would appear. The problem is one of requiring communities to house identifiable populations, now excluded, which are also functionally related to particular communities. Since exclusionary zoning is often closely related to municipal fiscal strategies to gain business and industry tax ratables, a standard which obliges municipalities to house the employees that result from tax ratable strategies would establish a functional linkage between a known number of households having identifiable income distributions and the responsible community. Requiring the zoning of communities to allow residential opportunities for the families of workers, the thrust of this chapter's opening quote from the National Committee on Urban Problems is intuitively appealing [17] and is also amenable to technical translation as a performance standard. As the President's Commission on Urban Housing has similarly concluded:

> The location of one's place of residence determines the accessibility and quality of many everyday advantages taken for granted by the mainstream of American society. Among these commonplace advantages are public educational facilities for a family's children, adequate police and fire protection, and a decent surrounding environment. In any case, a family should have the choice of living as close as possible to the breadwinner's place of employment.[18]

By concentrating on a better matching of residence and workplace, this standard also serves to reduce commuting burdens and overall metropolitan-level transportation costs. Since the income of workers and their households span the middle 90 percent or so of all income levels in the metropolitan area, allowing residential access to workers in communities where employment and the nonresidential tax base are located improves consumer and citizen sovereignty and creates an opportunity for whatever benefits might accompany income class mixing in more heterogenous communities.

In keying the standard exclusively to households which receive earned income from workers, one is dealing with about 92 percent of nonfarm families, or about 86 percent of all families and unrelated individuals on a nationwide basis.[19] It must be readily admitted that by specifying the standard in this manner, most of the eight to 14 percent not covered are easily as needy as worker's households. Little effective impact may, in fact, be sacrificed simply because the $3,200 median income of these 10 percent, or so, households is so low that few could afford even the least expensive new housing which could be built in the absence of exclusionary zoning. This point is no more than a restatement of the limited direct effect exclusionary zoning has on the poorest families. Therefore, a performance standard to limit or reduce the effects of exclusionary zoning will not materially improve the situation of many nonworking families nor, of course, will it improve significantly the situation in which the poorest working families find themselves. These needy families must be helped in more direct, positive ways, but substantial effects can be realized for families of moderate or greater means by devising a performance standard for zoning.

DEVELOPING THE WORKPLACE-RESIDENCE PERFORMANCE STANDARD

The next step involves the elaboration and specification of the general workplace-residence standard in sufficiently precise terms so that income and housing data, which are implicit in zoning ordinances, may be analyzed to detect and measure instances of exclusionary zoning.

To begin, if all the households of workers which would be generated by the nonresidential provisions of a zoning code are to have access to the communities where they work, the residential provisions of that code must allow houses of the type and cost which all the households can afford. This means, of course, that each community must have as many houses as worker's households, and that the profile of housing rents and prices must correspond with the household income profile of workers.[20] The fact that some workers could not afford the market price of the least expensive, unsubsidized new housing does not relieve municipalities of their responsibility in zoning land for these families. Since the workers could live in towns which have public housing or other housing subsidy programs, other towns should not be rewarded for their refusal to establish public housing authorities. The self-serving argument that zoning, per se, does not limit residential opportunities of the most impecunious worker

families cannot be used by these communities to justify zoning only enough
land to house the families of workers who can afford market prices of housing.

The developed portions of communities on the urbanizing fringe of
metropolitan areas have, on the average, more housing units than workers who
are household heads. Therefore, many of these communities would need to zone
their residential districts so that all workers' households can afford the prices
and rents of an equal number of housing units, but the remaining housing units
in the community could be of any type or price. Recall, however, that certain
of these municipalities may be more favorably located for commercial and
industrial development than others. Therefore, it is quite conceivable that the
economic base in some might well employ more household heads than could
be housed physically, even if all housing were of the kind and density which
workers can afford.

As the standard is formulated currently, municipalities would be
required to cut back their nonresidential zoning so that the total of workers'
households are just equal to housing units. Depending upon the amount and kind
of commercial or industrial development which would occur in the municipality
in the absence of the implied one-housing-unit per one-worker-per-household
restriction, some net loss of regional tax base and employment could result, and
the productive efficiency of firms which did manage to locate elsewhere in the
region could suffer. Consequently, it seems prudent to allow those few municipalities with superior locations to exceed the one-to-one ratio of worker household heads to housing units, provided that *all* of their housing units are affordable to a cross section of working household heads.[21] This proviso eliminates
the possibility of a municipality "creaming" the highest paid workers in determining the cost profile of its housing requirements. However, the refinement
does not constitute a loophole through which other communities would try to,
or could, squeeze. First, a community would have to be fairly sure that its
actual development potential would approach or exceed one employed household head per housing unit; otherwise it would be much better off to zone
more modestly for nonresidential development and build a sound residential
tax base with "extra" high priced housing units which are unencumbered by
workers' requirements. Second, communities which know their nonresidential
development potential is low could not expect to zone heavily for such development and lightly for worker housing, in the hope of maintaining an effective
holding action until the market for high priced housing ripened. This is so
because the performance standard applies to each zoning ordinance as amended
at every point in time; communities are accountable now or later for all their
workers. Finally, by allowing communities to zone for more working household
heads than housing units, it is extremely unlikely that the total balance of
actual housing opportunities and workers' households is jeopardized. One need
only consider the universal propensity of developing towns to zone for far more
combined development of all kinds than is actually needed at any given time.

It is highly probable that overzoning for all uses would result in more affordable housing opportunities than the actual number of workers' households.

Thus far, the performance standard has established that municipalities must devise their zoning ordinances in such a way that their workers can afford the housing allowed. It is of utmost importance that the rents and prices of housing, which are due only to residential provisions of zoning, are distinguished from the rents and prices which typically do, or could, obtain under identical zoning because of other factors. In other words, the price or rent of the least expensive unit which can be built within the terms of any given zoning ordinance should be used to determine whether or not workers have residential access to a municipality. If prices or rents above the minimum are used, then denial of access, which is really due to other factors, would improperly be attributed to zoning. Consequently, the performance standard should detect lack of access in terms of the number and proportion, by income level, of workers' households which are deprived of residential opportunities because of the lack of appropriate types or the minimum cost of housing. By placing the emphasis upon effective denial of access, the performance standard detects the "preclusive" element in zoning ordinances which necessarily results in exclusion; the performance standard specifically seeks to identify zoning which is carried on "to prevent or hinder by necessary consequence or implication, deter action of, access to, or enjoyment of"[22] the fruits of residency. Finally, the performance standard must be capable of detecting exclusionary mixes of household income and the prices and rents of housing. For example, it is obvious that a township which allows only two-acre lots would violate the performance standard substantially, but if there is some percentage of housing on two-acre lots which could be afforded by a number of worker households, the township would not, therefore, violate the standard. Accordingly, it is important that the performance standard is sufficiently sensitive to assess the magnitude of exclusion, and to identify which particular provisions of the zoning ordinance must be changed to guarantee workers and their families the opportunity for residential access.

NOTES

1. National Committee on Urban Problems, *Building The American City* (Washington: Government Printing Office, 1968), p. 243.
2. In Norman Williams, Jr., and Thomas Norman, "Exclusionary Land-Use Controls: The Case of North-Eastern New Jersey," *Lands Use Controls Quarterly,* Vol. 4, No. 4 (Chicago: American Society of Planning Officials, 1970), the authors have done considerable spadework for a subsequent study in which ". . . the various restrictions revealed by the state's [New Jersey] study would be

translated into actual housing costs, in order to demonstrate precisely the impact of each device and to see which devices are most damaging," fn., p. 3.

3. Linda Davidoff, Paul Davidoff and Neil N. Gold, "Suburban Action: Advocate Planning for an Open Society," *Journal of the American Institute of Planners,* XXXVI, No. 1, 1970, p. 17–19.

4. For a partial sampling of this literature, review citations and references which accompany the last section of Chapter 2, titled "Reform The Tool." A report which viewed housing mixture more broadly than the elimination of exclusionary zoning is Morton Lustig, et al, *Standards For Suburban Housing Mix,* (Philadelphia: Fels Center of Government, University of Pennsylvania, 1971).

5. A rather widespread view alleges that social classes in physical proximity are conducive to the development of an open society, but others claim that physical proximity of social classes is a symptom of an open society rather than a precondition to it. For a discussion of the desirability and feasibility of socioeconomic residential mixing, see Advisory Committee to the Department of Housing and Urban Development, National Academy of Sciences–National Academy of Engineering, *Freedom of Choice in Housing,* (Washington: National Academy of Sciences, 1972), pp. 35–44. Compare also early (Suburban Growth) and late (New Towns) Herbert J. Gans on residential mixing in, respectively, *People and Plans,* (New York: Basic Books, 1968), Part III, and "The Possibilities of Class and Racial Integration in American New Towns," in *New Towns: Why – and for Whom?,* Harvey S. Perloff and Neil C. Sandberg, eds. (New York: Praeger, 1973).

6. "Integration is no longer unquestionably accepted as a fundamental tenet of the American ethic. There are black leaders who believe deeply that the black man's future lies in economic development of the urban ghetto, control of its educational institutions, and amassing more political power in the central city. Integration is irrelevant to such thinking. There are whites who are supportive of the black quest for self-development and greater control over central city resources, some seeing this as a genuine need of blacks, others seeing it as a way of maintaining white distance from blacks." Mary Brooks, "Exclusionary Zoning," *Planning Advisory Service Report Z54,* (Chicago: American Society of Planning Officials, 1970), p. 39.

7. Wallace F. Smith, "Filtering and Neighborhood Change," in *Economics and Housing,* Michael Stegman, ed. (Cambridge: MIT Press, 1970), p. 70–72.

8. See Siegan's discussion of land market competition and antitrust laws in "Chapter 6: Zoning Reduces Competition," *Land Use Without Zoning* (Lexington, Mass.: Lexington Books, 1972), pp. 135–140.

9. Kenneth J. Arrow, *Social Choice and Individual Values* (New York: John Wiley and Sons, 1951).

10. Peter H. Weiner, "The Constitutionality of Local Zoning," *Land Use Con-*

trols Quarterly, ASPO–UCLA student article competition, (American Society of Planning Officials: Chicago, 1970), Vol. 4, No. 4, p. 55, as abstracted from Vol. 79 Yale Law Journal, p. 896 (1970). This important phenomenon was, of course, identified nearly two decades ago by Norman Williams and others, but none elaborated this precise argument in quite the detail or so deliberately for an explicit constitutional attack on zoning as that contained in Mr. Weiner's article.

11. In recognition of these and related hardships, a bill titled "Workers' Residential Rights Act," which would provide rights of residential access to workers who wish to live where they work, was submitted to the State of Illinois General Assembly. Harold Washington, et al, "Workers' Residential Rights Act," House Bill 4566, *1972 Final Legislative Synopsis and Digest* (Springfield: Legislative Reference Bureau, 1973), p. 1139.

12. See Morton Lustig, Janet R. Pack, Edward M. Bergman, Kent Eklund, and Arnold Goldstein, *"Standards For Housing in Suburban Communities Based on Zoning for Work,"* (Philadelphia: Fels Center of Government, University of Pennsylvania, 1972), Chap. V–A, for one solution to the methodological difficulties inherent in a standard based upon equalized journeys to work.

13. See Julius Margolis, *Metropolitan Fiscal Disparities: Problems and Policies,* A Report to the Metropolitan Council of the Twin Cities Area (Philadelphia: Fels Center of Government, University of Pennsylvania, 1971).

14. See Walter Isard, *Location and Space Economy* (New York: John Wiley and Sons, 1966).

15. Daniel K. Mandelker, in a personal communication, reminded the author of a British approach to the sharing of fiscal resources. The Town Development Act of 1952 was designed to empower large cities to provide a "public dowry" for the workers and their families who were exported to newly developing areas which lacked essential public services. "Such financial help was to be provided as would be 'necessary to get the job going'. At the present time this consists of a housing subsidy and a 50 per cent grant towards the cost of main sewerage, sewage works and water works required for the development." J.B. Cullingworth, *Town and Country Planning in England and Wales,* (London: Allen and Unwin, 1970), p. 254–255.

16. Miami [Ohio] Regional Valley Planning Commission, *A Housing Plan for the Miami Valley Region—A Reprint* (Philadelphia: Housing Association of Delaware Valley, 1971).

17. The inability of analysts in social science research to remain totally neutral, or "value free," and the inadvisability of trying to do so is discussed by Martin Rein in "Social Policy Analysis as the Interpretation of Beliefs," *Journal of the American Institute of Planners,* Vol. XXXVII, No. 5, pp. 297–310.

18. President's Committee on Urban Housing, *A Decent Home,* (Washington: Government Printing Office, 1968), p. 13.

19. U.S., Bureau of Census, "Income in 1969 of Families and Persons in the United States," Series P–60, No. 75, Table 29 (Washington: Government Printing Office, 1970).
20. Note that, as presently formulated, the standard requires one affordable housing unit per household with a working head. This represents a refinement over other more mechanical formulas suggested in the past, which vaguely required a house per worker, a equation which was apparently oblivious to multiple-worker households and other factors affecting household composition and labor force participation.
21. This refinement is further recognition of the need to avoid unduly simple or mechanical formulas of the sort mentioned in the preceding footnote. More particularly, it assumes that municipalities require a degree of discretion as to their mix of uses and control over types of development, so long as it does not constitute an exclusionary practice.
22. Definition of preclude in G & C Merriam Co., *Webster's Third New International Dictionary of The English Language* Springfield, Mass.: 1964), p. 1785.

Part II

Analyzing Exclusionary Zoning Ordinances

Chapter Four

Looking at Suburban Zoning Ordinances

A unique feature of *Hawkins* is that the plaintiffs effectively used
statistical evidence to impress upon the court the gravity of disparity
[in the provision of municipal services] . . . . Yet, the proponents of
the conclusion reached in Hawkins might be misled by the apparent
simplicity of the statistical evidence approach [sufficient for a small,
well-segregated municipality like Shaw, Mississippi, in the *Hawkins*
case]. Attempts to apply *Hawkins'* procedure to a large city may
well prove more than a complainant bargained for. The expense of
compilation alone is bound to discourage others who seek a similar
remedy.[1]

The first part of this volume sought to sketch the dimensions of exclusionary
zoning as it is generally conceived and to offer a more precise rendering of a
performance standard by which particular instances of exclusionary zoning
might be so judged. That performance standard would require zoning ordinances
to allow for comparable mixes of worker household incomes and the prices and
rents of available housing. However, before one can safely proceed with the
comparisons sanctioned by this performance standard, careful analysis of an
ordinance's provisions must be undertaken to estimate reliably and efficiently
the income, price and rent data imbedded in a locality's zoning. Following the
caveats surrounding the use of statistics in *Hawkins,* care must be taken to
assure that the mode of analysis used to elicit data from the narrative, figures
and maps typically found in zoning ordinances are applicable economically
and uniformly to the codes of municipalities which may vary considerably in
size and in potential for exclusion. Accordingly, a number of analytic procedures
were developed in Chapters 5 and 6 which (1) extract raw, quantified land use
relationships from the ordinances, and (2) make use of simplified algorithms
and secondary data materials, readily available for most metropolitan areas,
which convert the raw, land use relationships into implicit income, price and
rent structures. To ensure that the analytic procedures are uniformly applicable

to different types of suburban ordinance, a sample of zoning ordinance in six developing townships was used to devise the analysis.

Zoning ordinances of six developing townships in Delaware County, Pennsylvania, a county in the southwest corner of the Philadelphia SMSA, were selected for two purposes. First, a sample of several townships was deemed necessary to capture a variety of zoning ordinances in terms of their logical construction and range of provisions. It is well known that, in general, zoning ordinances have evolved considerably over the past fifty years, but particular townships currently enforce ordinances of differing vingages—a fact which further necessitates examining a variety of ordinances so that analytic procedures may be devised to elicit data uniformly applicable to the standard. Second, a sample of developing townships is also desirable to ensure that the analytic techniques are designed to handle various mixes of employment generating uses, as well as residential uses. The reliability of techniques which are capable of extracting the income, price and rent data from the ordinances of townships with varying modes of potential development is thereby enhanced.

The actual sample of townships chosen was based on criteria which assured a cross section of developing townships at various points in their historical development and potential future development. These criteria are: 1960 to 1970 growth in households, population, and population density, as compared with SMSA and county growth, and gross capacity for future growth.[2] The townships of Aston, Birmingham, Concord, Edgmont, Middletown and Thornbury meet the criteria as stated. The zoning provisions of these six townships pose a variety of complex, technical difficulties which foster the development of analytic procedures sufficiently sensitive to estimate the underlying data which will eventually allow us to discern the real—as opposed to apparent—differences in exclusion of the zoning ordinances under examination.

It would seem prudent at this time to set an empirical stage for the analytic chapters which will follow. To that end, a cursory view of the major land use provisions found within each of the six townships' zoning ordinances is provided in Table 4-1.

It can be seen in this table that all allow commercial uses within their boundaries and that all but one of the townships allow some form of industrial development. However, the ratio of land area zoned for residential use to land area zoned for nonresidential use varies dramatically from a low of about 2.5:1 to over 50:1. Four of the townships, though, cluster about 11:1. On the surface, one might be tempted to speculate that Aston Township is more likely to be engaged in fiscally motivated zoning, but the township may consider itself situated in a location that heavily favors nonresidential use. Firm conclusions about the presence of exclusion in Aston, or in any of the other townships, cannot, of course, be reached until household incomes and the prices

Table 4-1. Major Land Uses of Township Zoning Ordinances

Use by Township	Area Devoted to Uses (sq. mi.)					
	Resi-dential	Com-mercial	Industrial	Other	All	$R \div (C + I)$*
Aston	4.25	0.39	1.32	0.00	5.90	2.49
Birmingham	7.74	0.56	0.19	0.35	8.84	10.32
Concord	12.56	0.78	0.61	0.00	13.78	9.04
Edgmont	5.71	0.11	0.00	3.92	9.74	51.91
Middletown	12.50	0.20	0.81	0.39	13.43	12.38
Thornbury	8.57	0.04	0.59	0.00	9.16	13.60

Source: Calculated From Township Zoning Ordinances

*$[R \div (C + I)]$ is the ratio of residential to commercial and industrial uses.

and rents of housing that are implicit in the zoning ordinances have been extracted.

In confining the analysis only to the townships' potential development as allowed by their zoning, we make the implicit assumption that existing development accords with the present zoning ordinance. If the existing uses, and intensities of use, on the developed portions of a township's land area are far different than that allowed by the present ordinance, then the relationships derived from a township's zoning code might indicate far more or less exclusion than could reasonably be expected in toto. Our assumption is probably quite sound for virtually undeveloped townships such as Thornbury and Edgmont, but less sound for the more fully developed townships. One could, of course, further confine the analysis to only those undeveloped land areas which are subject to the ordinance's provisions and then compare the exclusion attributable to the ordinance with the observable exclusion inherent in existing development patterns. The relatively straightforward task of ascertaining current degrees of exclusion on developed land need not concern us here. While it is clear that current patterns of exclusion must be identified for remedial actions to proceed, remedial actions are inherently ineffective and deficient over the long term, due to the long, built-in lags which precede recognition, response and corrective measures. Those portions of metropolitan areas which are substantially developed at present will doubtless require remedial action, but it is our position that the opportunity should be seized to mitigate future exclusionary development that is likely to arise from present zoning practices of minor civil divisions in which the bulk of all urban development will occur by the end of this century.[3]

We also take the zoning ordinance to represent the current position of each township with regard to its development policy, and assume that the township is accountable for any exclusion thereby engendered. Accordingly, it follows that exclusionary zoning will be ascertained without reference to municipal intent or strategy, that is, whether exclusion is deliberate or merely a useful, incidental tactic to employ in a township's overall development decision processes.[4] Since, as any student of land use planning or zoning well knows, "zoning is merely a tool of planning,"[5] why, then, must a particular ordinance at any given period of time contain nonexclusionary provisions when the long-range plan upon which it is based is itself nonexclusionary? First, long-range plans, exclusionary or otherwise, are no assurance that development can be properly guided by an interim ordinance. Since a given ordinance, although interim in total calendar time, may be in effect at a time of intense development pressure, the ordinance might well structure the bulk of development despite the presence of the long-range development plan. On the other hand, an ordinance may be in effect during the *only* period of development activity and, while structuring only a small proportion of developable land, effectively replace the plan which envisioned much more total development over a longer period of time. The presence of a plan as a guide to enacting zoning ordinances which are designed to carry out the plan cannot anticipate the future thrust and staging of development, an event which often dissolves the tool relationship of zoning to planning. However, even if it were possible to devise a set of zoning ordinances which could faithfully guide development in accordance with a comprehensive plan, there is no sound reasoning by which an interim exclusionary ordinance can be justified. Nonexclusionary zoning, as technically defined in Chapter 3, is based upon functional relationships between employment generating uses and residential uses of land. While it is quite true that development of each of these uses may take place at varying rates, the timing of which may require a rather sensitive and adjustable system of land use guidance controls,[6] the mere fact that the pace of potential development could itself result in a dysfunctional relationship does not justify institutionalizing that dysfunction in the zoning ordinance. In short, every township zoning ordinance, and its amendments, should allow for nonexclusionary mixes of work and residence throughout the period of urbanization.[7] This stricture also applies to the modifying effects of variances, special use permits, and special exceptions which riddle contemporary zoning administration.[8] It might, in fact, be argued that the tactics employed by both townships and developers [9] which result in deviations from the original ordinance would become stabilized were nonexclusion to be strictly enforced.

In summary, we have argued that evidence of exclusion is best identified by systematically analyzing the zoning ordinances of a sample of developing townships. We further argue that the current zoning ordinance of a township is its most appropriate development policy statement, and that such policy must be continuously nonexclusionary during the period of rapid metropolitan growth now under way to avoid exclusionary development patterns and the need for painful, ineffective remedies later on. In the following two chapters we shall examine in great detail the zoning ordinances of six townships, so as to estimate the spectrum of household incomes and housing prices or rents implicit in the provisions of these ordinances.[10]

NOTES

1. R. Dennis Anderson, "Toward the Equalization of Municipal Services: Variations on a Theme by *Hawkins," Journal of Urban Law,* Vol. 50, No. 2, November 1972, pp. 187–88.
2. See Appendix A for detailed description of how these criteria were applied in order to choose the six townships for study.
3. Projected growth has been estimated somewhere between 55 percent to 145 percent of the urban development existing in 1960. For a discussion of the arguments underlying these diverse growth rates, see Anthony Downs, *Urban Problems and Prospects* (Chicago: Markham, 1970), pp. 6–10.
4. Some political economists have explained exclusionary behavior as the logical consequence of individuals who "rationally" seek homogenous communities so as to optimize their access to and costs of public service packages. One of them more reasoned attacks on such legitimating rationalizations for exclusionary behavior is Peter G. Brown, "Cities and Suburbs: The Exploitation Hypothesis," *Maryland Law Forum,* Vol. II, 1972, p. 128–134
5. Since this issue is so thoroughly discussed in both zoning and land use planning literature, there is little point in rehearsing at length the many positions taken. Useful overviews may be found in Richard F. Babcock, *The Zoning Game* (Madison: University of Wisconsin Press, 1966), pp. 120–125; Mandelker, *The Zoning Dilemma* (New York: Bobbs-Merrill, 1971), pp. 57–63; American Society of Planning Officials, *Problems of Zoning and Land Use Regulation* (Washington: National Commission on Urban Problems, 1968), pp. 28–30.
6. David G. Heeter, "Toward a More Effective System for Guiding the Use of Land," *Zoning Is Planning,* C.W. Forest, R.K. Joy, eds. (Urbana–Champaign, Ill.: Bureau of Community Planning, University of Illinois, 1969), pp. 56–70.
7. As Herbert Franklin has similarly argued, "A local development timing ordinance does not respond to regional housing needs unless, at a minimum, it can be shown that the development plan encourages the provision of housing for the number of employees with existing or anticipated jobs in the jurisdiction. . . .", *Controlling Urban Growth–But For Whom: The Social Impact of Development Timing Controls As Illustrated By The Ordinance of Ramapo, New York* (Washington: Metropolitan Housing Program, Potomac Institute, Inc.) 1973 prepublication draft, p. 47.

8. For a comprehensive review of these and related problems, see *Problems of Zoning and Land Use Regulation*, pp. 24–51.

9. Municipal strategies have been essentially summarized as three: "When in doubt, let 'em do it," "Pretend that you know best," and "Wait till you see what happens." Any one of these options might be employed at certain points in time, depending upon the technical competence and sophistication of local development officials, the pressures for development, and the level of uncertainty about potential types of development. For an elaboration of these strategy options, see Task Force on Land Use and Urban Growth, *The Use of Land: A Citizens' Guide to Urban Growth,* A Task Force Report by the Rockefeller Brothers Fund (New York: Thomas A. Crowell), 1973 prepublication copy, pp. 183–192. In responding to such a variety of municipal postures and the underlying layers of supporting public opinion, developers have devised a series of counter strategies. In particular, see Clan Crawford, Jr., *Strategies and Tactics in Municipal Zoning* (Englewood Cliffs, N.J.: Prentice-Hall, 1969), and Malcolm D. Rivkin, "Diplomacy Planning: What It Is," *Urban Land,* Vol. 32, No. 4, April 1973, pp. 4–9.

10. It bears repeating that we are *not* projecting or predicting future patterns of employment and residence, but rather that we wish to assess the joint effects of employment and housing configurations were they to develop precisely in accordance with a sample of zoning ordinances on the Philadelphia SMSA suburbanizing fringe. For an excellent overview of a methodology which *does* project both employment and residential growth, consult Franklin J. James and James W. Hughes, *Economic Growth and Residential Patterns: A Methodological Investigation,* (New Brunswick, N.J.: Center for Urban and Policy Research, 1972).

Chapter Five

Zoning Ordinances and Housing Prices in Suburban Townships

> The popularity of the homogeneity concept is indicated by the results of a questionnaire administered in 1961 to a random sample of Philadelphia suburbanites. In answer to the question "Do you favor using zoning laws to keep out of your community the type of people who usually build cheaper houses on smaller lots?" only 14 of 116 respondents replied "No."[1]

This is the first of two essentially methodological chapters, each of which is designed primarily to demonstrate how one might convert the narrative of a zoning ordinance into a set of quantifiable relationships. The task at hand in this chapter is to determine measurable dimensions of the probable prices and rents of housing which lie imbedded within zoning ordinances.

ZONING ORDINANCE DATA

Since the thrust of the inquiry is to relate residential zoning to housing prices, all zoning factors are examined which affect the size of dwelling units, land area and types of residential uses permitted in the townships under study. The following factors, all contained in the zoning ordinances, were examined:

1. Districts permitting residential use, including commercial districts allowing residences of any kind.
2. Residential uses permitted, by district; this category contains the types of dwelling unit allowed in each residential district.
3. Minimum lot size permitted, by residential district and dwelling type, if relevant, expressed in acres or square feet.
4. Maximum building coverage, as a percent of total lot.
5. Front yard minimum depth requirements, in feet.

6. Side yard minimum width requirement, in feet. Some ordinances list both individual side yard and aggregate size yard width minimums.
7. Rear yard minimum depth requirements, in feet.
8. Minimum street frontage of lot, in feet.
9. Maximum height permitted, if any, in feet or number of stories.

All of the above are standard items which most zoning ordinances contain and which were found in the zoning ordinances of the six study townships.[2]

The purposes for which the residential zoning information was collected were to determine the amount and types of housing that could be developed in the townships under study, if the townships became completely developed under the zoning regulations in force as of May, 1971. The information gathered from the zoning ordinances in the six townships is briefly summarized here to suggest the range of housing types and lot sizes permitted.

Only one township of the six permits other than single-family detached dwellings in a nonapartment residential zone. That municipality permits only single-family semi-detached housing, in addition to detached dwellings. All six townships have provisions for at least two districts restricted to single-family dwellings, the main difference between the two being the minimum required lot size. The smallest of the minimum lot area requirements occurs in one of Edgmont's three residential districts, which requires 4,775 square feet (hereafter sq. ft.), or approximately one-eighth acre.[3] The next largest is 10,000 sq. ft., slightly under one-quarter acre. The smallest of the townships' "premium" or large-lot residence districts is in Aston where the minimum lot is 20,000 sq. ft., or one-half acre. The largest minimum lot requirements are two-acre districts, which are in three of the six townships.

The largest and smallest minimum lot requirements for single-family dwellings in each township are:

Township	Largest	Smallest
Aston	20,000 sq. ft. (approx. 1/2 acre)	10,000 sq. ft. (approx. 1/4 acre)
Birmingham	2 acres	1 acre
Concord	1 acre	15,000 sq. ft. (approx. 1/3 acre)
Edgmont	60,000 sq. ft. (approx. 1-1/2 acre)	4,775 sq. ft. (approx. 1/8 acre)
Middletown	80,000 sq. ft. (approx. 2 acres)	20,000 sq. ft. (approx. 1/2 acre)
Thornbury	2 acres	60,000 sq. ft. (approx. 1-1/2 acre)

The widest range of lot sizes and the lowest specified minimum lot size are offered in Edgmont. Lots of one acre or more are allowed in most of the residential districts, while 5,000 sq. ft. is approximately the smallest lot size permissible for single-family dwellings in the area, and it is available in only one township of the six.

Virtually all single-family residential districts in the six townships limit development to detached dwellings. For example, only Middletown allows single-family semi-detached housing, with a minimum lot of 5,000 sq. ft. per family. Also, only Middletown allows row houses; the other municipalities forbid them in the general provisions of their ordinances, and Middletown's row housing provisions are contained in a Planned Residential Development (PRD) amendment only recently (1970) passed that applies to the same residential district in which semidetached single-family houses are allowed. The PRD "rows" are limited to groupings of six units, arranged more in a cluster than in a linear row. The minimum size of each lot is 4,000 sq. ft.

Four of the six townships allow multiple dwellings and/or apartments, in addition to single-family dwellings, but only in commercial districts.[4] These are Middletown, Edgmont, Aston and Concord Townships. Apartments are permitted by special exception in the commercial districts of Edgmont and Aston. Three townships, Middletown, Birmingham and Concord, have also created apartment districts. The latter two created these zones for a particular developer.

Thus far, the types of residential development or housing units allowed by zoning ordinances, and the permitted densities of housing in specified districts, designated by minimum lot sizes per unit, have been mentioned. The remaining piece of data from the ordinances which is needed to analyze the number of housing units and the distribution of housing costs is the maximum allowable number of each type of housing unit. To derive the maximum number of units by type and density in each township's residential district, one must divide the total net available land area in a residential district by the minimum lot size of the units allowed in that district. First, however, the gross land area of each residential district must be known. To determine the gross land area of each district, it is necessary to measure the zoning maps using a planimeter, since this information is seldom given either in the zoning ordinances or on the maps. Measurements completed, net land area available for residential development can be found by deducting a certain percentage for streets and other nonsite uses from the gross land area. A general rule of thumb used by developers for converting raw land parcels into building lots is about 0.80 to 0.90.[5]

The number of dwellings that can be developed is calculated by dividing the net residential land area by the minimum allowed lot size in each use district as given in the zoning ordinance. Apartment developments also have an implicit amount of site area per apartment unit. It is possible to ascribe a minimum lot per apartment, even though the zoning ordinance does not present the information in precisely that form. Middletown, for example, prescribes that "total land area for each family dwelling unit shall not be less than the following:

1. Dwelling with 1 bedroom—3,500 sq. ft.
2. Dwelling with 2 bedrooms—4,500 sq. ft.
3. Dwelling with 3 bedrooms—6,000 sq. ft."

An average of 4,500 sq. ft. per unit was chosen based on the prevalence of two-bedroom apartments found to exist in the five townships. Table 5-1 summarizes the several stages through which the type of housing allowed in each of the township's residential districts, and the total land area in the district, are translated into the maximum potential number of housing units allowed.

While the format of Table 5-1 clarifies the calculation procedures and facilitates subsequent analyses, it also tends to somewhat obscure the demonstrable and overwhelming preponderance of large-lot, single-family residential zoning. When each township's housing units are regrouped according to minimum lot size categories, the full impact of large-lot zoning can be better appreciated. Table 5-2 portrays the number and proportion of township housing units by lot size category and gross land area.

It is only too clear where this potential inventory of housing units will likely rest on the price and rent spectrum.[6] The two largest minimum lot size categories (three-quarter acre lots or greater) account for 87 percent of all residentially zoned land in townships and about 54 percent of their potential units. Conversely, less than 14 percent of all township land zoned for residential use is devoted to small-lot or multi-family housing in the highest density (one-quarter acre lots or smaller) categories which produce about 27 percent of all housing units.[7]

However, rather than speculate further about probable housing prices, additional analysis is necessary as this data only identifies housing units in terms of their physical or structural characteristics, whereas housing prices or rents are typically defined in terms of both tenure and structure.

STRUCTURE TYPE AND TENURE IN
RESIDENTIAL ZONING DISTRICTS

Standardizing residential zoning provisions in a system of lot size categories only provides one with uniform information about the physical or structural characteristics of a potential housing stock. Knowledge about how the stock is likely to be occupied, i.e., about the tenure-structure linkages, necessary so as to estimate the supply characteristics which households may face in a hypothetical housing market. The requirements of worker households,[8] at each income level, for rental and owner-occupied units will be estimated in subsequent chapters. Accordingly, the pool of housing units in structure of each type allowed within residential zoning districts must now be split into rental or owner sectors. It would be erroneous to consider all single-family units as owner-occupied and to consider multi-family units as only renter-occupied. Condominiums and cooperatives are not identifiable in zoning

Table 5-1. Summary of Residential Zoning Provisions for Six Developing Townships, 1971

District	Gross Land Area (sq. ft.)		Net Land Area (sq. ft.)	Minimum Lot (sq. ft. per dwelling)	Potential Number of Dwelling Units
Aston					
(1) R–A	63,317,374	0.84	53,186,594	20,000	2,659
(1) R–A1	2,651,022	0.84	2,226,858	11,250	20
(1) R–B	52,485,722	0.84	44,088,007	10,000	4,409
					7,088
Birmingham					
(2) R–1	200,606,044	0.88	176,533,319	87,100	2,027
(2) R–2	14,054,133	0.86	12,086,554	43,560	277
(2) R–A	874,467	0.80	699,573	3,630	192
					2,497
Concord					
(3) R–1	44,923,428	0.86	38,634,148	43,560	887
(3) R–2	226,560,247	0.86	194,841,812	43,560	4,473
(3) R–3	13,101,549	0.84	11,005,301	15,000	734
(3) R–2D	62,516,244	0.86	53,763,970	43,560	1,234
(3) R–A	1,953,056	0.80	1,562,444	3,000	521
(3) R–AH	816,244	0.80	652,995	1,200	544
					8,393
Edgmont					
(4) R–A	150,917,078	0.88	132,807,029	60,000	2,213
(4) R–B	7,586,065	0.86	6,524,016	9,270	704
(4) R–C	525,577	0.84	441,485	4,780	92
					3,009
Middletown					
(5) R–1A	73,417,509	0.88	64,607,408	80,000	808
(5) R–1	178,672,526	0.86	153,658,372	40,000	3,841
(5) R–2	76,725,011	0.84	64,449,009	20,000	3,222
(5) R–3	8,212,501	0.84	6,898,501	10,000	690
(5) R–4	5,534,999	0.80	4,427,999	5,000	886
(5) R–4A	3,082,501	0.80	2,466,001	5,000	493
(5) R–A	2,677,502	0.80	2,142,002	4,500	476
					10,416
Thornbury					
(6) RA	210,257,646	0.88	185,026,729	87,100	2,124
(6) RB	21,509,505	0.88	18,928,364	60,000	315
(6) QAB	6,929,838	0.25	1,732,459	87,120	20
					2,459

ordinances, nor is it possible to distinguish, a priori, garden apartments from townhouses strictly on physical and structural characteristics which are permitted. These newer tenure-structure relationships add to the current confusion surrounding tenure-structure uncertainties as expressed in widely varying proportions of owner- vs. renter-occupancy in single-family units among municipalities at a point in time, or during successive periods of time, for individual municipalities.

Table 5-2.   Minimum Lot Size Categories by Gross Land Area, Number of Housing Units and Township, 1971

Township Districts by Minimum Lot Size Category (Sq. ft.)	Gross Land Area (Sq. ft.)	Percent	Housing Units	
			Number	Percent
60,000–87,120				
(2) R–1	200,606,045		2027	
(4) R–A	150,917,079		2213	
(5) R–1A	73,417,509		808	
(6) RA, RB, QAB	238,691,990		2459	
All	663,632,623	36.2	7507	22.2
30,000–43,560				
(2) R–2	14,054,133		277	
(3) R–1, R–2, R–2D	738,999,920		6594	
(5) R–I	178,672,526		3841	
All	931,726,579	50.8	10712	31.6
15,000–20,000				
(1) R–A	63,317,374		2659	
(3) R–3	13,101,549		734	
(5) R–2	76,725,011		3222	
All	153,143,934	8.3	6615	19.5
9,270–11,250				
(1) RA–1, RB	55,136,745		4429	
(4) RB	7,586,065		704	
(5) R–s	8,212,502		690	
All	70,935,312	3.9	5823	17.2
1,200–5,000				
(2) R–A	874,467		193	
(3) R–A, R–AH	2,769,301		1065	
(4) R–C	525,578		92	
(5) R–4, R–4A, R–A	11,295,004		1855	
All	15,464,350	9.8	3205	9.5
Total	1,834,902,798	100.0	33862	100.0

The potential stock of each township must be allocated realistically to tenure categories on a basis of known structure-tenure relationships. Once this is done, prices and rentals can be assigned to tenure categories and, eventually, the resultant housing expenses compared with the incomes of households having known tenure preferences. The present task requires only that a reasonable procedure be devised for converting a known profile of structure types into a probable profile of tenure categories. The U.S. Census of Housing cross tabulates renter and owner tenure characteristics with one unit and two or more unit structures, and the census structure classification is comparable to single- and multi-family residential zoning categories. In 1970, the structure-tenure relationship for existing housing in all six suburban townships showed: (1) between 97 and 99 percent of all owned units were single-family; (2) between 43 and 87 percent of all rental units were also single-family.[9] It was decided that the six-township aggregate structure-tenure relationship would be applied to each township since peculiarities within an individual township—due to its unique stage of development which might not hold over time—would tend to be absorbed in the total relationship.[10] Further, the six-township relationship is not significantly different from that observed for individual townships, and it may be somewhat more representative of tenure-structure characteristics in average developing fringe townships (see Table 5–3).

In principle, for every 100 single-family unit allowed in zoning codes, one might expect that approximately nine would be rental stock. Similarly, 24 of every 100 multi-family units might be owned housing. However, since there is a far greater likelihood of a single-family dwelling unit on a small- to medium-size lot in the $15,000 to $30,000 price range being rented than the more expensive housing on acre lots or larger, the nine percent rental factor was arbitrarily only applied to single-family houses on lots of 20,000 sq. ft. or less. Conversely, the homeownership rate of 24 percent was applied only to multi-family housing with average lot sizes of 3,000 sq. ft. per dwelling unit on the site, a decision rule which allocated all the units in the sole high-rise apartment zone exclusively to the rental tenure category.

Some might argue that these two simplifying assumptions are not sufficiently supported by evidence. The obvious response is: (1) assumptions that costly single-family homes are seldom part of rental inventories or that high-rise apartments are seldom owned seem quite reasonable in the absence of definitive data, and (2) the only other alternative is to assume all single-family housing is owned and all multi-family housing is rented, both assumptions being demonstrably false.

One must then assign the homeownership rate to the number of units in each structure and lot-size class, as per the above discussion. The results which translate housing units by structure into housing units by tenure are found in Table 5–4. As one might expect, the probable tenure opportunities

Table 5–3. Tenure and Structure Type of Existing Housing Units in the Six Developing Townships, Delaware County, Pennsylvania, 1970

Tenure		One	Percent	Two or more	Percent	All	Percent
		Units in Structure					
Own	Number	7,777	98.1	151	1.9	7,928	100.0
	Percent	90.0		24.0		86.4	
Rent	Number	774	61.9	477	38.1	1,251	100.0
	Percent	9.1		76.0		13.6	
All	Number	8,551	93.2	628	6.8	9,179	100.0
	Percent	100.0		100.0		100.0	

Table 5-4.   Housing Units in Delaware County, Pennsylvania Township Residential Districts by Minimum Lot Size and Tenure, 1971

Township and Residence Zone	Minimum Lot Size	Total Units	Percent Owned	Rented Units	Owned Units
Aston					
(1) R-A	20,000	2,659	90.9	242	2,417
(1) R-A1, R-B	10,000–				
	11,500	4,429	90.9	403	4,026
		7,088	90.9	645	6,443
Birmingham					
(2) R-1	87,100	2,027	100.0	0	2,027
(2) R-2	43,560	277	100.0	0	277
(2) R-A	3,630	193	24.0	147	46
		2,497	95.0	147	2,350
Concord					
(3) R-1, R-2, R-2D	43,560	6,594	100.0	0	6,594
(3) R-3	15,000	734	90.9	67	667
(3) R-A	3,000	521	24.0	396	125
(3) R-AH	1,200	544	0.0	544	0
		8,393	88.0	1,007	7,386
Edgmont					
(4) R-A	60,000	2,213	100.0	0	2,213
(4) R-B	9,270	704	90.9	64	640
(4) R-C	4,775	92	90.9	8	84
		3,009	97.6	72	2,937
Middletown					
(5) R-1A	80,000	808	100.0	0	808
(5) R-1	40,000	3,841	100.0	0	3,841
(5) R-2	20,000	3,222	90.9	293	2,929
(5) R-3	10,000	690	90.9	63	627
(5) R-4, R4-A	5,000	1,379	90.9	125	1,254
(5) R-A	4,500	476	24.0	362	114
		10,416	91.9	843	9,573
Thornbury					
(6) RA, RB, QAB	60,000–				
	87,120	2,459	100.0	0	2,459
All	–	33,862	92.0	2,714	3,148

are heavily weighted in the direction of ownership, ranging from 88 to 100 percent. The average ownership rate for all the township's zoned housing is 92 percent, as compared with the average ownership rate of 86 percent for the township's existing housing. The difference between the two ownership rates is due primarily to the extraordinarily high proportion of undeveloped land zoned for housing units which are restricted to three-quarter acre lots and larger.

PRICE AND RENT OF HOUSING UNITS

It has become disappointingly obvious to many that house prices and rents cannot be lowered drastically by any single improvement in the realm of housing production, financing or sales. And it has been convincingly demonstrated that if subdivision regulations and building codes (construction, plumbing and electrical) were completely rewritten to remove the "fat", the final cost of a given housing type would not plummet. Operation Breakthrough,[11] the official inquiry into volume and cost bottlenecks of national housing production, uncovered no key area in which significant savings were possible. Moreover, unless a very sophisticated land market model could demonstrate that per-unit land costs would drop appreciably due to a greater proportion of undeveloped land area being devoted to an increased number of higher-density housing units, very little could be expected, despite optimistic predictions, from changes in zoning on per-unit land costs and house prices. However, this tentative conclusion should not mislead one into thinking that zoning has a benign effect upon new housing prices and rents. Even if it is acknowledged that cost reductions would be modest for the land and structure components of housing, significant cost reductions could be realized simply by altering zoning codes to allow a different mix of housing components, one which is affordable to a much larger segment of the population. In particular, row houses or efficiently designed "planned unit development" housing, at about 10 units per acre, would greatly broaden the market for new homes in some communities. They could be sold for about $20,000–25,000, whereas a single-family detached house on one acre could not sell in 1970 for less than $35,000–40,000. Assuming families can afford 25 percent of their incomes for housing, and that a gross housing expense multiplier of 7.0 accurately converts the purchase price of a new home into annual carrying costs,[12] a household income of $20,000 (received by only 13 percent of households whose head works in the six townships) would be necessary to buy the one acre single-family structure, and a household income of $11,400 (received by about 48 percent of worker households in the six townships) would suffice for the row house. This simple example demonstrates the sizable potential direct effect zoning can have on residential prices and household access. In addition, to the extent that less restrictive zoning expands as well as redirects new construction, filtering and favorable land market effects could well lower even further market prices and rents of the entire metropolitan housing inventory.

We must establish in this section of Chapter 5 the prices and rents of housing by the residential density categories, as found in zoning ordinances. Although other zoning requirements, such as front and side yard setbacks and frontage requirements can, conceivably, alter the cost of comparable units in a given density class, these "dimensional" requirements are functionally related to lot size, which is the single most important cost variable.[13] Whatever the lot size might be, the rents and prices of housing which are estimated for each residential zoning district should be the lowest possible, rather than typical or average prices and rents, for two reasons. First, the cost of housing due to the zoning restrictions per se must exclude potential residents, not some higher schedule of prices or rents due to preferences for larger houses, costlier construction, more equipment, etc. Second, by adhering firmly to the lowest possible prices and rents, one minimizes the chance of jeopardizing the potential for implementing the performance standard. If there are reasonable grounds to believe that the housing allowed by any given zoning ordinance was calculated as being more costly than necessary, few jurists, administrators or legislators would risk using the performance standard as a basis for reform of exclusionary zoning.

Price of Owner-Occupied Housing

The total number of potential owner-occupied, single-family dwelling units in each residential density class was determined earlier in the chapter by examining township zoning ordinances and Census of Housing data. The value of housing in each density class also must be determined so that the presence and magnitude of residential exclusion implied by the price configuration of each municipality's expected housing stock may be assessed.

There are three ways to determine the probable values of housing in various density classes: (1) synthetically calculate the component costs of each type of housing found in each density category and then aggregate total unit cost for a final sale price, (2) determine the local sales prices of each type of housing in each density category from area builders, or (3) determine the value of existing owner-occupied housing in each density category.

In estimating the cost of housing through synthetic component pricing, one must have sound knowledge about the styles and design of units which are generally preferred in the marketplace, and of local builder practice which varies from the norm, due to local material or labor economies, in the construction of preferred units. Once the type of unit is known, nationally derived indices of component costs[14] in per unit terms (e.g., costs per square foot of a single-story frame house on slab, etc.) would be adjusted to reflect regional cost factors of standard component construction. The total cost of all components represents structure costs only. To structure costs, one must also add the cost of developed lots of appropriate size, prices of which vary widely due to the unique locational advantages and market dynamics associated with raw land parcels. Because the information required is very great and difficult to localize, this approach was not used.

The second way of estimating prices of housing units is to examine the recent sales prices of housing by lot size. Prices of recently sold houses can be determined by examining public records. The sale value of housing in townships is entered in the Delaware County Assessor's Office, but the data are not useful because of lack of uniformity in recording the structure and lot size characteristics of units and because of the difficulties encountered in clerically separating the sale of newly constructed houses from all houses recently sold in the township. Although the State of Pennsylvania also maintains a record of all real property sales in somewhat more consistent detail for tax equalization purposes, the detail in these categories is not sufficient to distinguish housing units built on different lot sizes; equally bad, newly constructed units are usually not included in the state's record if an assessment has not been made by the time the initial purchaser first receives title to the property. This, obviously, excludes some unknown proportion of recently constructed housing which is not resold and recorded within a very short span of time. The Federal Housing Administration also collects data on the price of houses sold with FHA Section 203 mortgage guarantees. While these data are occasionally assembled and released in the detail required here,[15] the Philadelphia Office of FHA stated that it had not disaggregated Philadelphia SMSA data in suitable detail, which, unfortunately, effectively eliminated this source from further consideration. Finally, recent sales data also may be found by asking builders to estimate the minimum sales price of housing which they currently produce on lots that conform with given residential densities. Four large-scale builders active in Delaware County were asked to estimate the minimum selling prices of their houses. The results are shown in Table 5-5.

The sample is disappointingly small with regard to the range of densities covered and, to a lesser extent, in terms of the possible structure types, particularly townhouses and semi-detached or twin units. But the sample is necessarily deficient simply because local builders seldom build houses of this type or density as they are increasingly, or completely, unable to find tracts of open land in developing suburban communities zoned for single-family semidetached, row and townhouse structures—or even for detached single-family structures at high densities, i.e., on one-eighth to one-quarter acre lots. Builder estimates are potentially very valuable because they are based upon

Table 5-5. Minimum Prices of New Housing in Delaware County by Density and Type of Housing, 1971

House Type	Density (Houses per Acre)	Structure Costs ($)	Land Costs ($)	Selling Price ($)
Row	19	–	–	19,900–20,000
PUD Type Plan	6	–	–	23,900
Detached	6	22,000	6,000	28,000
	2–3	28,950	6,000	34,950
	2	25,300	9,700	35,000–45,000

Source: Interview with builders Frank Facciolo, Edward Anters, Richard Kelley, and David Slott on October 25,1971, conducted by Morton Lustig and Kent Eklund of the Fels Center of Government Staff, University of Pennsylvania.

actual, firsthand experience. That value is seriously eroded, or possibly lost, when builders are asked to step outside the realm of their current experience and estimate "likely" prices of housing units of structure type and densities which, if zoning allowed, might be built in developing townships. In an attempt to round out the local builder sample, a survey of national builders conducted periodically by the National Association of Home Builders was examined. [16] The data presented are timely and appropriate, but they apply only to the nation or to very large geographic regions, e.g., the Middle Atlantic states. A preface to the study noted, however, that data for metropolitan areas could be made available at processing costs, upon request to the Home Builders' Staff economist; unfortunately, an inquiry made about Philadelphia SMSA or suburban county data met without success.[17]

A third way of estimating house prices is to obtain information directly from owners of recently constructed housing. The most comprehensive source of this sort is the 1970 Census of Housing. The Census Bureau records the year in which structures were built and the value of single-family houses, as estimated by the owner, located in relatively small geographic sections (blocks, enumeration districts, tracts) of minor civil divisions. By selecting those areas of Delaware County townships in which most owners describe their units as having been recently constructed, e.g., 1968 to 1970, one can derive a sample of newly built single-family houses. If the total number of houses is divided by the number of acres within each of the census data collection districts, classes of residential density may be derived for which house values are known. As with the other approaches, this one has a number of shortcomings. The most obvious problem is that census data are available only once a decade, which limits their usefulness during the intervening years, although the 1970 census is close enough to the period with which this study is concerned to be useful. Another problem has to do with the reliability of owner estimates of house age and value, both of which must be known to estimate prices of recently built houses. It is often claimed that census respondents tend to underestimate values to avoid tax reassessments or that they simply err in estimating the age of their house. However, since the most recently constructed housing is already assessed at the transaction price, thereby posing no imminent danger of reassessment, and the house's recent vintage is more likely to be known by its first or second owner, the underestimates of value and random estimates of age normally expected from all owners might not apply as fully, or at all, in the case of newer housing.

Although it was indicated above that residential density in terms of houses per net acre (or its reciprocal, average lot size per house) could be calculated, there is the possibility of misclassifying a district in terms of its actual density. If a census district is not completely developed, its gross area cannot be reduced by a percentage factor to arrive at the correct aggregate of all lot areas. Also, if the housing in a district is developed at several vastly different densities, it would be misleading to use the values recorded in that district as characteristic of the average density computed for the entire district. Special pains must be taken to adjust for the net developed land area in districts which are not completely developed and to "weed out" districts with widely varying lot sizes.

All of the approaches are necessarily deficient in their ability to estimate the prices of every kind of house in localities whose zoning allows only a small segment of the potential housing market. Since some residential uses are prohibited outright, there is no sure way of knowing housing prices of those residential uses in the absence of market transactions. Each approach takes as given the existing cost of land which is known to vary across municipalities due to its unique location or the total supply of land in a metropolitan area for each allowed residential use or the array of municipal services and taxes available within the municipality. Although the location "value" of land is relatively fixed, in trying to estimate the land costs for residential uses which are not currently allowed, one cannot assume that per unit land costs for currently allowed uses will remain stable. That is, in trying to estimate the hypothetical prices of certain houses in localities which do not now allow them, current market information is always deficient because final house prices are dependent upon land costs. Since the cost of land for each use is a function of current supply and demand and of the capitalized value of public wealth (fiscal capacity, municipal services) in private property, positing the presence of residential uses (i.e., by estimating prices for houses) which are not now allowed will alter the market conditions and land costs. Nothing short of an extremely sophisticated model of the land and housing market can resolve this basic flaw, but, at the very least, care should be exercised to observe the relative differences in land costs and final house prices across major sectors of a metropolitan housing market.

Of the three, actual sales data are doubtless more reliable, particularly those obtained from builders because they are active in the current market and require the most realistic and current information to remain competitive. Moreover, builder data is usually obtainable for specific sub-metropolitan areas which other sales data cannot always isolate. Ideally, one would prefer to have all sources, including price indices and census data, available to estimate house prices in a given circumstance but, more realistically, one or two must usually suffice.[18] The present study is no exception. The only available information is the builder data described earlier, and the census data which will require some manipulation to be useful. The remainder of this section of the chapter will deal with blending builder and census data to arrive at plausible estimates of house prices.

As mentioned earlier, the Census of Housing data require some screening and simple statistical manipulation to be useful. To begin, relatively fine-grained value distributions are available for enumeration districts (EDs) and block groups from the first count release of 1970 Census of Housing data in Delaware County. Homogeneous residential development patterns, as observed from aerial photographs, can be grouped according to residential density patterns. First, however, the gross residential density of EDs must be calculated. Because portions of an ED's total land area may be undeveloped, a tracing of the residentially developed portion, as shown on aerial photographs, is transferred to census maps of EDs and then measured by planimeter to accurately determine the gross residential density of an ED's developed land area. The range of observed gross residential densities is then converted to equivalent lot area sizes, which were found in the township zoning ordinances by use of the gross-to-net area conversion factors discussed earlier.

Allowed minimum lot sizes and observed gross residential densities are equated as follows:

Minimum Lot Size Allowed by Zoning Ordinances (sq. ft.)	*0-5,000*	*10,000- 11,250*	*15,000- 20,000*	*30,000- 43,560*	*60,000- 87,120*
Observed Gross Residential Density in EDs (Houses per Acre)	5.30 and greater	3.00- 5.29	1.55- 2.99	0.75- 1.54	0.74 and less

The value of housing in gross residential density categories can now be related to zoning categories. Values for 69 EDs, containing over 19,000 owner-occupied housing units in suburban Delaware County, were found by the procedure described above. However, the values do not take into account the units' size, condition, age or general quality. Nor does the value of units occupying lots of various average sizes reflect the least costly unit which might have been built. Table 5-6 portrays the net result of these deviations from the least costly new unit, derivations which are reflected by representation in the several intervals of a value distribution. The virtual lack of units having values of $10,000 or less, with little more than one percent of the houses on small lots (5,000 sq. ft. or less) being valued at less than $10,000, reflects the conscious effort to choose EDs which experienced recent growth on the developing fringe of Delaware County.[19] It is, therefore, likely that most of the older housing has been omitted, although one cannot be certain about the actual vintage. When compared with Delaware County's entire value distribution, of which the ED sample constitutes about one-sixth, markedly higher values for ED sample units are apparent, as shown in Table 5-7.

Even though the sample may represent fairly recent additions to Delaware County's inventory, there may well be a significant number of dwelling units in each gross residential density category with values which could not be reproduced in the current housing market. In particular, 17 percent of the units built on lots of 5,000 sq. ft. or smaller were valued at $15,000 or less, yet

Table 5-6. Value Distribution of Owner-Occupied Houses by Minimum Lot Area, Delaware County, Pennsylvania, 1970

Minimum Lot Area (sq. ft.)	Value of Owner-Occupied Units ($)								All Units	Median Value
	0–4,999	5,000–9,999	10,000–14,999	15,000–19,999	20,000–24,999	25,000–34,999	35,000–49,999	50,000 and Over		
0 5,000	4 / 0.10	47 / 1.21	599 / 15.43	1273 / 32.78	1217 / 31.34	704 / 18.13	34 / 0.87	4 / 0.10	3882 / 100.0	20,100
10,000 11,250	4 / 0.04	85 / 0.78	932 / 8.52	2242 / 20.49	3686 / 33.68	3304 / 30.19	574 / 5.25	116 / 1.06	10,943 / 100.0	23,000
15,000 20,000	0 / 0.00	6 / 0.19	50 / 1.62	245 / 7.97	784 / 25.52	1153 / 37.54	694 / 22.59	139 / 4.52	3070 / 100.0	28,900
30,000 43,560	0 / 0.00	7 / 0.53	18 / 1.36	25 / 1.88	85 / 6.40	317 / 23.87	499 / 37.58	377 / 28.39	1328 / 100.0	41,400
60,000 87,120	0 / 0.00	0 / 0.00	5 / 2.78	5 / 2.78	8 / 4.44	26 / 14.44	51 / 28.33	85 / 47.22	180 / 100.0	48,500
Total	8 / 0.00	145 / 0.01	1604 / 8.26	3790 / 19.53	5780 / 29.78	5504 / 28.36	1852 / 9.54	719 / 3.70	19,403 / 100.0	

*Range of lot sizes actually found in the zoning ordinances of the six sample townships.

Source: Census of Housing, first count enumeration, District or Block Group data used to derive this summary table. See Lustig, "Standards for Housing," Appendix 2–9, pp. 56–60 for census data in detail.

Table 5-7.   Value Distribution of Owner-Occupied Houses Located in ED Sample and Delaware County, Pennsylvania, 1970

House Values ($)	ED Sample (Percent)	Delaware County (Percent)
0–4,999	0.00	.64
5,000–9,999	0.01	8.26
10,000–14,999	8.26	26.76
15,000–19,999	19.53	25.15
20,000–24,999	29.78	15.62
25,000–34,999	38.36	14.39
35,000–50,000	9.54	6.34
50,000 and Over	3.70	2.81
	100.00	100.00
Total Houses	19,403	123,908
Median Value	$23,726	$17,850

builder interviews revealed that $20,000 was about the lowest price for which they could bring a unit to the market. The median value for all units in the same gross residential density class was calculated at about $20,100, virtually the selling price cited by builders. Similarly, the median value observed for houses on lots in the 30,000 to 43,560 sq. ft. range was about $41,400 as compared with $40,000, the midpoint of a $35,000 to $45,000 price span noted by builders. The fragmentary evidence available suggests that medians are a fair proxy for minimum sale prices.

Even though (1) the median values for each of the gross residential density categories increase in a logical, stepwise progression, and (2) median values show agreement with prices based on known builder practice, reliance upon medians alone as a surrogate for the price of housing across the residential density gradient might not be the best choice. Builder prices were estimated as of July 1971, which was nearly two years later than the 1969 earnings and income data used in the following chapter to determine the household income of workers. Also, three of the medians are sufficiently close to the dividing lines between value intervals so that taking only the interval in which the median falls entails the needless risk of accepting an interval which may be $5,000 to $10,000 too high or too low. Therefore, it was decided arbitrarily to use the interdecile range around the median (40th to 60th percentile) to adjust for the possibility of slightly lower 1969 prices and to control, somewhat, the possibility of extremely sensitive estimates of median values.[20] These procedures should not be interpreted as a direct claim that the 40th to 60th percentiles of census value distributions are highly correlated with the minimum sales price range of new construction. If the latter were known, or could be otherwise determined, recourse to census data would be unnecessary, although the correlations might themselves prove interesting. However, since only census materials are available for all density classes, and since a given segment of the value distribution for properties of central tendency either agrees with the fragmentary market evidence from builders or "behaves" much like theoretical market operations would suggest, the census value surrogate for the cost of new housing is a reasonable choice. Table 5–8 portrays the interdecile values for each density class category.

Table 5–8. Minimum Lot Sizes by Media and Interdecile House Values of Housing in Developing Townships, Delaware County, Pennsylvania, 1970

House Value ($)	Minimum Lot Sizes (Sq. ft.)				
	5,000	10,000 11,250	15,000 20,000	30,000 43,560	60,000 87,120
					(60) 52,600
50,000					
					48,500 (50)
45,000				(60) 45,400	
					43,200 (40)
40,000				41,400 (50)	
35,000				37,400 (40)	
30,000			(60) 31,600		
			28,900 (50)		
			26,300 (40)		
25,000			(60) 24,500		
			23,000		
20,000	(60) 21,700 20,100 (50) 18,500 (40)		(50) 21,500 (40)		

When the interdecile range is used to assign housing units to value categories, it can be seen from Table 5-9 that the full $15,000 to $50,000-plus value distribution (roughly the minimum-to-maximum cost range of a new house) is included.[21] However, that entire distribution will only be present in townships which also have the requisite range of gross residential classes in their zoning ordinances. The potential number of owner-occupied houses by gross residential or zoned lot size class is shown for each township in Table 5-4, which summarizes the earlier analysis of structure and tenure. Applying the value categories from Table 5-9 to those housing units, the value distribution of all owned units in each township is obtained as shown in Table 5-10.[22]

Only Aston and Thornbury Townships do not have potential housing in the lowest value category, although all of Aston's is in the second and third lowest categories, whereas Thornbury's is in the highest two categories. Birmingham and Edgmont Townships have potential housing in all but the $25,000 to $34,999 category, but unlike Edgmont, Birmingham's units are primarily concentrated in the two highest value categories. Finally, Concord and Middletown Townships both have housing in the four lowest value categories; where Concord has none in the highest, Middletown has $50,000-plus value housing but also has a more even representation in all value categories than does Concord. Without benefit of household income comparisons, it appears that Thornbury and Birmingham Townships are more likely to violate the worker-access standard than are the others but, again, further analysis will be needed before conclusive statements can be made.

Rents of Renter-Occupied Housing

Since both single- and multi-family structures share significant portions of the rental stock, rent schedules for two different kinds of structure must be developed which reflect housing expenses comparable with imputed values for owned housing. Rents for single-family houses will be calculated from the price of houses on the same size lots, as determined in the preceding section. The rents of multi-family structures will be estimated directly from census

Table 5-9. Percent Houses by Value Interval and Density Class in Delaware County, Pennsylvania, 1970

Gross Residential Density Class	$15,000– 19,999	$20,000– 24,999	$25,000– 34,999	$35,000– 49,000	$50,000– plus	
5.30 and greater	0.50	0.50	0.0	0.0	0.0	100.0
3.00–5.29	0.0	1.00	0.0	0.0	0.0	100.0
1.55–2.99	0.0	0.0	1.00	0.0	0.0	100.0
0.75–1.54	0.0	0.0	0.0	1.00	0.0	100.0
0.74 and less	0.0	0.0	0.0	0.67	0.33	100.0

Table 5-10. Value of Owner-Occupied Houses by Gross Residential Density and Township, 1970

Houses by Gross Residential Density	House Value ($)					
	15,000–19,000	20,000–24,999	25,000–35,999	35,000–49,999	50,000–plus	All
Aston Township						
5.30–plus	–	–	–	–	–	0
3.00–5.29	–	4,026	–	–	–	4,026
1.55–2.99	–	–	2,417	–	–	2,417
0.75–1.54	–	–	–	–	–	0
0.74 and less	–	–	–	–	–	0
All	0	4,026	2,417	0	0	6,443
Birmingham Township						
5.30–plus	23	23	–	–	–	46
3.00–5.29	–	–	–	–	–	0
1.55–2.99	–	–	–	–	–	0
0.75–1.54	–	–	–	–	–	277
0.74 and less	–	–	–	1,358	699	2,027
All	23	23	0	1,635	699	2,350
Concord Township						
5.30–plus	62	63	–	–	–	125
3.00–5.29	–	–	–	–	–	0
1.55–2.99	–	–	667	–	–	667
0.75–1.54	–	–	–	6,594	–	6,594
0.74 and less	–	–	–	–	–	0
All	62	63	667	6,594	0	7,386
Edgmont Township						
5.30–plus	42	42	–	–	–	84
3.00–5.29	–	640	–	–	–	640
1.55–2.99	–	–	–	–	–	0
0.75–1.54	–	–	–	–	–	0
0.74 and less	–	–	–	1,483	730	2,213
All	42	682	0	1,483	730	2,937
Middletown Township						
5.30–plus	684	684	–	–	–	1,368
3.00–5.29	–	627	–	–	–	627
1.55–2.99	–	–	2,929	–	–	2,929
0.75–1.54	–	–	–	3,841	–	3,841
0.74 and less	–	–	–	541	267	808
All	684	1,311	2,929	4,382	267	9,573
Thornbury Township						
5.30–plus	–	–	–	–	–	0
3.00–5.29	–	–	–	–	–	0
1.55–2.99	–	–	–	–	–	0
0.75–1.54	–	–	–	–	–	0
0.74 and less	–	–	–	1,648	811	2,459
All	0	0	0	1,648	811	2,459

rent distributions with procedures very similar to those used for estimating single-family house prices.

Rents in Single-Family Housing

Rents of single-family dwelling units, by residential density, can be derived, theoretically, from the house values developed earlier. That is, the value of housing units which are likely to be rented in each density class has a corresponding rent that can be estimated. Earlier, seven-to-one ratio of unit value to annual carrying costs for new construction (gross housing expense multiplier) was found to be a stable and useful rule of thumb and it will be used here for converting values of single-family houses to rentals. Therefore, dividing unit values by 84 (multiplier of 7.0 X 12 months) will yield an estimate of monthly gross rents. Since it was assumed earlier that single-family units on lots of 20,000 sq. ft. or smaller would comprise the probable rental pool of such units, the 40th and 60th percentile values of each "eligible" density class were divided by 84 to determine the equivalent rent intervals subtended. When this technique is applied, the schedule of rents shown in Table 5-11 results.

Houses at densities of 5.30 and higher would rent for between $220 and $258, or roughly in the $200 to $250 rent interval. Densities from 3.00 to 5.29 would bring rentals from $256 to $292, i.e., the $250 to $300 range. Houses of 1.55 to 2.99 density would rent in the over $300 range. The number of rented, single-family houses by density class in each township will be assigned to the rent intervals mentioned above.

Table 5-11. Equivalent Rents and Values for Single-Family Houses by Gross Residential Density, 1970

| Resi-dential Density | Rents and Values (Percentile) | | | | | |
| | 40th | | 50th | | 60th | |
	Rent ($)	Value ($)	Rent ($)	Value ($)	Rent ($)	Value ($)
5.30 or More Houses Per Acre	220	18,500	239	20,100	258	21,700
3.00–5.29 Houses Per Acre	256	21,500	274	23,000	292	24,500
1.55–2.99 Houses Per Acre	313	26,300	344	28,900	376	31,600

Rents in Multi-Family Housing

Rents for units in multi-family structures can be estimated directly from the Census of Housing by summing the rent distribution in census blocks or tracts for all structures having two or more units which are shown by the census to be of recent vintage. However, the fourth count census tapes which contain this specific data were not released at the time this analysis was conducted, although the first count tapes were available; therefore, some additional steps are required to make the first count census data useful.[23] The first count census tapes give rent distributions for all housing units in an ED, but do not directly identify the age or structural characteristics of the units. Those EDs which had 15 or more units with cash rents and which experienced substantial growth in rental units since the 1960 Census of Housing are examined to include only the rents in relatively new multi-family structures. However, some of the rental units in these EDs may well be rented single-family houses. To screen out EDs in which rental units are not primarily multi-family, those EDs having the lowest number of single-family units lacking reported house values as a percentage of all cash rental units are retained on the assumption that when this percentage is low most rental units are in multi-family structures.[24] When the percentages of "other than owner-occupied" single-family units are calculated for all EDs, they range from about five percent to over 100 percent.[25] The lowest 15 percentage points in the range, i.e., EDs with up to 20 percent of single-family houses lacking house values, were arbitrarily selected to represent EDs in which the bulk of all rental units are likely to be found in multi-family structures. The 2,108 rental units in this range constitute about 43 percent of the rental units in all ranges; they had a median rent of $157 with rent distributions of:

Percent Single-Family Houses Lacking House Values (0–20) percent

All Cash Rentals ($)	40	40–60	60–80	80–100	100–120	120–150	150–200	200	Median Rent
2,108	11	7	13	48	137	704	1031	157	157

In the absence of definitive fourth count census data on rents in multi-family structures, the 0–20 percent category's rent distribution will be taken as an acceptable surrogate for multi-family rentals. Relying again upon the 40th through the 60th percentile of rents in that distribution to determine the minimum equivalent rent intervals, the 40th percentile ($147) is very near the extreme upper end of the $120–$149 interval and the 60th ($166) is well within the $150–$199 interval. With the median anchored at $157, logic suggests

Table 5-12. Percent of Housing Unit Rents in Developing Townships, Delaware County, Pennsylvania, by Density and Structure Type, 1970

Rental Units by Structure Type and Density	Rent Intervals				
	$120-149	$150-199	$200-249	$250-300	$300-plus
Single Family					
5.30 dwelling units per acre	0.0	0.0	100.0	0.0	0.0
3.00–5.29 dwelling units per acre	0.0	0.0	0.0	100.0	0.0
1.39–2.99 dwelling units per acre	0.0	0.0	0.0	0.0	100.0
Multi-family (All)	33.0	67.0	0.0	0.0	0.0

Table 5-13. Rents of Units by Structure and Township, 1970

Rental Units by Structure and Township	Rents ($)					
	120-149	150-199	200-249	250-300	300-plus	All
Aston						
Single-Family	0	0	0	403	242	645
Multi-Family	0	0	0	0	0	0
All	0	0	0	403	242	645
Birmingham						
Single-Family	0	0	0	0	0	0
Multi-Family	49	98	0	0	0	147
All	49	98	0	0	0	147
Concord						
Single-Family	0	0	0	0	67	67
Multi-Family	310	630	0	0	0	940
All	310	630	0	0	67	1,007
Edgmont						
Single-Family	0	0	8	64	0	72
Multi-Family	0	0	0	0	0	0
All	0	0	8	64	0	72
Middletown						
Single-Family	0	0	114	63	293	470
Multi-Family	120	242	0	0	0	362
All	120	242	114	63	293	832
Thornbury						
Single-Family	0	0	0	0	0	0
Multi-Family	0	0	0	0	0	0
All	0	0	0	0	0	0

that all but a very small fraction of multi-family units be assigned to the $150–$199 rent interval. However, rather than risk erring in a direction which might be interpreted as exaggerating the degree of exclusion by overestimating 1969 rental costs in multi-family housing, it was decided that one-third of all multi-family units be allocated to the $120–$149 rent interval. Consequently, two-thirds of all multi-family units allowed in each township's residential zoning ordinance are considered to have rentals of between $150 and $199, and rentals of $120 to $149 apply to the remaining one-third.

Having estimated separate rent schedules for single-family and multi-family housing, Table 5-12 portrays the joint allocation of all rental units by structure and density to the appropriate rent intervals. When Table 5-10 is used to allocate the rental housing units in township zoning ordinance to a probable rent distribution, the total rent distribution for each township is derived as shown in Table 5-13. The final array of rents and values of all housing units attributable to each township's zoning for residence will eventually be compared with the requirements for rental and owner housing by households of various income levels. The following chapter will concern itself with the formidable task of estimating the size and income distribution of worker households implied by the zoning ordinance.

NOTES

1. James G. Coke and John J. Gargan, *Fragmentation in Land Use Planning and Control,* Research Report No. 18, National Commission on Urban Problems (Washington, D.C.: Government Printing Office, 1969), p. 14.
2. For a detailed description of these items as found in the six-township study, as of May, 1971, see Morton Lustig, Janet R. Pack, Edward M. Bergman, Kent Eklund, and Arnold Goldstein, "Standards for Housing in Suburban Communities Based Upon Zoning for Work," Appendix II–8 (Philadelphia: Fels Center of Government, University of Pennsylvania, 1972), pp. 47–55.
3. Minimum lot sizes are needed to estimate the total number of units allowed in these two districts, but Edgmont's ordinance, unlike other townships, does not specify the minimum lot sizes allowed for development in its "B" and "C" districts. However, if one assembles the minimum size components of front, side, and back yards, plus the minimum building coverage of 750 sq. ft., the following minimum lot sizes may be derived:
     B. District: 9,270 sq. ft.
     C. District: 4,775 sq. ft.
4. However, since commercial activities generate sufficiently high revenues to outbid all but the highest density, luxury-type residential uses, little

residential development could be expected. The miniscule percentage of land in commercial districts now devoted to residential use also suggests that commercial districts should not be considered as potential reservoirs of housing. See Appendix B for a full discussion of the considerations which lead to this conclusion.

5. Net available land area is comprised only of the parcels of real estate associated with housing units, thereby excluding streets, parks, schools, etc., normally found in "residential" neighborhoods. Rahenkamp, Sachs, Wells and Associates, Inc., a land planning firm active in the Philadelphia SMSA, estimates that two lots of 18,000 sq. ft. (36,000 sq. ft. total) can be realized from each raw acre (43,560 sq. ft.), a relatively efficient conversion factor of 0.84. Assuming greater efficiency is gained at lower densities, due to relatively less land consumption for public use, and less efficiency at higher densities, the following conversion factors for each finished lot size range have been used: 0–5,999 sq. ft. = 0.80; 6,000–9,000 sq. ft. = 0.82; 10,000–24,999 sq. ft. = 0.84; 25,000–59,000 sq. ft. = 0.86; 60,000–plus sq. ft. = 0.88.

6. A very similar analysis of zoned lot sizes and housing prices for a different sample of Delaware County Townships from 1956 to 1960 may be found in James G. Coke and Charles S. Liebman, "Political Values and Population Density Control," *Land Economics,* 37 (1961), pp. 347–361.

7. Compare the results of Table 5–2 with the findings of a parallel analysis for urbanizing counties in the neighboring state of New Jersey wherein 14 percent of all residential land was zoned for lots up to 20,000 sq. ft. as contrasted with 22 percent of the land in our sample of six Pennsylvania townships. See "Table VII–Minimum Lot Size Requirements For Single-Family Zoned Residential Land by County," *Land Use Regulation: The Residential Land Supply* (Trenton: New Jersey Division of State and Regional Planning, 1972), p. 15.

8. The term "worker household" is understood to be a family or household unit in which the head is employed in the townships studied and the head's earnings contribute to total household income.

9. U.S., Bureau of Census, 1970 Census of Housing (print-out of housing variable 38 from second count data supplied by Delaware Valley Regional Planning Commission: U.S. Census, Summary Tape Processing Center, Philadelphia, March 16, 1972.)

10. These relationships are, of course, based upon current market preferences for the existing stock. The relationships might change somewhat if the performance standard drastically alters the stock characteristics through zoning. In the absence of firm knowledge about such a potential change, it is doubtless better to rely upon present relationships.

11. For an early, but comprehensive, guide to the literature, see U.S., Department of Housing and Urban Development, *Operation Breakthrough, Mass Produced and Industrialized Housing: A Bibliography* (Washington: Government Printing Office, 1970).

12. Mr. Harry Carroll, Jr. of Jackson-Cross Company, a Philadelphia-based real estate appraisal firm, stated in a telephone conversation that, as of July, 1972, new suburban garden apartment or multi-family housing had gross income multipliers of between 6 and 7, with 7 being the rule of thumb. For the type of assumptions commonly made when calculating and using gross income multipliers, see Richard V. Ratcliffe, *Real Estate Analysis* (New York: McGraw Hill, 1961), pp. 128–30.

13. "The requirements for lot size and frontage were found to operate together. The generalization can be made that the larger the lot size required, the wider the required frontage. This holds true at the municipal, county and study levels," *Land Use Regulation: The Land Use Supply,* p. 20.

14. The Dow, Boeckh, and Bureau of Labor Statistics indices are the most widely used. For discussion of their coverage and applicability, see McGraw–Hill Information Systems Company, "A Study of Comparative Time and Cost for Building Five Selected Types of Low-Cost Housing," pp. 3–52, and Ralph J. Johnson, "Housing Technology and Housing Costs," *The Report of the President's Committee on Urban Housing–Technical Studies,* Vol. II (Washington: Government Printing Office, 1968), pp. 55–144. See also Craig Swan, "Labor and Material Requirements for Housing," *Brookings Papers on Economic Activity,* No. 2 (Washington: The Brookings Institution, 1971), pp. 347–382.

15. The St. Louis office of FHA released data on land cost, cost per lot, average lot front footage, improvement cost per lot, total site cost, and total house plus lot cost for houses built in five residential zoning districts ranging from 6,000 sq. ft. to 43,560 sq. ft. per lot in St. Louis County, Missouri. These data were made available to Neil Gold and Paul Davidoff in preparing "The Supply and Availability of Land for Housing for Low- and Moderate-Income Families," President's Commission On Urban Housing, *Technical Studies,* Vol. II (Washington: Government Printing Office, 1968), p. 365.

16. Michael Sumichrast and Sarah A. Frankel, *Profile of the Builder and His Industry* (Washington: National Association of Home Builders, 1970).

17. A letter dated February 18, 1972, from Michael Sumichrast, staff vice president, National Association of Home Builders, stated that the request for data tabulations had been received and that further information regarding the request would be forthcoming; however, the NAHB did not provide the data requested, nor did it state reasons why the data were not released.

18. This bit of realism illuminates the need to develop more systematically the public data which are currently generated in tax assessment, in the issuance of building permits, and in the guaranteeing of mortgages, in order to monitor the pulse of housing production and supply at local and metropolitan levels.

19. The fourth count census data which contain information about the age of

houses had not been released at this writing. Therefore, enumeration districts were chosen from census tracts in the most rapidly developing townships which were not substantially developed in the 1960 Census of Housing. Some of the value dispersion found in Table 5–8 can, therefore, be traced to the inclusion of some EDs with older housing stocks.

20. A very similar approach was employed to estimate the minimum rent necessary to occupy "adequate housing" from a distribution of rents paid for all rental housing, in John D. Heinberg, *The Transfer Cost of A Housing Allowance: Conceptual Issues and Benefit Patterns* (Washington: Urban Institute, 1971), p. 24–25.

21. For example, the $18,500–$21,700 range of the highest density class falls within the $15,000–$19,999 and the $20,000–$24,999 value categories. Since the median is virtually on their dividing line, 50 percent of all 5,000 or less sq. ft. lot housing is assigned to the $15,000–$19,000 value category, and 50 percent to the $20,000–$24,999 category. When two value categories are spanned and the median value falls well within one of them, that one is assigned 67 percent of the density classes' housing units and the other category receives 33 percent. Finally, when the full 40th–60th percentile range falls entirely within one value category, that value category receives all the housing of the appropriate residential density class.

22. If, for example, only the median census value in Delaware County townships was used to determine the proper value interval, the estimated price of new houses would have been higher for houses built on the smallest lots and lower for houses built on the largest lots. These particular lot sizes happened to have median house values very close to a dividing line between value intervals; by introducing the interdecile range as a measure of central tendency, the risk of choosing a single, incorrect interval from a distribution having arbitrary dimensions is somewhat reduced.

23. For an official discussion of the difference between the several census counts, consult Bureau of Census, *Census Users' Guide,* Vols. I and II, (Washington: Government Printing Office, 1970).

24. Values are also not reported when single-family homes are on a 10-acre or larger lot, and when houses adjoin or are part of commercial and professional establishments. Therefore, some portion of the calculated percentages might indicate more single-family houses as being rented than actually are, i.e., some low, but finite, percentage could very well obtain with *no* houses being rented and a percentage of over 100 could obtain if all or nearly all rentals were single-family houses.

25. See Appendix C for further discussion and the relevant census data.

Chapter Six

Zoning Ordinances and Worker Household Incomes in Suburban Townships

> As rapid residential expansion occurred, suburban county planners emphasized industrial development, primarily for taxes but also— in Bucks and Delaware [Pennsylvania counties], where employment declined sharply in 1955—for payrolls.[1]

In the preceding chapter, we were able to convert the provisions of residential districts in township zoning ordinances to a stock of housing units in a relatively straightforward manner. There is some overlap between the residential housing analysis and the procedures required to estimate worker households from zoning ordinances. First, a small fraction of all employment is accounted for by government and service-related workers who are invariably needed to service the potential population housed in the residential districts. Therefore, the estimate of households from the residential provisions establish a base to which commonly available ratios of workers to households are applied, a procedure discussed at some length in the first major section of this chapter. Second, the commercial and industrial districts, within which the bulk of employment is generally found, are initially analyzed in much the same way as are the residential districts: the district size is measured from the zoning maps and reduced to net developable site area, the allowed uses are codified, and the controls on density evaluated to estimate maximum "yield" of allowed uses from the net developable site area. Lastly, we shall apply an appropriate, localized schedule of earnings and incomes to workers in the various jobs, much as we applied rent and price schedules to the various types of housing.

However, similarities in the analysis of residential districts and commercial and industrial districts are more superficial than substantial. This becomes clearer when it is recognized that several residential districts are often provided in a township, within each of which the residential development is predominantly the highest density allowed. This is in contrast to commercial and industrial districts which are fewer in number and within which all of the permitted uses might develop in many possible mixtures. Residential districts could be expected to yield a determinate number of housing units because all are assumed to develop at the maximum density allowed. However, the delicate web of controls over land use intensity of commercial and industrial uses is virtually tailored to all the potential uses, because certain of these uses have unusual parking, loading and space characteristics. These are features lacking in residential districts which must be taken account of explicitly when analyzing the commercial and industrial provisions of an ordinance. The nuances of multiple intensity controls, then, render the maximum "yield" of employment-creating uses to be a partial function of their mix. Finally, where the analysis of residential districts produces a stock of housing units directly from the ordinance, the equivalent unit of analysis, i.e., worker households, can emerge only from the multistage process of extracting raw ordinance data, allocating uses to the zoned land, and converting zoned land to developable floor area and workers. These major differences call forth an analytic effort significantly different in approach and scope.

     Since the primary purpose of this chapter is to estimate the number of worker households and their income, it will be necessary to develop a consistent linkage between the narrative of a zoning ordinance, which controls only the type and land-use intensity of various commercial and industrial establishments, and the income characteristics of workers. That linkage, or common thread, is the Standard Industrial Classification of economic uses allowed in districts, for which considerable data on space utilization, labor force and income statistics are available. A general approach emerges in which systematic SIC linkages are developed from land and floor area uses, through job and labor force characteristics, culminating in worker earnings and household income. There are three stages of this approach which comprise a like number of major sections in the chapter. These major sections and the steps within each are, very briefly, these:

1. The Zoning Ordinance, SIC Activities, and Potential Employers
    Collect and organize essential zoning ordinance data in terms of a system
    of SIC equivalents, i.e., codification of all uses permitted by SIC, site
    intensity (or density) restrictions in the form of maximum floor area to
    land area ratios applicable to certain identifiable SICs or groups of SIC,
    and total district area zoned for SICs.
2. Potential Zoning District and Township Employment
    Develop a land area and employment allocation model which combines
    the ordinance data from [1. above] with floor area to job conversion ratios,
    regional job distribution and labor force coefficients relating jobs and
    workers to estimate total site area, floor area, and employment by SIC.
3. Earnings and Household Income of Township Workers

Estimate the earnings distribution of workers in each SIC, and the resultant number of households and household income, by use of SIC specific occupational coefficients, earnings distributions and means, and household income distributions.

Each of the major sections contains sufficient analysis and discussion of a single subject to merit separate chapter headings, but for the purposes of this volume the subjects treated do not easily stand alone.[2] Each is an essential link of a complete analytic chain that requires the context of a larger chapter to establish continuity of purpose and to foster overall understanding. Although Chapter 6 is, consequently, much longer than the other chapters, we feel that special delineation of the major sections will serve to divide the chapter into digestible portions.

THE ZONING ORDINANCE, SIC ACTIVITIES, AND POTENTIAL EMPLOYERS

The bulk of potential employment in developing townships will be located in commercial and manufacturing districts. However, employment in agriculture, private household professions, and government is found primarily in residential districts. The estimate of potential employment in commercial and industrial districts will be related to the land area and the permitted uses in each such district; the estimate of potential employment in residential districts will be related to total potential households.

ANALYSIS OF COMMERCIAL AND INDUSTRIAL DISTRICTS

The range of economic activities, the intensity of those activities allowed within a district, and the size of the district determine the potential number and kind of jobs. In this section, we analyze the zoning ordinances of the sample of six developing townships [3] to demonstrate how data implicit in the code's provisions and relevant to these three important use restrictions may be directly estimated or inferred. The need for inference is generally indicative of poorly designed or inadequate codes.

Size and Identification of Zoning Use Districts

Each of the six townships under study has one or more business-commercial or industrial-manufacturing districts (total of 18) within which the bulk of potential employment would be located. To aid in future identification of the 18 districts, each was initially given a two-digit code, wherein the first digit represents the township name and the second digit identifies particular districts within that township. A simple convention, listing the business-commercial districts first and the industrial-manufacturing districts last, was adopted for the second digit of each township.

88

None of the township ordinances indicated the land area in its zoning districts. It was therefore necessary to measure zoning map districts by planimeter. The most detailed zoning maps available were used to measure district size which was expressed in square feet of land area for ease of subsequent conversion to floor area. Since some of the land area would be consumed for nonsite purposes (e.g., utility easements, streets and roads), a suitable factor [4] was applied to gross district land area to derive net developable site area. Table 6-1 summarizes the relevant code identification, township major activity and land area for each district.

It is important to note here the significance of district 36 for which no land area is shown in Table 6-1. Even though district 36 exists in the text of Concord Township's zoning ordinance and is subject to an explicit set of use and development intensity controls, the district has not been placed on the zoning map (although it is shown on the future land use plan). This is a typical "floating zone" which is not placed on the map until a developer makes a request for a specific, acceptable location.

Accordingly, district 36 is not used in the estimation of type or amount of employment generated by Concord Township industrial zoning.

Table 6-1. Employment Districts: Type, Size Identification, and Township, 1971

Identification	Township and Type of District	Land Area (sq. ft. net)*
11	Aston Township, Business	7,748,272
12	Aston Township, Shopping Center	460,801
13	Aston Township, Industrial	31,363,433
21	Birmingham Township, Business	11,695,046
22	Birmingham Township, Light Industrial	4,607,649
31	Concord Township, C-1 Commercial	3,674,702
32	Concord Township, C-2 Commercial	7,103,602
33	Concord Township, C-2A Commercial	1,798,290
34	Concord Township, C-3 Commercial	3,744,247
35	Concord Township, Light Industrial	14,332,924
36	Concord Township, Planned Industrial Park	0
41	Edgmont Township, Business	2,198,881
51	Middletown Township, Business	2,289,423
52	Middletown Township, B-1 Business	1,906,876
53	Middletown Township, Special Use	11,513,254
54	Middletown Township, Manufacturing	7,573,502
61	Thornbury Township, Commercial	928,103
62	Thornbury Township, Limited Industrial	14,018,303

*Land area is 0.85 and 0.75 of gross land area for industrial-manufacturing and business-commercial districts, respectively, to reflect nonsite uses of district land area (see Chapter 6, note 4).

It may be of interest to note that in Concord Township's future land use plan, district 36 is allotted approximately 5,300,500 sq. ft., which would take 334,000 sq. ft. from the present C–3 district and 4,979,800 sq. ft. from the present R–2 district. At the time district 36 finally ceases to float and settles on a known site, it, too, would be included in the analysis.

Allowed Uses in Commercial and Manufacturing Districts

Over the past forty to fifty years of zoning experience, ordinances have evolved in their several dimensions, including the categorization of allowed economic uses. The earliest codes had a long, fairly detailed list of forbidden uses, i.e., anything not on the list was, presumably, allowed. Often the prohibited uses were described in such archaic or literary terms that one required an unabridged dictionary to discover the actual product or production technique in question. Very often, development of these prohibited uses was not even remotely possible; they were sometimes technologically obsolescent and, occasionally, a single use was variously identified and prohibited by every known synonym. When a municipality employs a list of prohibited uses, the list tends to be remarkably similar to other municipalities' lists, in both content and in order of listing, whether the ordinance is one currently in effect or an older, outdated version.

A major refinement of the "laundry list" of prohibitions is an enumeration of specifically allowed uses expressed in terms more descriptive of contemporary economic processes. This tends to be a much less ambiguous approach.

At about the same time that allowed uses were being specifically designated, ordinances also began to incorporate performance criteria relating to the conduct with which those allowed uses must carry on their operations. The "allowed" uses were accepted only on condition that they would not violate certain measurable criteria relating to noise, smoke, heat, glare, traffic and other environmental or nuisance factors. Imposition of performance criteria tends to limit the longer list of enumerated uses but, when viewed more broadly, it logically should allow other nominally prohibited uses if they, too, can meet the performance standards. Accordingly, the most recent ordinances give a detailed list of allowed or similar, uses, all subject to a set of specified performance criteria. Sometimes the allowed uses are tersely described as "light industry," which includes any use which does not employ general classes of production techniques or otherwise violate the blanket performance standards.

All of these forms of use description were present in one or more of the eighteen commercial and industrial districts in the six developing townships. Somehow, a uniform system of allowed uses had to be developed which

(1) reduced the several use systems to a common denominator, (2) pertained to products or processes characteristic of identifiable industries and employers, and (3) was consistent with other classification systems for which statistical data relating to employees, payrolls, space consumption, etc. were available. Correspondence with knowledgeable officials and organizations supported the conclusion, based on a literature search, that no such system had been proposed or analyzed.[5]

It thus became necessary to develop rules for classifying economic activities in a single system and to decide which system to use. General industrial categories such as construction, durable manufacturing, nondurable manufacturing, wholesale trade, retail trade, services, etc., used by the census and, in varying forms, by land use planners, are so broad that they lack precision. Among the more detailed systems in use, there are only two known possibilities from which to choose: the Standard Land Use (SLU) coding system designed jointly by the Department of Housing and Urban Development and the Bureau of Public Roads, or the Standard Industrial Classification (SIC) system developed by the U.S. Bureau of the Budget (upon which the SLU is primarily based). While the SLU is attractive because it codifies all remotely conceivable uses of land for purposes economic or otherwise, it is much less specific than the SIC for certain activities defined precisely by zoning ordinances. More importantly, the only detailed industrial statistics available are gathered and organized in terms of SIC. The procedures which were used to translate economic activities allowed by ordinance into equivalent SICs may be found in Appendix D.

Maximum Permitted Intensity of
Manufacturing and Commercial Activity

Suburban development restrictions are focused mainly on maximum lot area coverage for buildings and for other uses, maximum story or building height, and a requirement for on-site loading space, plus customer and employee parking. These restrictions are not applied uniformly within districts to all kinds of economic activity; uses such as gasoline filling stations and professional office buildings obviously require different treatment. By tailoring use restrictions to types of economic activity, planners use zoning to control indirectly the intensity of use, where developable floor area is generally considered as the best index of intensity.

These differences of regulation create problems for one engaged in estimating the maximum, developable floor area allowed by code as a proportion of land area. That is, if a tract of land can be developed for any of several allowed uses, how does the net conversion ratio of land area to maximum floor area vary according to the particular use in question? As in all other matters, we would like to determine whether floor area ratio (FAR) conver-

sion factors can be calculated for particular SICs which are likely to occupy
the land. Such a calculation entails systematic consideration of all development intensity controls and their ultimate expression as a single ratio of land
area to floor area for particular SICs or classes of SIC.

Without question, this is the most complex step in translating
zoning ordinance narrative into data useful for estimating the type and scale of
potential employment implicit in a zoning district. The first major difficulty
of this step is combining the many forms of intensity control specified for each
district into a simple, but conceptually sound, algorithm for the estimation of
the matrix of land area to floor area conversion ratios, within which the ratio
for any particular SIC might be found. The second problem is concerned with
reducing the various quantitative and verbal expressions of standards and requirements found in the 18 district regulations, to standardized data which
can be entered directly in the algorithm designed to convert code-implicit
data to ratio coefficients of floor area to land area.

First, the algorithm will be described in terms of how it enters and
weights standardized code data to arrive at a final Floor Area Ratio (FAR).
As mentioned earlier, the important kinds of control over development intensity are:

1.   the maximum percentage (A) of lot area which can be covered by build-
     ings;
2.   the maximum percentage (B) of lot area which can be covered by build-
     ings, parking space, and loading space;
3.   the maximum, allowable height of buildings (C) as measured in floors (f);
4.   SIC-related ratio (j) of parking area to floor area for specific commercial or
     service establishments which generate extraordinary parking demands; and,
5.   a constant ratio (k) of parking area to floor area, which is required of all
     uses to accommodate employee parking, customer parking or loading space.

In general, restrictions A, B and C constitute an overall intensity envelope
which all SICs must observe. The intensity of site development is further restricted by j and k, which compel particular classes of SIC, either explicitly or
by virtue of common space utilization characteristics, to devote a portion of
the site area to nonbuilding purposes thereby further reducing the maximum
FAR. By use of the following formula,[6] A, B, C, f, j and k may be reduced
to a matrix of *FAR*s which pertain to all possible classes of SIC within a particular district:

$$FAR = \frac{B}{\frac{1}{f} + j + k}$$

subject to: where:

1) $\dfrac{FAR}{f} \leqslant A$ $0 < A < 1$

2) $\dfrac{FAR}{f} + j(FAR) + k\,(FAR) \leqslant B$ $0 < B < 1$

                                                         $f = 1, 2, \ldots C$

3) $f \leqslant C$ $0 < j < +\infty$

                                                         $0 < k < +\infty$

     The column dimension of the resultant matrix is comprised of a series of j and k combinations which apply to establishments with varying work force sizes per unit of floor space, or to establishments specifically identified in the ordinance. Each of these combinations is defined as a floor area class (FAC), and they are 16 in number. Individual SICs, or classes of SIC, are associated with one of the 16 $FACs$, either because floor space per worker is known for SICs or because specifically cited establishments, e.g., gasoline stations, have readily assessable SIC equivalents.

     The row dimension is scaled by a range of building floors, the upper limit of which is constrained by C as stipulated in the ordinance. Since the nature of economic activity and the design of buildings for particular SICs is often a more binding constraint on the number of floors than that enacted by ordinance . . .C, $FARs$ were calculated in the matrix for a range of fs up to $f = C$.[7] This would then allow the effective constraint to determine which row (or f value) is best suited to unique SICs. Therefore, to locate the appropriate cell and its FAR value for any particular SIC, one need only know which floor area class it is in and the characteristic number of floors in buildings that house that SIC.

     The two constraints governing the percentage of lot coverage were earlier defined as A and B, where A is the maximum percentage of a given site which can be covered by buildings, and B is the maximum percentage of the site which can be covered by buildings plus other use-related site development. Of the 18 districts studied, all but three commercial or business districts stipulated maximum values for A and B. Commercial districts which did state values of B averaged about 0.84 (most in the 90 percentiles), and commonly allow full use of the site except for ornamental plantings or other token site amenities. Five other districts, two industrial and three commercial-business, did not limit B, but did set a maximum for A, the building coverage. A and B values were calculated for all 18 districts,[8] the results of which are shown in Table 6-2.

     Estimates of j and k are the next task. These are either variable (j)

Table 6-2. Values for A and B and Their Determination

Districts	A	B
11	0.30[c]	1.00[b]
12	0.25[c]	1.00[b]
13	0.25[d]	0.50[c]
21	0.40[d]	1.00[b]
22	0.30[d]	0.30[d]
31	0.55[d]	0.95[a]
32	0.25[d]	0.92[a]
33	0.35[d]	0.93[a]
34	0.20[d]	0.92[a]
35	0.40[d]	0.80[c]
36	0.30[d]	0.60[d]
41	0.30[d]	0.70[d]
51	0.30[d]	1.00[b]
52	0.25[c]	1.00[b]
53	0.33[d]	0.66[b]
54	0.50[d]	0.75[d]
61	0.20[d]	1.00[b]
62	0.25[d]	0.75[d]

[a] $B = 1.00 - 0.10 (1 - A/1.10)$

[b] Assume $Y = 1.00$, i.e., lack of a stated maximum in the ordinance is "rational."

[c] Derived from other similar districts for which values were specified (average or ratio derivation).

[d] Taken directly from ordinance in percentage terms.

or constant (k) proportions of gross floor space to be provided at ground level, which invariably consume site area, often at the cost of building coverage.[9] Neither are shown in the township ordinances as proportions of gross floor space but are, instead, couched in terms which can be converted to a proportion. The requirement may be stated in two ways. One specifies the number of spaces for one or more employees (and the size of the space): for example, one automobile parking stall of 300 sq. ft. for each main shift employee. Another form requires a stated number of square feet of parking space for each square foot of floor area. Estimates, which are summarized in Table 6-3, were made of each district's parking standards.

The product obtained by multiplying the parking space size by the number of spaces per employee gives the required square feet of parking per employee. If parking space per employee is divided by floor area per employee, we obtain the k factor. Using industrial zoning district 36 as an example, its parking space size (300 sq. ft.) is multiplied by the spaces per worker (0.67) which yields 200 sq. ft. per employee.[10] If the 200 sq. ft. is then divided by 150 sq. ft., the floor area per worker in floor area class (FAC)1, the k factor is computed as 1.30. By continuing this process for the floor areas in each *FAC*, a table of k values is generated which summarizes the ordinance

Table 6-3. Parking Standards for Industrial Zoning Districts

Industrial Zoning Districts	Number of Parking Spaces Per Person[b]		Parking Space Size (sq. ft.)
13	Adequate	= 0.75[a]	Adequate = 300[a]
22	3.4	= 0.75	200-plus = 300[c]
35	1:1	= 1.00	350
36	2:3	= 0.67	200-plus = 300
53	1:1	= 1.00	200-plus = 300
54	1:1	= 1.00	200-plus = 300
62	Adequate	= 0.75[a]	Adequate = 300[a]

[a] Values assigned on basis of other districts' requirements.

[b] Number of spaces reduced to a per single employee basis to standardize differing specifications.

[c] Requirement of 200 sq. ft. for parking stall, plus maneuvering space, is treated as a total of 300 sq. ft.

requirement that all the SICs in each FAC must provide parking space for their employees equal to their total floor space multiplied times k. Table 6-4 summarizes the employee parking k values for each of the four basic employee parking requirements observed in the manufacturing districts and identifies those districts which use or were assigned one of the four parking requirements.

Another possible k-type value was computed in those instances when the zoning ordinance for a business-commercial district made no distinction between SICs, either directly by name or indirectly through characteristic space consumption, by requiring a fixed proportion (generally 300 to 400 percent) of floor area to be set aside for both customer and employee parking. Typical requirements are stated in the form "x square feet of parking space are to be provided for each square foot of gross floor area." Five of the eleven business-commercial districts made this blanket requirement, two made no specific parking requirements at all, and four used a variable parking requirement (j) which will be discussed in a subsequent section. One of the districts (no. 11) without a specific parking requirement was in a township with another business-commercial district (no. 12) which did specify the fixed parking requirement. Fixed-type requirements were also found in four townships' districts, as compared with variable requirements in two townships' districts. Because of the preponderance of districts which employed the k-type requirement, we adopted a k-type requirement for those business-commercial districts which lacked specific parking provisions. A value of 4.00 for k was assigned to those districts lacking requirements, because three of the five districts with fixed requirements stipulated 4.00 as the value for k, and because the mean value of k for all five districts was 3.90. Table 6-5 summarizes a final set of k values pertaining to combined customer and employee parking in seven of the eleven business-commercial districts:

Table 6-4. *k*-Values of Parking Requirements

Floor Area Class	Mean Floor Space Per Worker	1:1 @ 300 sq. ft. Parking Per Worker	k	3:4 @ 300 sq. ft. Parking Per Worker	k	2:3 @ 300 sq. ft. Parking Per Worker	k	1:1 @ 350 sq. ft. Parking Per Worker	k
1	150	300	2.00	250	1.67	200	1.30	350	2.33
2	250	300	1.20	250	1.00	200	0.80	350	1.40
3	400	300	0.75	250	0.63	200	0.50	350	0.88
4	650	300	0.47	250	0.39	200	0.31	350	0.53
5	950	300	0.32	250	0.26	200	0.21	350	0.37
6	1300	300	0.23	250	0.19	200	0.15	350	0.27
7	1850	300	0.16	250	0.14	200	0.11	350	0.18
8	2700	300	0.11	250	0.09	200	0.07	350	0.13
Districts		53, 54		13, 22, 62		36		35	

Table 6-5. k-Values for Combined Customer and Employee Parking in Business Districts

District	11	12	21	33	51	52	61
k	4.00*	4.00	4.00*	4.50	3.00	4.00	4.00

*Value assigned on basis of values in other districts.

The last "constant" space requirement observed in zoning codes for the 18 districts obliges establishments to set aside a fixed proportion of their gross floor area for loading space. Three business-commercial districts (nos. 31, 32, 34) in one township require that one loading space of 12 X 30 feet (360 sq. ft.) be set aside for every 2,000 sq. ft. of floor space. On average then, the k value for loading space is 360 sq. ft. ÷ 2,000 sq. ft., or 0.18.

As noted above, four business-commercial districts (three of which were in one township) tailor customer parking provisions to certain kinds of establishment.[11] That is, the floor area alone is considered to be less important than the type of enterprise in determining parking space requirements for customers. This particular type of parking factor is labeled j. Several of the enterprises cited in the township ordinances, e.g., bowling alleys, private clubs, tourist or rooming houses, were considered so unlikely to be a significant portion of total development in the townships under examination that j values were not calculated for them. It is quite conceivable that in certain regions where tourism is an important part of the economic base, j values should be calculated for these particular uses.

Of the many possible uses singled out in the codes for specific treatment, eight general categories eventually were found to be most important. Because the SICs which comprise these eight customer parking categories must also accommodate their employee parking, both j and k values are to be calculated for the districts in question.

The SICs within a given j category occasionally will have somewhat different Floor Area Class designations because they differ in the amount of floor space per worker. To simplify the calculation of parking obligations for all SICs within a single j category, an average parking space per worker, weighted by the Philadelphia SMSA suburban employment in each SIC, is calculated for each j category. The Floor Area Class corresponding to that average floor area per worker is, in turn, used to select the appropriate k to be used in the FAR algorithm.

Having devised the set of eight categories, the amount of customer parking space which the ordinance requires must be calculated as a proportion of each j category's mean floor area, so that j values are expressed in terms comparable to values of k. Table 6-6 summarizes the j categories, their constituent SICs, the FAC which is assigned to each j category, and the values for j. By expressing the values of j and k in comparable terms, we are now in a position

Table 6–6.   Floor Area Per Worker by Type of Enterprise, FAC, j Values and Zoning District

j Category Number	Type of Enterprise	Floor Area per Worker			FAC	j Values	
		SICs	SIC	j Category		Districts 31, 33, 34	District 41
1	Wholesale	5000	682	682	4	0.33	0.33
2	Retail	5200 5300 5400 5500 5600 5700 5900	766 271 534 502 532 878 444	472 (average)	3	3.00	0.40
3	Restaurant	5800	270	270	2	6.00	6.00
4	Hotel	7010	875	875	5	1.06	0.71
5	Auto Service Station	7500	3454	3454	8	1.50	0.60
6	Cinema	7830	681	681	4	5.00	5.00
7	Hospital	8060	202	202	2	0.33	0.40
8	Office	7390 8010 8020 8030 8100 8900	305 317 269 283 195 312	300 (average)	2	0.33	0.60

to use the *FAR* algorithm for ordinances which selectively apply site area requirements to particular SIC activities. That is, columns 1–8 of the *FAR* matrix are devoted to the k type (constant site area to floor area) parking requirement for all uses in a *FAC*, and columns 9–16 apply to specifically cited SIC activities which must provide for both j and k parking requirements.[12]

The last important piece of data which must be derived from the township zoning provisions for commercial and industrial districts is the maximum number of building floors allowed. Zoning ordinances which contain height restrictions are more likely to specify maximum building height in feet than in floors. The allowed height in feet is not always readily convertible into a number of floors; the fact that some districts gave the height restriction in both feet and floors indicates that certain townships are aware of this ambiguity. For those townships which restrict building height to foot measurements alone, we found it necessary to convert feet to floors. Table 6–7 describes resultant height restrictions in floors for the 18 districts.

Because the height per floor ranged from 12.5 to 17.5 feet in the observed districts (the entire range being present in one district, depending on

Table 6–7. Height Restriction in Floors and Feet, by District and *FAC*

Districts	FAC	Floors	Feet	Feet per Floor
11	All	(4)[b]	65	e
12	All	(4)[b]	(65)[a]	e
13	All	(2)[b]	30	e
21	All	(4)[b]	50	e
22	All	(4)[b]	50	e
31	d	2	35	17.5
32	d	2	35	17.5
33	d	2	35	17.5
34	d	2	35	17.5
35	All	(4)[b]	65	e
36	1–15	2	35	17.5
	16	4	50	12.5
41	All	3	45	15.0
51	All	c	c	e
52	All	c	c	e
53	All	c	c	e
54	All	c	c	e
61	All	(2)[b]	35	e
62	All	(3)[b]	40	e

[a] Assume height restriction the same as for Aston business district no. 11.
[b] Equivalent number of floors @ 15 ft. ± 3 ft. per floor.
[c] No height limitation given.
[d] All, except Filling Stations (*FAC* 13) where 45 ft. is maximum height.
[e] Not applicable.

the type of building), a conversion factor of 15 feet ± 3 feet per floor was used which we believe provides a reasonable estimate of maximum floors for districts where only a "foot maximum" height restriction was given. It should be mentioned that districts which restricted neither total feet nor story height were not assisgned a proxy height, unlike our treatment of other omissions in zoning ordinances, for the following reasons. First, we assumed that the township which allowed all of its four-use districts to develop without height maximums could not have "overlooked" this omission and, therefore, the township probably considered such restrictions unnecessary. Second, the characteristics of certain SIC activities automatically preclude multiple-story buildings because of production process, storage and distribution practices, or display and sales techniques, thereby rendering many height restrictions superfluous. The third reason height restrictions are, or could be explained as, logically unnecessary is that the cumulative effect of all other intensity restrictions (A, B, k, j) combine to such a degree that adding floors increases the land-use intensity, as measured by FAR, very little if at all. For example, if a hypothetical business district requires three square feet of parking for each square foot of floor area, and if parking is provided at ground level, changes in the number of floors have the following results:

Total Site Area

Building Height in Floors	Percentage Covered by Building	Percentage Covered by Parking Area	Use Intensity as Measured by Floor Area Ratio
1	25 percent	75 percent	0.25
3	10 percent	90 percent	0.30
10	3 percent	97 percent	0.32

Add other typical restrictions on ground area coverage (including parking structures), off-street loading spaces, setbacks, and it is even clearer that unrestricted changes in height have very limited effect on the effective floor area ratio.

ANALYSIS OF RESIDENTIAL DISTRICTS

Total potential employment within our suburban townships is the sum of employment located in districts zoned for work (commercial and industrial), and other employment found in residential districts. Accordingly, we use data from the residential provisions of a zoning code to estimate individual and household population size, to which certain kinds and amounts of other employment are attributed by use of population service ratios.

Table 6-8. Summary of Township Residential Zoning Districts by Potential Dwelling Units and Population

District	Number of Dwelling Units or Households[b]	Persons Per Household	Number of Persons
(1) R–A	2,659	3.3	8,776
(1) R–A1	20	3.3	67
(1) R–B	4,409	3.3	15,549
	7,088		23,392
(2) R–1	2,027	3.3	6,688
(2) R–2	277	3.3	916
(2) R–A	193	2.0	385
	2,497		7,989
(3) R–1	887	3.3	2,927
(3) R–2	4,473	3.3	14,761
(3) R–3	734	3.3	2,421
(3) R–2D	1,234	3.3	4,073
(3) R–A	521	2.0	1,042
(3) R–AH	544	1.5	816
	8,393		26,040
(4) R–A	2,213	3.3	7,304
(4) R–B	704	3.3	2,322
(4) R–C	92	3.3	304
	3,009		9,930
(5) R–1A	808	3.3	2,665
(5) R–1	3,841	3.3	12,677
(5) R–2	3,222	3.3	10,634
(5) R–3	690	3.3	2,277
(5) R–4	886	3.3	2,922
(5) R–4A	493	3.3	1,628
(5) R–A	476	2.0	952
	10,416		33,755
(6) RA	2,124	3.3	7,010
(6) RB	315	3.3	1,041
(6) QAB[a]	20	3.3	66
	2,459		8,117

[a]Eventual conversion of present quarry district, which allows residences assumed to be 25 percent of district acreage.
[b]Totals taken from Table 5-1.

Holding Capacity of Households in Residential Districts

Just as it was assumed that the size distribution of SIC employment is computed at 100 percent development of land in manufacturing and commercial districts, the size of the population in residential districts, for estimating attributed employment, is also based upon complete residential development. However, the task is simpler for residential districts because the intensity and use of residential development can be estimated directly from the code without the difficulty of dealing with a mix of uses. While it is true that less dense residential development is nearly always allowed in residential districts of higher maximum densities, and a mix could therefore conceivably occur, the manner in which the real estate market operates strongly limits this as a possible complication.

The procedure is relatively straightforward [13] and involves estimating the number of households which would occupy the fully developed land in each residential district at the maximum density allowed. The 24 residential districts found in the six-township sample are identified by the designation used in each township's code, and are preceded by the same number (in parentheses) earlier used to identify townships; thus, the Residential-*A* district in Aston Township is listed in Table 6-8 as (1) R-A.

Since the potential number of housing units in township residential districts was calculated in Chapter 5, the figures may be taken directly from Table 5-1 for use here. Housing or dwelling units are the facilities in which households reside, so that by definition the total number of dwelling units equals the total number of households. Once the potential number of households or dwelling units in each residential district is known, an average number of persons per household [14] is multiplied by that number to estimate the total potential number of persons.

Having determined the potential household and individual population of each district at capacity, the districts are summed for township totals. Because agricultural employment is, in general, inversely proportional to population density, the total population of each township will be divided by the land area of the township to determine an index of land development. This index will be used later to adjust the township's land-percentage share of total county agricultural employment up or down, relative to the county index. Table 6-9 summarizes all the residential data needed to estimate employment in public and other service employment.

Table 6-9.   Summary of Potential Households and Population, by Township, 1971

Township	Number of Households	Number of Persons	Sq. Miles	Households Per Sq. Mile	Persons Per Sq. Mile
Aston	7,088	23,392	5.90	1,201	3,965
Birmingham	2,497	7,989	8.84	283	904
Concord	8,393	26,040	13.78	609	1,890
Edgmont	3,009	9,930	9.74	309	1,020
Middletown	10,416	33,755	13.43	775	2,513
Thornbury	2,459	8,117	9.16	268	886
All	33,862	109,223	60.85	556	1,795

NOTES

1. Charles E. Gilbert, *Governing the Suburbs* (Bloomington, Indiana: Indiana University Press, 1967), p. 187.
2. These three sections were previously released as individual chapters in Morton Lustig, Janet R. Pack, Edward M. Bergman, Kent Eklund, Arnold Goldstein, *Standards for Housing in Suburban Zoning Based Upon Zoning for Work* (Philadelphia: Fels Center of Government, University of Pennsylvania, 1972), an official study report upon which this book is based. This author has altered his text somewhat, due to a minor change of emphasis, but the analysis contained within remains essentially unchanged.
3. All the township zoning ordinances were those in effect as of May, 1971.
4. For industrial-manufacturing districts, net developable area was assumed to be equal to 0.85 gross district land area. Assumption based on G.I. Whitlatch, *Industrial Districts, Their Planning and Development* (Industrial Development Division, Georgia Institute of Technology, n.d.), 15–25 percent loss of gross acreage to rights-of-way and utility easements; and R.E. Boley, *Industrial Districts, Principles and Practice,* Technical Bulletin, No.44 (Washington: Urban Land Institute, 1962), 10–27 percent land losses averaging 16 percent in recently established industrial districts.

   A factor of 0.75 was chosen for business-commercial districts, based on information from Edward Schlosser, Assistant Director, Delaware County Planning Commission. The factor is in accordance with general rules of thumb and is logically lower than the industrial-manufacturing factor cited above, due to added traffic generation and consequent street consumption of land.
5. Letters of May 11, 1971, to the National Industrial Zoning Committee and to the American Industrial Development Council and replies from Jack Meister, Librarian, May 26, 1971, and Richard Preston, Executive Vice President, May 28, 1971, of the AIDC.
6. The formula has been written as a computer algorithm, the program and sample output of which may be found in Appendix E.
7. To account operationally for the number of floors characteristically associated with certain SICs, fs from 1 to 10 were entered in the formula. The result is a full 16×10 matrix of FARs with the row dimension scaled by a range of 1–10 floors. The maximum number of floors allowed in the district limit the value which FARs can take at the point where $f = C$. The FAR recorded at that point is then merely repeated for the remaining fs up to $f = 10$, which is but another way of applying a maximum height restriction on FARs for SICs which typically occupy buildings with more floors than are allowed in these townships. See Appendix F.
8. See Appendix F for the assumptions and procedures involved in estimating A and B values from township zoning ordinances.

9. Ground level provision is assumed because total building/structure coverage must be $\leqslant A$, and parking structures are uneconomical in all but a very few, high-intensity uses. Where parking structures are feasible, the assumption of ground level parking is "conservative" in the sense that ground level parking minimizes potential floor space, workers, and "demand" for moderate- or low-cost housing.

10. The calculation of parking standards is fleshed out in Appendix G.

11. See Appendix H.

12. Refer to Appendix I for additional detail on deriving values of j which are comparable to values of k, and the 16 combinations of j and k which define the column dimension of the *FAR* Matrix. For a more precise rendering of how the *FAR* algorithm chooses any one of these 16 columns when calculating the *FAR* for a particular SIC, refer to the computer program in Appendix E.

13. An early attempt to estimate land holding capacity was made by the Detroit City Planning Commission in *Population Capacity: A Study Determining the Number of Dwelling Units and the Population Detroit's Neighborhoods May Be Expected to Have When Major Proposals Expected to Occur by 1980 are Completed*, 1954.

14. Persons per household are given for the following types of residential districts: single-family detached and attached—3.3 persons/hh; garden apartment or low-density apartment—1.5/hh. These figures are averages for U.S. Census of Housing persons per structure tabulations where: single-family attached and detached residences are assumed to be all one-unit structures, both owned and rented; garden or low-density apartments are assumed to be owner-occupied structures with two or more units, plus renter-occupied structures with two to 20 units; high-rise, high-density apartments are assumed to be structures with 20 or more units. Because appropriate data from the 1970 census were unavailable at the time this analysis occurred, figures shown here are for 1960, as derived from the Bureau of Census, *Metropolitan Housing: Philadelphia, Pennsylvania, N.S. SMSA* (Washington: Government Printing Office, 1960), Table A–6, pp. 137–38.

POTENTIAL ZONING DISTRICT
AND TOWNSHIP EMPLOYMENT

In the last section we developed a list of permitted work-related activities in three-digit SIC categories for each zoning district of the townships under study. A procedure was also devised for estimating the floor area ratio (floor area divided by land area) for each kind of permitted activity. The additional factors required in estimating the number of workers by SIC and by district, are briefly described as follows:

1. In a given district it is not likely that all permitted activities will have equal numbers of workers and it is, therefore, necessary to estimate the probable shares for each SIC. We assume that the relative shares of employment by SIC, in any district, will be the same as the relative shares of employment for those same SICs which are currently active in the four Pennsylvania suburban counties of the Philadelphia Standard Metropolitan Statistical Area.
2. Different industries require different amounts of floor area per worker, and industries differ in the number of shifts using the same floor space. These factors must be considered in relating the number of workers to the land area zoned for manufacturing or business. The floor area per worker and number of work shifts, by SIC, were taken from a recent report for the U.S. Department of Transportation, which was based on a national sample.[15]
3. The manner in which these factors are used is best explained by an illustration (Table 6-10), in which we assume that a manufacturing district allows three SIC industries, A, B and C, of which only A and B are found in the surrounding region, although industry D is also present in the region. The illustration is a step-by-step summary of a computerized algorithm which translates the raw zoning ordinance data taken from Section A of this chapter into final estimates of the labor force by SIC.

This gentle, simplistic exercise conceals a thorny theoretical question. Since we are assuming that areas of vacant land are now filled with

Table 6-10.   Summary of Algorithm for Deriving Employment by SIC: An Illustration

		SIC A	*SIC B*	*SIC C*	*SIC D*	*Total*
a.	SIC permitted in district	YES	YES	YES	NO	
b.	Workers in 4-county area*	10,000	6,000	0	20,000	16,000
c.	Ratio, main shift to total workers*	1.0	0.50	–	–	
d.	Workers requiring floor space ($b \times c$)	10,000	3,000	–	–	13,000
e.	Floor area per worker, sq. ft.*	200	333	–	–	
f.	Floor space, 1000s sq. ft. ($d \times e$)	2,000	1,000	–	–	3,000
g.	Floor area ratio (FAR)*	0.25	0.50	–	–	
h.	Land required, 1000s sq. ft. ($f \div g$)	8,000	2,000	–	–	10,000
i.	Percent distribution of land by SIC	80	20	–	–	100
j.	Total land available in the zoning district, sq. ft.*					600,000
k.	District land division by SIC, sq. ft. ($i \times j$)	480,000	120,000	–	–	600,000
l.	District floor area, sq. ft. ($k \times g$)	120,000	60,000	–	–	180,000
m.	District main shift workers ($l \div e$)	600	180	–	–	780
n.	District total workers ($m \div d$)	600	360	–	–	960
o.	Employment rate, i.e., (1 – unemployment rate)*	0.95	0.90	–	–	
p.	Total district labor force ($n \div o$)	630	400	–	–	1,030

*Assumptions for the example

hypothetical SICs, we have to decide whether to assume that the filling has been taking place over some span of time during the past, that it takes place in a single miraculous day, or that it will take place in the future. There is nothing inherently better about one of these assumptions than another, but the implications for the estimating process are important enough to mention. If it is assumed that the tracts have filled up through past time, it is reasonable to assume that all the kinds of industry to be found in those tracts will be similar to industrial patterns presently found throughout some larger area. If it is assumed that the tracts have been filled in a day, the kinds of industry selected should be weighted toward the kinds that are growing rapidly, since the total stock of industry includes some that may bulk large at present, even though declining. If it is assumed that the tracts are filled in the future, the kinds of industry selected should be weighted by predictions of future growth.

In order to use available employment data as the estimating base, we have adopted the assumption that the vacant work areas developed through past time.[16]

The steps in the estimating process will now be reviewed in detail.

EMPLOYMENT COEFFICIENTS FOR COMMERCIAL AND MANUFACTURING DISTRICTS

Local Employment Distribution by SIC

As depicted in step b of Table 6-10, the employment algorithm requires a "reference base" distribution of SIC employment to determine the mix of SIC employment in each commercial and industrial district. Once it is known from the zoning code which SICs are allowed in a given district, only those which are also found in some larger reference area are allocated a portion of the district's land area. The amount of land devoted to any particular SIC is made proportional to that SIC's share of total reference area land in the permitted SIC groups. One could scarcely allocate land area in a district among all permitted uses, whether they exist in the reference area or not; there is no conceptually defensible way of allocating district land to allowed SICs which cannot be found in the reference area. In order to provide a basis for allocations of district land area to all conceivable allowed SICs, one might well be forced to use the U.S. total SIC mix, with a consequent loss of important employment differences between, say, Anchorage, Phoenix, Philadelphia, or Honolulu. We find it most reasonable to allocate land in individual zoning districts to allowed SICs in relation to their regional employment mix, the data for which are readily available.

In selecting the appropriate reference area, one might consider the entire SMSA or some portion of it. An entire SMSA distribution of SICs is a poor choice when center city distributions of SIC employment are significantly different than those of suburban counties. The SIC employment distribution found in sections of the SMSA most like the area in question would be more useful. Although we considered Delaware County and the combined four Pennsylvania suburban counties of the Philadelphia Metropolitan area as alternatives, the four-county area was selected because it provided wider SIC coverage and was less distorted by the heavy waterfront industries which characterize Delaware County.

The availability of reliable, current SIC employment data is limited to counties, SMSAs, and states in the U.S. Department of Commerce annual publication, *County Business Patterns.* Since the publication is a statistical by-product of employment and payroll information reported on U.S. Treasury Form 941, about 70 percent of total, paid civilian employment is included; many agricultural, domestic service, railroad, government, and self-employed workers are excluded. Employment of federal, nonpostal workers and state employees outside major SMSA center cities and state capitols should also be estimated for the surrounding region and added to the *County Business Patterns* (*CBP*) totals for distribution purposes. The remaining kinds of employment are attributed to each township on the basis of its land area, zoned residential district holding capacity, and potential population. The set of coefficients needed for attributed employment is, therefore, quite different and will be the subject of the next major subsection.

Returning to the matter of *CBP* as a source of employment distributions, there are two important complications which must be resolved in order to use data from the publication for appropriate SICs. One complication, mentioned earlier in the first section, is that central administrative office and auxiliary (CAO and *A*) units are not specifically designated in *CBP* as being associated with particular SICs. Instead, the total employment in all CAO and *A*s is given for an entire industry group, such as nondurable manufacturing. For our purposes, it is essential to obtain a finer breakdown because some CAO and *A* subgroups are permitted by township zoning ordinances and other subgroups are not. For reasons mentioned earlier in this chapter, CAO and *A*s were coded with proxy SIC designations and the estimated employment for each kind of CAO and *A* is added to the employment total of its related SIC industry.[17] The net effect of this adjustment is to give a more realistic regional employment distribution of activities which are often specifically allowed (and eagerly sought) through zoning regulations, but which lack SIC designation and cannot be readily found in *CBP* tables.

The second complication encountered in the use of *CBP* is caused by the Census Bureau policy of not releasing data which might disclose a single firm's actual employees and payroll; figures are suppressed when a very small number of firms, usually at the three- or four-digit SIC level, are found within a county. Even when the actual number of employees in an industry is omitted, *CBP* does indicate the number of firms in each of eight employment-size classes from which an imputed number of employees can be derived.[18] A simple illustration will help clarify the nature of this difficulty. For SIC 369, miscellaneous electrical equipment and supplies, there are six firms, but total employment figures are suppressed because the group is dominated by two large firms. The accompanying table, giving the number of firms by size groups for each industry, has the following information for SIC 369:

Employment Size Group	*Number of Firms*
1–3	2
4–7	0
8–19	2
20–49	0
50–99	0
100–249	1
250–499	1
500 or more	0
	6

Multiplying the midpoint of each size group by the number of firms in that group gives a total estimated employment of 580 for SIC 369. Sometimes (as in this case) the total can also be derived by subtraction if the two-digit total and all other three-digit totals are given.

SIC	36		2,561	employees
	362	1,489		
	366	127		
	367	257		
			− 1,867	
	369		694	

Taking Delaware County as an example, *CBP* reports total employment of 135,129 persons (excluding CAO and A). Using the above methods, we estimate there were 45,800 employees in the three-digit industry groups affected by the nondisclosure rule, approximately 34 percent of the county total. When our estimates are added to the published subtotal for three-digit groups which do have employment figures in *CBP*, the combined total is 131,643, or 97.4 percent of the published county total. The remaining 2.6 percent is presumably accounted for by some inconsistencies in *CBP* detail, and by errors introduced in estimating employment for SICs affected by the nondisclosure rule.

Having made these necessary adjustments to the *County Business Patterns*-SIC employment distribution, the only remaining task before a final employment distribution can be coded for use in the employment estimating algorithm is that of determining regional government employment. All state employment outside of capital cities is assumed to be locationally independent, i.e., its ultimate location was determined by forces other than primary need for its service in the local area. There are exceptions, such as state police barracks, etc., which do service a particular region, but even these are usually free to locate nearly anywhere within large service areas comprising the region.

State employment in counties is available for 1967 from Table 20, Volume 3, U.S. Bureau of the Census, *Compendium of Public Employment, 1967 Census of Governments.* However, these figures are subject to some change over time so that the more recent estimates are preferred. Since most states must know the geographic location of their employees for payroll and other personnel-related purposes, it is quite common for them to keep such information up to date, even if it is not published. For example, the Commonwealth of Pennsylvania supplied a computer print-out of employees as of January 11, 1971, by county and civil service status, noting the number of employees residing in the county and the number headquartered in the county; we used the work location figures. Table 6–11 compares the published figures by 1967 Census of Governments and the 1971 figures from the Commonwealth of Pennsylvania.

Table 6-11. State Employees by County and Source of Data

	Delaware County	*Four-County*
1967: State Employment	2,186	9,713
January 11, 1971: State Employment in Residence	2,293	10,588
January 11, 1971: State Employment Headquartered	2,963	10,931

Table 6-12. Federal Civilian Employment by County, 1969

Employment	*Delaware County*	*Four-County*
Total	2,130	11,646
Postal	1,586	5,039
Nonpostal	544	6,607

Comparable figures must also be estimated for federal employment in counties. Fortunately, excellent statistics of federal employment by geographic area are maintained and published by the U.S. Civil Service Commission. Referring to the commission's publication, *Federal Civilian Employment by Geographic Area* (pamphlet SM 68-04, page 58), federal employment figures for both Delaware County and the four-county area are readily obtained, as shown in Table 6-12.

All that remains is the assembly of adjusted *CBP* employment by SIC and totals of employment for state and federal nonpostal employment, coded as SIC 920 and SIC 912, respectively, to construct a table of regional employment distributions.

Square Feet of Floor Space Per Worker

This single link in the entire analytic chain which translates zoning ordinance data into estimates of employment is the most crucial. Only by knowing the relationship between physical space and labor production tasks can land area be translated into jobs and earnings. For this important ratio to be useful in the present study, square feet per worker must be known at the three-digit level for SICs which have located in developing, low-density areas. A review of the literature revealed either very general or "dated" relationships,[19] which proved to be inadequate in building a systematic, detailed analysis of employment-derived earnings and household income. Fortunately, a key piece of research into these detailed relationships by Edward Ide and Associates, only recently published,[20] fits precisely into the present methodology. Unlike earlier sources, this report contains square foot per worker data, gathered during the late 1960s, for detailed SIC activities, with a slight sampling bias toward developing, suburban areas; in short, the data appear to be ideal.[21]

The Ide Report includes specific data for about 215 of the 250 three-digit SICs found in the four-county area. Since SICs which were not found in the surrounding area (or are not allowed in any of the zoning districts) automatically drop out of the algorithm, estimated ratios are required for only about 35 three-digit SICs. Although a telephone survey of local establishments might pin down the floor area estimate with the greatest accuracy, useful proxies can be taken from the data itself. In general, one can adopt the ratio of a "similar" three-digit activity for the three-digit activity which lacks a ratio of floor area to worker. This proved to be the technique of choice for eight three-digit SICs as shown in Table 6-13.

Another estimating procedure is to use the known floor area per worker at the two-digit level, for example, use SIC 32 to represent SIC 321. This was done for the remaining SICs which lacked ratios in the Ide Report. Although floor area to worker ratios are given, or may be estimated, for the 250 four-county, three-digit SICs from the Ide Report alone, revised estimates should be considered when local floor space usage in other regions is known to be at variance with national averages because of climate, labor supply, stock of industrial space, etc., or when better estimates are obtainable from other sources.[22]

Main Shift to Total Job Ratio

Because the final number of workers employed in each SIC is of prime importance, it is essential that the number of jobs generated by a given

Table 6-13. Estimates of Floor Area per Worker for Selected SICs

Missing SICs	Similar SICs	Floor Area Per Worker (sq. ft.)
2360 (Children's Outerwear)	2330 (Women's and Misses' Outerwear)	471
3020 (Rubber Footwear)	3060 (Fabricated Rubber Products, NEC)	442
4950 (Sanitary Services)	4940 (Water Supply)	251
5320 (Mail Order Houses)	5310 (Department Stores)	231
6030 (Mutual Savings Banks)	6020 (Commercial and Stock Savings Banks)	100
6120 (Savings and Loan Associations)	6020 (Commercial and Stock Savings Banks)	100
7270 (Garment Pressing, Alteration, Repair)	7210 (Laundries and Dry Cleaning Plants)	259
7940 (Miscellaneous Amusement, Recreation Services)	7910 (Dance Halls, Studios, and Schools)	433

amount of floor space be enlarged by a factor which accounts for multiple work shifts. The number of jobs accounted for by total floor space and the floor area per worker represent only the workers on the main shift. Many industries operate more than one shift, due to continuous production technique, heavy product demand, or long hours of service (such as suburban department stores).

A deck of original data cards containing the relevant information was made available to us by Edward Ide and Associates, and by the Federal Highway Administration. From this original data, we were able to calculate ratios of main shift to total workers, by two- and three-digit SIC. (The Ide Report apparently did not calculate or publish this detailed statistic). In the course of making these calculations, a few anomalies were detected in the values recorded for certain establishments; i.e., for some SICs one term or the other (main shift employees or total employees) lacked a numerical value, mechanically producing a ratio of zero or infinity. When only one value was given, that establishment was automatically assigned a ratio of 1.00 (that is, main shift workers divided by total workers =1). In a few cases, where the reported number of main shift workers exceeded total workers, the values were reversed prior to calculation of the ratio on the assumption that they must have been miscoded. [23]

Single Job Holding Rate

The total number of jobs is nearly always larger than the total number of workers holding jobs, because workers in certain occupations and industries hold more than one job. In order to avoid double counting workers, the total number of jobs generated by an SIC must be adjusted to reflect the likely number of workers who hold only those jobs. [24]

The U.S. Department of Labor, Bureau of Labor Statistics, estimates multiple job holding rates for major occupational and industrial categories. A multiple job holding rate for a particular industry describes what percentage of workers employed by that industry *in their primary jobs* take additional jobs in other industries. A better figure for our purposes is the proportion of total jobs in each industry held by workers as their secondary jobs. Once this percentage is determined, it is subtracted from 1.00 to arrive at the "single job holding" rate, which accounts for those who work only in that industry and hold secondary jobs elsewhere.

Occasionally, the Bureau of Labor Statistics analyzes multiple job holding in depth and releases the detailed statistical information in its series *Special Labor Force Reports.* The most recent issue dealing with multiple job holding did not calculate the secondary job holding rates for industries, but it did include the total number of secondary jobs held in each industry. This data allows the calculation of a secondary job holding rate and its complement, the single job holding rate. Table 6–14 summarizes the pertinent computations.

Table 6-14. Derivation of Single Job Holding Rate For SICs and Industries, 1969

Industry Groups	SICs	Total Employment (000s)	Primary Jobs Number in (000s)	Primary Jobs Percent	Secondary Jobs Number in (000s)	Secondary Jobs Percent	Derived Single Job Holding Rate
Mining	10,11,12, 13,14	506	37	7.3	–	–	100.0
Construction	15,16,17,	4,054	300	7.4	144	3.6	96.4
Durable Goods	19,24,25,32 33,34,35,36, 37,38,39	12,250	637	5.2	160	1.3	98.7
Nondurable Goods	20,21,22,23, 26,27,28,29, 30,31	8,386	369	4.4	124	1.5	98.5
Transportation Public Utilities	40,41,42, 44,45,46,47, 48,49	4,829	281	5.7	188	3.9	96.1
Wholesale Trade	50	2,467	116	4.9	72	2.9	97.1
Retail Trade	52,53,54,55 56,57,58,59	10,026	381	3.8	653	6.5	93.5
Finance, Insurance, Real Estate	60,61,62,63, 64,65,66	3,368	128	3.8	132	3.9	96.1
Business and Repair	73,75,76	1,777	96	5.4	152	8.5	91.5
Educational Services	82	5,815	420	7.1	228	3.9	96.1
Professional Services	80,81,89	5,730	259	4.6	293	5.0	95.0
All Other Services	70,72,77,78, 79,80,84,86	2,359	92	3.9	216	9.2	90.8
State/Local Public Administration	92,93	2,089	234	11.2	152	7.3	92.7
Federal Public Administration	9120	1,469	72	4.9	8	0.5	99.5
Postal Service	9110	721	75	10.4	24	3.3	96.7

Source: U.S. Bureau of Labor Statistics, *Special Labor Force Reports: Multiple Job Holders in May, 1969* (Washington: Government Printing Office, 1970).

Employment Rate

The single job holding rate introduced the demographic reality of actual workers, rather than total available jobs, to the analysis, but one final coefficient is required. Since the presence of worker unemployment in various industries (and their constituent SICs) tends to underestimate the size of a resident population of workers, both employed and unemployed, the total size of the labor force must be estimated. The procedure necessary to estimate the size of the labor force is very straightforward. The first step involves simple subtraction of an industry's unemployment percentage from 100 to determine its "employment rate." The number of employed workers is then divided by the employment rate to derive the size of the labor force for each industry and SIC. Table 6–15 assigns two-digit SICs to each of the industries for which an unemployment rate is known and the employment rate is determined.

Summary

The six coefficients derived from secondary data sources, as discussed in this section, are not uniformly available at three-digit SIC detail. Fortunately, it was possible to establish three-digit detail for the most critical coefficients: regional employment distribution and floor area per worker. However, potential sources of interindustry variation are introduced by use of the four remaining coefficients of two-digit SIC detail, which translate estimates of shift jobs into the labor force. A concerted effort was made to assure that the most universally available coefficients, in greatest SIC detail, were used, but as better data sources (primarily the 1970 census) become available, they should be used to update, localize and increase the SIC detail of all coefficients. The final version of these coefficients was assembled on a single set of coding sheets prior to card punching for use in the algorithm as shown in Appendix M.

EMPLOYMENT FOUND IN
RESIDENTIAL DISTRICTS

Some kinds of employment are typically found in districts zoned for residence. The facilities involved consume a very small portion of total residential land, and the estimating procedure is therefore based on population size rather than land area. Government employment, which provides public services to a local population, is the most obvious example. The population of residential districts constitutes a base which is then multiplied by a ratio of government employees to population. In addition to local government, we will also estimate employment in the federal postal service, private households, and agriculture.[25]

Local Government Employment

Looking first at local government, there is employment in even the smallest civil division which provides municipal functions and services, plus

Table 6-15. Employment and Unemployment Rates of Industries and SICs, 1969

Industries	SICs	Unemployment[1] Percent	Employment[1] Percent
Mining	10,11,12,13,14	2.8	97.2
Construction	15,16,17	6.0	94.0
Primary Metal	33	2.2	97.8
Fabricated Metal	34	3.2	96.8
Machinery	35	2.2	97.8
Electrical Equipment	36	3.0	97.0
Transportation Equipment[2]	37	3.3	96.7
Other Durable Goods	19,24,25 32,38,39	3.8	96.2
Food and Kindred	20	4.5	95.5
Textile Mill	22	4.2	95.8
Apparel	23	5.9	94.1
Other Nondurable Goods	21,26,27,28,29 30,31	2.5	97.5
Railroads	40	1.6	98.4
Other Transportation	41,42,44,45 46,47,49	3.0	97.0
Communications	48	1.5	98.5
Wholesale and Retail Trade	50,52,53,54 55,56,57 58,59	4.1	95.9
Finance, Insurance, Real Estate	60,61,62,63,64 65,66	2.1	97.9
Professional Services	80,81,89	2.3	97.7
All Other Services	70,72,73,75,76 78,79,82,84,86	4.7	95.3
Public Administration[3]	91,92,93	1.8	98.2

1. U.S. Bureau of Labor Statistics, *Special Labor Force Report: Employment and Unemployment in 1969*, no. 129 (Washington: Government Printing Office), Table 4–10.

2. Weighted mean of motor vehicle and all other transportation equipment.

3. From U.S. Bureau of Labor Statistics *Handbook of Labor Statistics*, (Washington: Government Printing Office, 1970), Table 78, p. 144.

employment in local school districts. There may also be county level employment to consider, but only if the minor civil division in question is also the county headquarters; none of the townships in our study is a county seat. Therefore the present analysis will be concerned only with local township and school district employment. Since only two of the six townships being examined were large enough to be reported separately in the *1967 Census of Governments, Employment of Major Local Governments,* Number 1,[26] it was decided that ratios of government employees to population would be more appropriately estimated from data on Pennsylvania townships by population-size class, which are published in *Compendium of Public Employment,* Number 2, Table 35.[27] The ratios of each population-size class were adjusted by a factor obtained by dividing total Delaware County jobs per 1,000 population by the equivalent Pennsylvania ratio. Table 6-16 presents the figures by population-size class.

Federal Postal Employment

The other form of government employment providing service to a local area is that of the Federal Postal Service. Ratios of postal employees to population can be derived from known 1970 census population of governmental units and published figures of postal employees as shown in Table 6-17.[28] Relative uniformity of the ratios would render any of them suitable for adoption, but Delaware County is chosen simply because it is the next largest government unit in which the townships are situated.

Private Household Employment

Residential units are the base from which household workers are calculated. Since private household workers form such a small occupational category, reliable estimates of its size within a region are difficult to establish,[29] and the multiplicity of employers involved precludes employer surveys.

Table 6-16. Ratio of Local Government Employment to Population, 1967

	Workers per 10,000 Population		
	Pennsylvania	*Adjustment Factor*	*Delaware County*
All workers	224		189
Adjustment factor: Delaware County, Pennsylvania Townships,		0.843	
0–9,999 population	239	X 0.843	202
10,000–24,999 population	176	X 0.843	147
25,000–49,000 population	192	X 0.843	163

Sources: Ratios for Delaware County are calculated from Table 20, *1967 Census of Governments, Compendium of Public Employment.*

Ratios for Pennsylvania were taken from Table 19 of the same report.

Table 6-17.   Postal Employees per 100,000 Population

	Delaware County	*4-County*	*Philadelphia SMSA*	*Pennsylvania*	*U.S.*
Federal P.O. Employment	951	5,039	19,913	43,613	739,064
Population 1970 (1000s)	415	1,917	4,819	11,794	202,534
Postal Employees per 100,000 Population	378	381	413	370	365

The small number of employees per employer, the casual nature of occupational entry and exit, and the extremely high proportion of part-time workers effectively excludes employers in this combination industry (SIC 88) and occupation from participating in state unemployment insurance programs and, therefore, employment figures are not reported in *CBP*.

      If one were to take the Philadelphia Bureau of Employment Security's estimate of private household workers in the Philadelphia labor market area for 1970 and adjust that estimate by the known change in total U.S. private household worker employment (47,000 $\times$ .52), approximately 24,500 workers result. Knowing that black females constitute a significant proportion of all private household workers,[30] it is then possible to determine the Pennsylvania counties' proportion of the Philadelphia SMSA's total (24,500) private household workers. In 1970, the black female population, 20 years old or more, in Bucks, Chester, Delaware, Montgomery, and Philadelphia counties was 231,800, or about 92 percent of the total (252,601) SMSA black female population. Applying the 92 percent proportion, about 22,500 private household workers would be expected to live in the Pennsylvania portion of the Philadelphia SMSA. The proportion of these 22,500 household workers working in the city vs. those working in the four suburban counties can be estimated by the location of residence and workplace of private household workers in the 1960 census of population.[31] Of total private household workers in the Pennsylvania portion of Philadelphia's SMSA, about 45 percent would work in ring Pennsylvania counties. Thus, about 10,125 private household workers (0.45 $\times$ 22,500) were employed by the 580,199 households in the four suburban-county area.[32] When this figure is expressed in terms of a household ratio, (10,125 $\div$ 580,199 $\times$ 1,000) there are about 17.5 private household workers per 1,000 residential households.

Agricultural Employment

      Finally, coefficients are needed to estimate each township's share of current county agricultural employment. Because the amount of agricultural employment possible is roughly proportional to the size of the township and inversely proportional to its density of development, these two factors will be used as coefficients in Table 6-18. First, the percent of total county land in each township was calculated (A and B, Table 6-18). Each township's land area percentage was then multiplied by total county agricultural employment to determine the township's crude share of agricultural employment (C), assuming the development densities (population per square mile) for the county and all townships are equal. However, knowing the development densities are not equal (D), county population per square mile was divided by the comparable density measure for each township to determine a relative density index (E). The density index for each township was, in turn, applied to its estimated "equal density" land area share of county agricultural (C) to arrive at a density-weighted estimate of agricultural employment (F). Because the sum of individual estimated township employment (500), exceeded the expected size of total employment calculated for the aggregate of all townships (214 × 1.812 = 388), the estimates in (C), were systematically diminished by multiplying each times 0.776 (388 ÷ 500), resulting in final agricultural employment by township (G).

PATTERNS OF EMPLOYMENT DERIVED FROM TOWNSHIP ZONING ORDINANCES

Earlier sections of this chapter examined in detail the manner in which estimates of employment were generated, and established the statistical underpinnings for such estimates. We are now in a position to present and briefly review the estimates of employment arising out of township zoning ordinances.

Employment in Manufacturing and Industrial Districts

It will be recalled that once the list of allowed SIC uses within a district is established, the employment algorithm allocates land area to each SIC on the basis of its observed employment representation in the reference area.[33] The several development restrictions which zoning ordinances impose upon particular SICs or classes of SIC in their use of that land then determines how much net floor area is likely. The algorithm allocates district land area to allowed SICs within a district, and since each district has its own list of allowed SICs and a particular floor to land area ratio for each SIC on that list, the potential yield of developable floor area can vary quite considerably. These differences are, of course, important from the viewpoint of employment generated, but they could also affect the physical bulk of plant or store size, and the consequent ad valorem tax base. Floor areas are then converted to main shift jobs by ratios of floor area per worker and, in turn, main shift jobs are translated through a series of steps through total jobs and total workers

Table 6-18. Agricultural Workers by Township, 1969

	A Square Miles	B Percent Land Area	C Employees	D Population per Square Miles	E Delaware County Townships	F Employees	G Employees
Delaware County	184.43	100.0	644*	3,254	—	644	644
Aston Township	5.90	3.1	20	3,965	0.821	16	12
Birmingham Township	8.84	4.8	31	904	3.600	111	82
Concord Township	13.78	7.5	48	1,890	1.722	83	61
Edgmont Township	9.74	5.3	34	1,020	3.193	109	80
Middletown Township	13.43	7.5	48	2,513	1.295	63	46
Thornbury Township	9.16	5.0	32	886	3.673	118	87
Six Townships	60.85	33.2	214	1,795	1.812	500	388

*644 agricultural workers includes 112 farm operators and 532 hired farm laborers. From Tables 3 and 14, Delaware County, Pa. U.S., Department of Commerce, *County Report Text*, Census of Agricultural, 1969 (Washington: Government Printing Office, 1971).

to arrive at the size of the labor force.[34] Table 6-19 summarizes for each industrial and commercial district the final yield of developable floor area (measured as the floor area to land area ratio) and helps to sort out the results obtained at each link along the analytic chain between main shift jobs and the labor force.[35]

Note that industrial districts tend to have considerably higher ratios of floor area to land area (FAR) than do commercial districts, i.e., 0.405 v 0.237, respectively, and that there are also significant differences in FAR among particular districts within the industrial and commercial groups. The number of main shift jobs generated by each district's floor area constitute only about 83 percent of the total labor force for all districts, both commercial and industrial. It would thus appear that the effort expended on tracing main shift jobs through the labor force, the employment statistic most directly related to a township's household population, was well worth the effort.

The patterns of floor area and employment for each of the districts provide a good overview of the results obtained by our estimating procedures, but they necessarily gloss over the probable mix of industrial and commercial establishments. One might advance the hypothesis that care exercised in the selection of uses which are allowed within districts is indicative of a development strategy designed to either enlarge the tax base or the earned incomes of resident workers. While it is much too cumbersome to tabulate potential employment by SICs for each township, it is worth trying to summarize the relationship of each district's total number of allowed three-digit SICs to other benchmarks, and then note any significant differences across districts. To this end, Table 6-20 was prepared.

Column (A) shows the total number of three-digit SICs possible in any given district, and the actual number of SICs allowed in each district is shown in Column (B). Column (C) gives the number of three-digit SICs, both allowed and existing, in the four-county reference area. Accordingly, (C/A) can be viewed as an effective measure of the potential SICs which could locate within a district. The arithmetic difference between (B/A) and (C/A) represents the percentage of allowed SICs which are not likely to materialize and, perhaps, reflects how realistically local townships define allowed activities. The definition process is also tested by (C/B), which might be thought of as the efficiency of choice. The patterns in Table 6-20 suggest that townships which were somewhat selective in defining the allowed uses in their districts (as depicted by (B/A) were relatively accurate in choosing activities that were potentially developable (C/B).

Total Township Employment

Employment in the 17 commercial and manufacturing districts need only be summed for the districts in any given township to arrive at the total township employment. Table 6-21 summarizes by district the total labor force

Table 6-19. Land Area, Floor Area, and Floor to Land Area Ratio, Main Shift Jobs, Total Jobs, Total Workers and Labor Force of Districts

Districts	Land Area	Floor Area	Ratio of Floor to Land Area $(FA \div LA)$	Main Shift Jobs	Total Jobs	Total Workers	Labor Force	Main Shift Job $\div$ Labor Force
Industrial								
13	31,363,424	10,497,352	0.335	22,614	27,235	26,736	27,654	0.818
22	3,936,900	1,631,290	0.414	3,328	3,950	3,878	4,005	0.831
35	14,332,924	7,167,817	0.500	15,626	18,448	17,793	18,448	0.847
53	11,513,254	4,840,979	0.420	10,750	12,740	12,399	12,805	0.840
54	7,573,502	3,990,763	0.527	9,194	10,780	10,559	10,951	0.840
62	14,018,303	5,400,531	0.385	12,375	14,973	14,761	15,283	0.810
All	82,736,307	33,528,732	0.405	73,887	88,126	86,126	89,146	0.829
Commercial								
11	7,748,272	1,642,034	0.212	3,811	4,628	4,347	4,508	0.854
12	460,801	98,864	0.215	230	279	262	272	0.846
21	11,631,551	2,465,875	0.212	5,600	6,782	6,369	6,605	0.848
31	3,674,702	1,281,583	0.349	3,406	4,115	3,872	4,000	0.852
32	7,103,602	1,762,962	0.248	4,197	5,259	4,925	5,109	0.822
33	1,798,290	324,598	0.181	840	1,010	950	981	0.856
34	3,744,247	858,165	0.229	1,598	1,897	1,780	1,852	0.863
41	2,198,881	665,310	0.303	1,511	1,830	1,718	1,782	0.848
51	2,289,423	621,810	0.272	1,412	1,710	1,606	1,666	0.848
52	1,906,876	404,258	0.212	918	1,112	1,044	1,083	0.848
61	928,103	194,744	0.210	442	536	503	522	0.847
All	43,484,748	10,320,203	0.237	23,965	29,158	27,376	28,380	0.844
Total	126,221,055	43,848,935	0.347	97,852	117,284	113,502	117,526	0.832

Table 6–20. Representation of All Three-Digit SICs in Districts

District	All SICs Possible (A)	SICs allowed by Ordinance (B)	Employment in Four-County SICs (C)	(B/A)	(C/A)	(C/B)
Industrial						
13	348	126	108	0.36	0.31	0.86
22	348	110	107	0.32	0.31	0.97
35	348	150	150	0.37	0.37	0.00
53	348	135	128	0.39	0.37	0.95
54	348	149	88	0.43	0.25	0.59
62	348	41	41	0.12	0.12	1.00
All	348	119	104	0.34	0.30	0.87
Commercial						
11	348	134	106	0.39	0.31	0.79
12	348	126	103	0.36	0.30	0.81
21	348	137	109	0.39	0.31	0.80
31	348	97	80	0.28	0.23	0.83
32	348	80	80	0.23	0.23	1.00
33	348	100	83	0.29	0.23	0.83
34	348	88	84	0.25	0.24	0.96
41	348	136	109	0.39	0.31	0.80
51	348	138	109	0.40	0.31	0.80
52	348	137	109	0.39	0.31	0.80
61	348	139	109	0.40	0.31	0.78
All	348	119	98	0.34	0.28	0.83

supported by the employment in each township. There is a wide variation in labor force size across the township; the largest labor force (32,344), commercial and industrial district workers, was in Aston Township and the smallest (1,782), in Edgmont Township. To lend a bit of perspective to each township's development policy, the total number of labor force members was compared with the total number of housing units allowed by the residential codes. On this basis, Thornbury Township allowed 6.4 workers (the highest) per potential housing unit and Edgmont 0.6 workers (the lowest). The two townships have entirely different development strategies, but additional knowledge about housing costs, other forms of employment, and the workers' household income distribution are required to judge the net effect of their residence and workplace zoning mix.

Table 6–21 presents district and township labor force figures for workers in commercial and manufacturing districts which were estimated by the employment algorithm. The township labor force also includes local government employees, postal workers, agricultural workers and private household workers.[36] When the coefficients for each of these kinds of employment are multiplied by their respective bases, and adjusted for the employment rate, the resultant labor force for each township is obtained as shown in Table 6–22.

Table 6-21. Potential Labor Force by Townships and District, and Housing Units by Township, as per Zoning Ordinance

Townships	District	Labor Force Number	Labor Force Percent	Housing Units	Ratio of Labor Force Members to Housing Units
Aston	All	32,344	100.0	7,088	4.6:1
	11	4,508	13.9		
	12	272	0.8		
	13	27,564	85.2		
Birmingham	All	11,330	100.0	2,498	4.5:1
	21	6,642	58.2		
	22	4,688	41.4		
Concord	All	30,390	100.0	8,393	3.5:1
	31	4,000	13.2		
	32	5,109	16.8		
	33	981	3.2		
	34	1,852	6.1		
	35	18,448	60.7		
Edgmont	41	1,782	100.0	3,009	0.6:1
Middletown	All	26,505	100.0	10,414	2.5:1
	51	1,666	6.3		
	52	1,083	4.1		
	53	12,805	48.3		
	54	10,951	41.3		
Thornbury	All	15,805	100.0	2,459	6.4:1
	61	522	3.3		
	62	15,283	96.7		

Table 6-22. Agricultural, Local Government, Postal, and Private Household Worker Labor Force, by Township

	Agriculture	Local Government	Postal	Private Households	Total
Aston	12	326	89	124	551
Birmingham	82	153	31	44	310
Concord	61	399	100	147	707
Edgmont	80	155	31	43	310
Middletown	46	518	130	182	876
Thornbury	87	155	31	43	316

The labor force from commercial and manufacturing districts (Table 6-21), is then combined with the labor force estimated from residential zoning districts (Table 6-22), as shown in Table 6-23. With the exception of Edgmont Township, the township labor force from residential districts ranged roughly between two and three percent of the total labor force, with a six-

Table 6-23. Total Township Labor Force by Type of District

Township	Commercial-Manufacturing District (Number)	Residential District (Number)	Total (Number)	Commercial-Manufacturing District (Percent)	Residential District (Percent)
Aston	32,344	551	32,895	98.3	1.7
Birmingham	11,330	310	11,640	97.2	2.8
Concord	30,390	707	31,097	97.7	2.3
Edgmont	1,782	310	2,092	84.1	15.9
Middletown	26,505	876	27,381	96.8	3.2
Thornbury	15,805	316	16,121	98.0	2.0
All	118,156	3070	121,226	97.4	2.6

township mean of 2.6 percent. On the whole, over 97 percent of potential township employment is traced to commercial and industrial zoning districts. Residential district employment was, however, 15.9 percent of the total in Edgmont and it was primarily due to Edgmont's relatively small commercial and industrial district employment, combined with a relatively large stock of housing units. Clearly, Edgmont Township has an overall development strategy quite different from the other five townships in that its total land area is about 16 percent of the total six-township land area, yet it has zoned that land to produce less than 2 percent of the six-township labor force and about 9 percent of its housing stock.

NOTES

15. Edward Ide and Associates, *Estimating Land and Floor Area Implicit in Employment Projections: How Land and Floor Area Usage Rates Vary by Industry and Site Variables,* Vols. I, II (Washington: Federal Highway Administration, U.S. Department of Transportation, 1970).

16. In the third section of this chapter, the regional mix of SICs was mechanically altered, in accordance with 1960 to 1970 growth trends, to simulate current and future potential mixes and to trace their impact on the number and income distribution of households with working heads. As noted in later discussions, the resultant household income figures were quite resistant to dramatically altered assumptions about differential SIC growth patterns.

17. See Appendix J for further detail on the procedures used to estimate SIC equivalents of CAO and *A*s.

18. Seven of the eight employment-size classes have an implicit mean employment which can be multiplied by the known number of firms in that class. By checking the total number of firms, and employees at the two-digit or industry level, it is possible to determine whether the estimate obtained at a three- or four-digit level falls within the

known range of possibilities; this is particularly important when one of the firms in question falls in the eighth employment-size class, which is open-ended and therefore has no upper bound.

19. Early studies of the industrial structure of the economic base of cities and regions typically examined only the number of workers per acre for major industrial categories (manufacturing, wholesale trade, etc.), occasionally separating ratios of central cities from those of surrounding areas; see for example, Balitmore (Md.) Regional Planning Council, *Industrial Land Development,* Technical Report No. 2, May, 1959. Employees per acre has also recently been used to demonstrate gross imbalances between land zoned for industrial and residential uses in a large region; see Middlesex-Somerset-Mercer (N.J.), Regional Study Council, *Housing and Quality of our Environment* (Princeton, N.J., December, 1970). Perhaps the most useful, but still relatively crude, findings were those generated by the Philadelphia City Planning Commission, *Comprehensive Plan for the City of Philadelphia,* 1960. Floor space per worker, as well as employees per site acre, were given for many two-digit SICs, by zones (three) of development intensity (Floor Area Ratio of building to site). Although the least intensive zone is probably not too different from developing suburban areas, technology has possibly eroded the relationships found in the late 1950s, and two-digit SIC detail is inadequate. Another study of Philadelphia's industry *(The Usefulness of Philadelphia's Industrial Plant: An Approach to Industrial Renewal, Arthur D. Little,* January, 1960) did specify sq. ft. per worker for many of Philadelphia's three- and four-digit industries, but some industries were omitted and technological change over a decade also tends to date these moving relationships.

20. Edward Ide and Associates, *Estimating Land and Floor Area Implicit in Employment Projections.*

21. Ibid., see Introduction, Vol. I; Appendix B, "Cooperative Mail Survey," Vol. II.

22. Once the floor area per worker is known for each SIC, the proper Floor Area Class can be determined. Knowing the Floor Area Class and the mean number of floors characteristic of buildings which house a given SIC, its land area to floor area ration (FAR) may be determined. The Ide Report contains both kinds of data. Additional detail on procedures required to estimate mean number of floors by SIC from the Ide Report may be found in Appendix K. Our estimates for the mean number of floors for each three-digit SIC are contained in Appendix L.

23. The ratio thus obtained reflects a set of relationships which existed during the late 1960s, a period of near full employment and near capacity output. The effect of strong economic activity would tend to produce relatively high ratios, on the assumption that extra labor would be hired during the short run to meet high aggregate demand. Thus, the ratios probably represent the upper end of a

range, within which the ratios might be expected to move rather quickly from boom to bust, or more slowly in response to changes in technology and production technique. Our estimate of these ratios may be found in Appendix L.

24. In translating main shift jobs to total workers, it is implicitly assumed that all jobs are occupied by someone as his primary or secondary job. However, a fraction of a percent of all jobs are unoccupied at any given point in time and, therefore, the estimate of total workers is a bit high. The use of job vacancy rates to adjust the estimated number of workers is not feasible at this time, due primarily to the incomplete coverage of industries; nor, perhaps, is it worth the effort, although the discrepancy should be noted.

25. Recall that state and federal employment, which does not service particular populations, is assumed to be locationally neutral and is, therefore, allocated to townships on the same basis as other private industries.

26. U.S., Bureau of the Census (Washington: Government Printing Office, 1967).

27. U.S., Bureau of the Census (Washington: Government Printing Office, 1967).

28. U.S. Civil Service Commission, *Annual Report of Federal Civilian Employment by Geographic Area, 1969,* Pamphlet SM 68–04 (Washington: Government Printing Office, 1969), p. 158.

29. If one were to accept the 1970 estimates from Philadelphia's Bureau of Employment Security (BES), there were approximately 47,000 household workers in the Philadelphia Labor Market Area (PLMA), an increase over 1960 census reported 38,565 employees, an increase in close agreement with total growth (22 percent) of the PLMA labor force from 1960 to 1970. However, the total number of private household workers in the U.S. is known by household sampling to be 48 percent smaller than the total reported for 1960, a divergence of 70 percent (22 percent + 48 percent) from Philadelphia's BES estimates.

30. In May, 1970, there were 1,538,000 private household workers in the U.S., 647,000 of whom were black females (42 percent), the largest single demographic category comprising the occupation. U.S. Department of Labor, *Employment and Earnings,* Vol. 17, No. 12, Table A–19 (Washington: Government Printing Office, 1971).

31. U.S., Bureau of Census, *Journey to Work,* Table 2, PC (2)–6B (Washington: Government Printing Office, 1960).

32. When the remaining 12,375 workers are expressed as a percent of the City of Philadelphia's black female population, the 6.1 percent figure obtained falls within a range of similar percentage calculations for poverty areas of nonsouthern cities (Chicago–5.3 percent; Los Angeles–14.8 percent; New York City–17.5 percent; Detroit–19.0 percent; four-city mean–13.2 percent) from U.S., Bureau of Labor Statistics, *Handbook of Labor Statistics* 1970 (Washington: Government Printing Office, 1970), p. 109. In other words, the estimate probably is not unreasonable.

33. As mentioned earlier in this major section, subtle, but interesting, differences

in employment estimates are produced by using an alternative reference area in the employment algorithm. For further information on the differences observed when the Delaware County reference area employment distribution was used in the employment algorithm see Appendix N.

34. See Appendix 0, which contains the computer program for our employment algorithm and estimate of the employment generated by the algorithm for District 62.

35. A final review of the analysis in this section of Chapter 6 brought to light a minor programming error in the very first step of the computing procedure, as illustrated in Table 6–10. A corrected program was used to reproduce all of the computations up to and including households by income distribution by district (See Appendix P). The errors proved to be exceedingly small and, having completed all subsequent analyses based on this step, we therefore did not go through the routine, but time-consuming, final steps of reconverting household income to housing type and cost, and then to zoning changes. Appendix P also gives the corrected figures, and the difference between corrected and initial estimates, for employment and household income.

In order to maintain consistency through all stages of the computations described in this volume, the text and appendix tables include the original error.

36. There are other kinds of employment often found in residential districts: rest homes, nursing homes, private schools and colleges, state and county institutions for adult and juvenile offenders, hospitals, and "home occupations" in which the residence is used in part for medical, dental, and other services. Although any one municipality may have a number of jobs in one or more of these activities, the large ones (such as hospitals, institutions, colleges) are not distributed widely among municipalities. Without a reasonable basis for estimating them for all municipalities, they were omitted from the computation of total workers.

EARNINGS AND HOUSEHOLD INCOME OF
TOWNSHIP WORKERS

Having determined the potential labor force by SIC for each township, the next step is to determine the associated household income distributions.[37] This section will deal with the procedures, assumptions and data which were developed to link SIC specific workers to an estimate of households and their wage related income.

DEVELOPING A WORKER HOUSEHOLD
INCOME ALGORITHM

Households often include more than one wage earner and household income often includes nonwage income, e.g., dividends, interest, social security payments, etc. Accordingly, our estimate of workers by SIC from Section B is not directly convertible to a distribution of households and their total income.

Earnings distributions, for example, are available only for major industry groups and occupations on a current basis for the U.S. as a whole, from the Bureau of the Census, *Current Population Reports, (CPR)* series.[38] These distributions are not localized to reflect differential compensation structures, nor are they given for all SICs, even at the two-digit level. The Bureau of Labor Statistics does publish average weekly earnings by detailed SICs on an annual basis for most labor market areas.[39] However, not all local SICs are included, and, of those which are, the reported earnings are only for production and nonsupervisory employees. This tends to understate average weekly earnings in proportion to the percentage of an SIC's supervisory or nonproduction work force. Even if the above difficulties could be resolved, it is the distribution of annual earnings which is important for our purposes, not the weekly average earnings.

As noted above, industry-related worker earnings and household income distributions in the *Current Population Reports* sample are available for only 14 broad industry groups. Since there are well over 100 possible

SICs in most township zoning districts, much of the SIC detail strived for earlier, in the analysis of zoning ordinances and in employment estimation, could be washed away if these broad industry level earnings and income distributions were applied. However, in 12 of the 14 industries *CPR* Also gives income and earnings distributions for each of four occupational groups which comprise the industry in question. These four occupational distributions within the total industry distribution provide the key to disaggregating a broad industry's distribution into its constituent SIC distributions. The additional piece of data required for this step is a set of industry-occupational coefficients. Once these are in hand, the proportion of the labor force in any three-digit SIC accounted for by each occupational group may be determined. The resultant number of workers in each SIC's occupational group is then distributed across its earnings and income distribution at the industry level. The total number of workers in each dollar category are then summed across occupational group distributions to derive a three-digit SIC earnings distribution. The following hypothetical example will serve to illustrate this process.

Assume:
a. Occupational Coefficients of three-digit SIC xxx where $Occ_1 = 0.10$, $Occ_2 = 0.20$, $Occ_3 = 0.30$, $Occ_4 = 0.40$
b. Labor Force of SIC xxx = 100 workers
c. Distribution of Earnings, by Occupations, for Industry x of which SIC xxx is a part, where:

Industry x

Occupations	Percent of Industry x in Occupations	Earnings					Mean Earnings ($)
		$0–5,000	$5–10,000	$10–15,000	$15–20,000	All	
Occ_1	25	0.10	0.20	0.30	0.40	1.00	12,500
Occ_2	25	0.20	0.30	0.40	0.10	1.00	9,500
Occ_3	25	0.40	0.30	0.20	0.10	1.00	7,500
Occ_4	25	0.30	0.40	0.10	0.20	1.00	8,500
All	100	0.25	0.30	0.25	0.20	1.00	9,500

Calculation:
The calculation of the earnings distribution for three-digit SIC xxx workers, from that of the more aggregated industry distribution, is illustrated by Table 6–24. The occupational coefficients for SIC xxx (column 1) are multiplied by the total labor force for SIC xxx (100), to derive SIC xxx's labor force by occupation (column 2). The number of workers in each occupation is then multiplied by the earnings percentage distribution (matrix 3) to derive the number of workers in each earnings group (matrix 4).

Table 6-24. Illustrative Calculation of SIC Earnings Distribution

(1) SIC Occupational Coefficients	(2) SIC Labor Force	(3) Industry Earnings Distribution ($)				(4) SIC Earnings Distribution ($)				(5) SIC ($) Mean Earnings
		0–5,000	5–10,000	10–15,000	15–20,000	0–5,000	5–10,000	10–15,000	15–10,000	
$Occ_1 = 0.10$	10	0.10	0.20	0.30	0.40	1	2	3	4	$12,500
$Occ_2 = 0.20$	20	0.20	0.30	0.40	0.10	4	6	8	2	9,500
$Occ_3 = 0.30$	30	0.40	0.30	0.20	0.10	12	9	6	3	7,500
$Occ_4 = 0.40$	40	0.30	0.40	0.10	0.20	$\frac{12}{29}$	$\frac{16}{33}$	$\frac{4}{21}$	$\frac{8}{17}$	$\frac{8,500}{\$\,8,825}$
$\overline{1.00}$	$\overline{100}$	$\overline{0.25}$	$\overline{0.30}$	$\overline{0.25}$	$\overline{0.20}$					
						0.29	0.33	0.21	0.17	

Earnings distributions for the townships were generated in this manner for all workers in each three-digit SIC. It must be recognized that they are based upon average earnings distributions for the U.S. as a whole, which may be at slight or considerable variance from the local earnings structure. We considered it unnecessary to adjust the U.S. distribution in this study since the average weekly earnings of durable and nondurable manufacturing industry employees (average earnings weighted by employment) in the U.S. were 98.5 percent that of mean Philadelphia SMSA earnings.[40] If, in other areas, greater variation in weekly or annual earnings is observed, it would be wise to localize the U.S. distribution.[41]

In order to move from the earnings distribution of workers to the income distribution of households, earnings must be adjusted to include unearned income, and the labor force size must also be adjusted downward to household totals to take account of multiple family earners. Both adjustments are made by analogy to U.S. data. The *Current Population Reports* data, referred to previously, include income distributions of household heads employed in the same 14 industries for which worker earnings are known. Using the observed relationships between the two U.S. distributions, we then converted our estimated worker earnings distribution to household income distributions.

To develop these relationships for our purpose, household to worker ratios were computed from the U.S. data by dividing the number of households in an income class, e.g., less than $5,000, by the number of workers in the same dollar earnings class, e.g., less than $5,000.

The calculation of a household income distribution is illustrated in Table 6–25, using the hypothetical earnings distribution derived above for SIC xxx, as described in Table 6–24.

Table 6–25. Illustrative Calculation of Household Income Distribution for SIC xxx

	All	*Earnings and Income Distribution*				*Mean*
		$0–5,000	*$5–10,000*	*$10–15,000*	*$15–20,000*	
Workers with Earnings (Number/Percent)	100	29	33	21	17	$ 8,825
Ratio of Households to Workers	0.70	0.17	0.33	1.19	1.77	0.70
Households with Income (Number)	70	5	10	25	30	$13,570
(Percent)	100	7.1	14.3	37.7	42.9	–

Note that the average ratio of households to workers is necessarily less than 1.00, a reflection of the presence of multiple-worker households; we assumed SIC xxx averaged 0.70 workers per household for purposes of this illustration, a ratio very close to that observed in the durable goods industry. The fact that incomes exceed earnings, e.g., 29 percent of earners vs. only 7 percent households in the $0–5,000 interval, . . ., 17 percent of earners vs. 43 percent of households in the $15,000–20,000 interval reflects, in part, multiple wages which accrue to households with more than one worker. It also reflects the unearned component of household income, e.g. rents, interests, profits, transfers. The aggregate income of the households in our illustration (70 · $13,570 = $949,900) exceeds the aggregate earnings of the workers (100 · $8,825 = $882,500) by $67,400, or by about $960 per household. This $960 represents the average amount of "unearned" income, i.e., income from sources other than wages and salaries or self-employment. Since Philadelphia SMSA earned income, as a percentage of total Philadelphia SMSA income, was found to be very close to that of the nation as a whole, we did not make any local adjustment for other forms of income.[42] The 1970 census provides up-to-date relationships between household earnings and income by which local income can be directly determined and which can be used to establish local benchmarks for subsequent adjustment of national distributions.

COEFFICIENTS FOR WORKER-HOUSEHOLD INCOME ALGORITHM

The task of calculating household income distributions for each town's labor force lies primarily in assembling the relevant data and translating it into coefficients which can be entered in the worker-household income algorithm. This section will trace the estimation of income coefficients in full detail, from original source to their final form, as recorded on coding sheets for input to the algorithm.

Worker Earnings Distribution by Industry

The availability of U.S. industry earnings distributions by occupational group has already been cited. The earnings distributions available from the *Current Population Reports* are published separately for male and female workers and are further distinguished by whether such workers were year-round, full-time workers or all workers with earnings in a given year. Since all workers who received earnings in a given year would more nearly approximate the labor force working in employment districts, we elected to use the "all worker" earnings distribution.

The breakdown by sex of each township's potential labor force is unknown and yet the township's entire labor force must be distributed among earnings categories which reflect implicitly the relative number of males and females in each earnings category. In the *CPR* data there are 14 earnings categories, 11 industries, four occupational groups and two sexes, all of which must be combined to weight the male and female earnings distribution for the derivation of potential worker earnings for each town. A simple computer program was designed which calculates the weighted industry-occupational coefficients.[43] Table 6–26 shows the earnings distribution for male and female workers, by occupational group, in the durable goods industries, by sex and as a combined weighted average.

Industry-Occupational Coefficients
Occupational coefficients for three-digit SICs are required to combine the four occupational groups' earnings distribution, by major industry, to derive an occupationally weighted three-digit SIC earnings distribution. The occupational coefficients of SICs are to be estimated in the same detail as the occupational groupings for which earnings distributions are published:

1. professional and managerial workers
2. clerical and sales workers
3. craftsmen and operatives
4. other workers

In 1960 the Bureau of Census published occupational coefficients for the Philadelphia SMSA, but only for 34 two-digit SICs, or clusters of two-digit SICs, as compared with about 350 three-digit SICs which could show up in township zoning ordinances. To obtain the needed three-digit SIC detail, we relied upon the national industry-occupation matrix, which contains the U.S. coefficients for 1960 and those projected for 1975.[44] This matrix of coefficients is also preferred to that from the 1960 census because it uses the Bureau of Labor Statistics' occupational definitions which are identical with the definitions *CPR* has adopted in its sampling.[45] In gaining SIC detail by use of the BLS occupational coefficients, one also gains more occupational detail than is required. However, it is a simple matter to collapse the nine major occupational categories into the four occupational groups for which *CPR* collects earnings and income data, as the published coefficients are additive and require no further manipulation. The projected 1975 coefficients were chosen over those for 1960 because the year for which most of the data in this study were collected (1970), and any subsequent year in which similar studies may be replicated, is closer to 1975 than 1960.
The only remaining difficulty in using the national matrix is the possible disparity between national and local coefficients, due to peculiarities of local occupational labor pools (skills, wage rates, demographic variables), the capital intensity of local production or the degree of product differentia-

Table 6-26.   Earnings of All Workers, Durable Goods Industries, U.S., 1969

Annual Earnings ($)	Male				Female				Weighted Average*			
	Occupation Group				Occupation Group				Occupation Group			
	1	2	3	4	1	2	3	4	1	2	3	4
0–999	0.9	3.4	3.1	13.4	2.7	8.9	14.5	51.6	1.0	6.0	6.0	16.0
1,000–1,499	0.4	2.5	2.0	5.0	0.0	3.8	6.2	10.7	0.0	3.0	3.0	5.0
1,500–1,999	0.6	1.1	1.3	5.1	0.0	5.2	4.7	7.2	1.0	3.0	2.0	5.0
2,000–2,499	1.0	1.9	1.7	4.6	3.6	3.6	6.8	6.4	1.0	3.0	3.0	5.0
2,500–2,999	0.9	3.1	1.4	2.3	1.9	4.8	5.2	4.8	1.0	4.0	2.0	2.0
3,000–3,999	1.0	2.0	5.4	10.8	5.4	10.3	17.8	8.6	1.0	7.0	8.0	11.0
4,000–4,999	1.5	5.0	6.0	9.0	7.4	17.8	15.8	5.1	2.0	12.0	8.0	9.0
5,000–5,999	3.3	8.4	8.2	10.1	15.0	18.5	15.4	2.8	4.0	14.0	10.0	10.0
6,000–6,999	3.9	9.9	11.9	11.9	19.2	13.5	7.8	1.6	5.0	12.0	11.0	11.0
7,000–7,999	5.1	13.9	14.9	10.9	13.4	8.8	3.2	0.6	6.0	11.0	12.0	10.0
8,000–9,999	14.3	21.7	22.6	12.2	19.4	4.1	2.2	0.3	15.0	12.0	18.0	11.0
10,000–14,999	37.8	21.0	19.3	4.4	11.2	0.7	0.4	0.3	36.0	10.0	15.0	4.0
15,000–24,999	24.2	4.7	2.1	0.3	0.9	0.0	0.0	0.0	23.0	2.0	2.0	0.0
25,000–plus	4.9	1.4	0.1	0.0	0.0	0.1	0.0	0.0	5.0	1.0	0.0	0.0
	100.0	100.0	100.0	100.0	100.0	100.0	100.0	100.0	100.0	100.0	100.0	100.0
Workers (000s) with earnings	2,180	867	6,890	913	147	1,076	1,962	70	2,327	1,943	8,852	983

*All percentages are rounded off to the tenth place, with zeros entered to facilitate visual comparison of weighted distributions.

Source: U.S., Department of Commerce, Bureau of the Census, *Current Population Reports*, Series P-60, No. 75, "Income in 1969 of Families and Persons in the United States" (Washington: 1970).

tion within nominally "identical" three-digit SICs. Any or all of these could
result in a given local three-digit SIC having a mix of occupational groups
at variance with the mix which would be attributed to it by use of national
coefficients. We therefore assessed the impact on income estimates which
might arise due to a potential disparity between the Philadelphia SMSA and
U.S. coefficients. First, U.S. occupational coefficients for 1975 were adjusted
by the ratio of Philadelphia to U.S coefficients in 1960 for SICs 20, 35, 53
and 73, all of which are important employers on both a local and national
level, and all of which tend to have substantially different occupational composition. The adjusted 1975 coefficients for Philadelphia which result are
then multiplied by the 1969 mean income for each of the industry's occupational groups and their respective products summed to derive the industry's
1969 mean income in Philadelphia. The locally derived mean income of
these industries was then compared with the U.S. mean income, which
was similarly derived but based instead upon the unadjusted U.S. coefficients.
[46] As Table 6–27 shows, the Philadelphia SMSA mean income ranged between 97.5 percent and 100.5 percent of U.S. mean income for the four
industries in question.

The mean income for all four industries combined for the Philadelphia SMSA (weighted by relative Philadelphia employment totals) was
about 99 percent of U.S. mean income. This is an insignificant disparity and
does not justify adjusting the U.S. occupational coefficient matrix to estimate
local Philadelphia SMSA earnings or income distributions. However, if
local occupational coefficients are quite different from U.S. coefficients, then
the detailed national matrix probably ought to be adjusted by use of the
1970 census.

Each three-digit SIC for which occupational coefficients are
known was entered in a matrix with dimensions of 350 SICs by four occupational groups. Major subdivisions within this matrix also served to identify
the appropriate aggregated industry group to which the published *CPR*

**Table 6–27. Mean Incomes of Households Whose Head Works in
Selected SICs, Using Adjusted and Unadjusted 1975 National Occupational
Coefficients**

Industries	Relative Philadelphia Employment	Philadelphia Adjusted Mean Incomes	Unadjusted National Mean Incomes	Philadelphia ÷ National
20	0.152	$11,053	$11,094	0.996
35	0.428	12,105	12,048	1.005
53	0.281	9,709	9,952	0.975
73	0.140	11,521	11,660	0.988
All	1.000	$10,911	$11,008	0.991

occupational earnings distributions apply.[47] These distributions are then used to derive earnings at the three-digit SIC level, as illustrated earlier in Table 6-24. However, *CPR* did not provide occupational breakdowns for agricultural, entertainment or private household workers. Therefore the earnings of workers in these categories were determined by using the average earnings distribution of the agriculture and entertainment industries and of the private household occupation, respectively.

Household to Worker Ratios

The earnings coefficients discussed above are then entered in the worker to household income algorithm in order to estimate three-digit SIC worker earnings. To convert workers to households and to combine work-derived earnings with income derived from other sources, thereby attributing it to households, a set of household to worker ratios is needed. Household to worker ratios, the use of which is illustrated in Table 6-25, are derived from *CPR* data as shown in Table 6-28 for 14 industries or industry subsets.

Even though the *CPR* data do not allow calculation of household to worker ratios at two- or three-digit SIC detail, it would be difficult to imagine a significant increase in interindustry variance of ratios were it possible to calculate SIC-specific ratios. For example, the average ratio among industries included values as low as 0.258 for private household services and as high as 0.871 for mining; the average ratio for all industries together ranged from

Table 6-28.   Ratio of Households to Workers in Dollar Earnings/Income Intervals by Industry, U.S., 1969

Industry	All	$0-999	$1,000-1,499	$1,500-1,999	$2,000-2,499	$2,500-2,999
Agriculture	0.604	0.101	0.426	0.428	0.688	0.861
Mining	0.871	0.073	0.000	0.156	0.619	0.250
Construction	0.789	0.105	0.154	0.326	0.426	0.482
Durable Goods	0.712	0.047	0.117	0.152	0.217	0.220
Nondurable Goods	0.559	0.048	0.135	0.132	0.130	0.295
Transportation, Communications, Public Utilities	0.697	0.058	0.086	0.207	0.188	0.213
Wholesale	0.694	0.092	0.094	0.186	0.304	0.282
Retail	0.422	0.028	0.032	0.091	0.154	0.198
Finance, Insurance, Real Estate	0.517	0.046	0.030	0.143	0.157	0.201
Business, Repair Service	0.613	0.049	0.134	0.306	0.276	0.369
Personal Service	0.331	0.065	0.341	0.484	0.506	0.625
Private Households	0.258	0.072	0.453	0.812	0.796	1.120
Professional and Related Service	0.433	0.059	0.121	0.175	0.221	0.258
Public Administration	0.668	0.035	0.067	0.240	0.348	0.325
All	0.558	0.061	0.153	0.291	0.262	0.341

Source: Computed from U.S., Bureau of the Census, *Current Population Reports,* Series P-60, No. 75, "Income in 1969 of Families in the United States" (Washington: 1970).

0.061 in the lowest earnings income group to 2.232 in the $15,000 to $24,999 class. As expected, those industries with the highest proportion of male workers (e.g., mining, construction) tended to have the highest average household head to worker ratios and the industries with greater proportions of female workers (e.g., private households, personal service, retail) had the lowest ratios. Over-all, the ratio for the nondurable goods industry most closely resembled that calculated as the all-industry average.

INCOME DISTRIBUTIONS

In moving from the number of SIC workers, which were calculated by the employment algorithm, to earnings and income distributions, the areal unit of analysis changes from the district to the township level. That is, district distinctions which were important in determining the number and mix of employment by SIC are now unnecessary, since the earnings distribution is applied directly to the total number of workers in each SIC regardless of the district from which they come. Accordingly, the distributions are for all workers, by SIC or industry, in the township.

The link between three-digit SIC earnings of workers and final income of households at the township level is illustrated by Table 6-29, which traces the transformation of the worker earnings distribution for a single three-digit SIC to the final household income distribution in Concord Town-

$3,000-3,999	$4,000-4,999	$5,000-5,999	$6,000-6,999	$7,000-7,999	$8,000-9,999	$10,000-14,999	$15,000-24,999	$25,000+
0.958	1.007	1.195	1.152	1.137	1.688	1.731	2.256	2.741
0.363	0.628	0.380	0.620	0.883	0.706	1.386	1.842	1.377
0.518	0.561	0.644	0.642	0.724	0.971	1.221	2.440	2.306
0.274	0.327	0.398	0.461	0.547	0.749	1.374	2.525	2.160
0.213	0.269	0.401	0.533	0.595	0.839	1.432	2.630	1.740
0.277	0.356	0.338	0.486	0.587	0.767	1.170	2.906	1.988
0.464	0.355	0.451	0.489	0.562	0.845	1.231	1.894	1.701
0.266	0.471	0.607	0.751	0.813	1.086	1.721	2.156	2.352
0.199	0.233	0.389	0.443	0.551	0.764	1.354	1.575	1.597
0.472	0.408	0.510	0.628	0.733	0.960	1.532	1.632	1.803
0.689	0.733	0.502	0.816	0.979	1.428	2.177	2.597	3.092
1.345	1.698	1.476	3.905	1.561	3.000	0.000	0.000	0.000
0.291	0.282	0.349	0.396	0.485	0.686	1.066	1.670	1.586
0.288	0.336	0.328	0.400	0.467	0.575	1.323	2.890	3.888
0.351	0.391	0.446	0.527	0.603	0.813	1.324	2.232	1.817

Table 6-29.   Illustrative Earnings to Income Calculation: Distribution of Earnings and Income for SIC 7390, Business and Repair Service Industry and All Industries for Concord Township

	$0–999	$1,000–1,499	$1,500–1,999	$2,000–2,499	$2,500–2,999	$3,000–3,999
Worker Earnings						
SIC 7390						
Number	506	159	92	105	67	177
Percent	20.1	6.3	3.7	4.2	2.7	7.0
Business and Repair Service Industry: SIC 73						
Number	634	199	117	133	87	227
Percent	19.8	6.2	3.6	4.1	2.7	7.1
Household Income						
Business and Repair Service Industry: SIC 73						
Number	31	27	36	37	32	107
Percent	1.6	1.4	1.8	1.9	1.6	5.4
All Industries						
Number	223	179	222	262	259	744
Percent	1.0	1.0	1.0	2.0	2.0	5.0

ship. The derived earnings distribution of SIC 7390 (Miscellaneous Business Services), and that published by *CPR* for its parent industry group SIC 73 (Business and Repair Services) are quite similar, and their medians, $4,690 and $4,750, respectively, are equally close. After summing the earnings distribution of all the three-digit SICs which comprise it, the Business and Repair Service industry's worker earnings distribution is then converted to its household income distribution via the household to worker ratios. This conversion results in a median income of $9,520 for 1,991 households, as compared with median earnings of $4,750 for that industry's 3,207 workers. Put another way, household heads represent 62.1 percent of all that industry's workers in Concord Township, as compared with 61.3 percent of all workers in the same industry for the U.S. The Business and Repair Service industry's households accounted for 12.1 percent of the 16,497 potential worker households in Concord Township, and its income distribution was slightly lower, overall, than the income distribution calculated for all potential worker households in the township; this fact is reflected by a median income of $9,520 for the industry vs. $9,860 for all potential households in the township.

Township Income Distributions:
Similarities and Differences

The chain of relationships from SIC worker earnings to township household income is substantially the same for each of the townships and differs

$4,000–4,999	$5,000–5,999	$6,000–6,999	$7,000–7,999	$8,000–9,999	$10,000–14,999	$15,000–24,999	$25,000+	All
219	197	158	161	203	251	172	41	2520
8.7	7.8	6.3	6.4	8.1	10.0	6.8	1.6	100.0
278	259	207	212	265	323	216	50	3207
8.7	8.1	6.5	6.6	8.3	10.1	6.7	1.6	100.0
113	132	130	155	254	495	351	91	1991
5.7	6.6	6.5	7.8	12.8	24.9	17.6	4.6	100.0
Median: $9,520								
847	1006	1096	1220	2359	4552	2831	697	16497
5.0	6.0	7.0	7.0	14.0	28.0	17.0	4.0	100.0
Median: $9,860								

only in the initial mix of workers by SIC generated by each district and, of course, their total number. The household income distributions for each of the six townships are shown in Table 6–30.

Significant differences in worker household income distributions across townships are observed: the median household income for all six townships, for example, was about $10,300, whereas Thornbury Township's median was about $670 higher, at $10,970, and Birmingham Township's $475 lower, at $9,825.

These differences are undoubtedly accounted for by differences in the relative numbers of workers in industrial and commercial districts within a township, which are, in turn, a function of the amounts of land allotted to each district and to the restrictions upon development. In an effort to determine the sensitivity of income distributions to these kinds of influence, Concord Township's SIC employment was recalculated, based on the following series of changes: [48]

1. the four-county reference area's SIC employment distribution was reweighted;
2. the matrices of Floor Area Ratio derived for other townships' districts which had the highest and lowest average FARs were substituted for the actual matrices of Concord's five districts to detect the differential effect of density controls;

3. a hypothetical rezoning of Concord Township's commercial district to a light industrial district was carried out in accordance with Concord's Township Plan.

These changes will alter the income distribution to the degree that the estimated mix of allowed SICs, or the intensity of SIC development, or the commercial vs. light industrial use mixture, respectively, affects Concord's household income distribution. Table 6–31 shows the income distributions which result from these "sensitivity" changes for Concord Township. As far as the income distributions are concerned, the most obvious thing about the results shown in Table 6–31 is that none of these changes affect the distributions very much. The total number of workers does change quite substantially, however.

Table 6–30.   Estimated Worker Household Income Distribution by Township

	$0–999	$1,000–1,499	$1,500–1,999	$2,000–2,499	$2,500–2,999	$3,000–3,999
Aston						
Number	154	133	158	208	231	675
Percent	1.0	1.0	1.0	1.0	1.0	3.0
Birmingham						
Number	80	84	80	94	93	259
Percent	1.0	1.0	1.0	2.0	2.0	4.0
Concord						
Number	223	179	222	262	259	744
Percent	1.0	1.0	1.0	2.0	2.0	5.0
Edgmont						
Number	22	46	22	23	20	49
Percent	2.0	5.0	2.0	2.0	2.0	5.0
Middletown						
Number	151	145	161	200	218	614
Percent	1.0	1.0	1.0	1.0	1.0	4.0
Thornbury						
Number	73	95	71	93	118	329
Percent	1.0	1.0	1.0	1.0	1.0	3.0
All						
Number	703	682	714	880	939	2,670
Percent	1.0	1.0	1.0	1.0	1.0	4.0

Controls which affect the density of development, e.g., the *FAR*s (floor area to land area ratios), have a very substantial effect on the potential number of worker households. Holding all other restrictions in Concord's zoning districts constant, substituting the lowest *FAR*s found among the six township's zoning ordinances would result in 11,452 worker households, compared with the 18,398 worker households which would result from substituting the highest *FAR*s. A shift in the use of land from a commercial district to a light industrial district produced the largest change in total worker households. This is a result of several factors: generally higher *FAR*s in the industrial district, greater worker to floor area ratios, and a higher proportion of household heads to total workers than is found in the commercial districts, where

$4,000–4,999	$5,000–5,999	$6,000–6,999	$7,000–7,999	$8,000–9,999	$10,000–14,999	$15,000–24,999	$25,000+	All
850	1,144	1,353	1,566	3,361	6,609	3,992	717	21,151
4.0	5.0	6.0	7.0	16.0	31.0	19.0	3.0	100.0
				Median: $10,560				
298	354	386	425	812	1,578	994	252	5,789
5.0	6.0	7.0	7.0	14.0	27.0	17.0	4.0	100.0
				Median: $9,825				
847	1,006	1,096	1,220	2,359	4,552	2,831	697	16,497
5.0	6.0	7.0	7.0	14.0	28.0	17.0	4.0	100.0
				Median: $9,860				
57	61	66	69	119	232	146	41	973
6.0	6.0	7.0	7.0	12.0	24.0	15.0	4.0	100.0
				Median: $9,875				
744	972	1,121	1,291	2,737	5,207	3,019	545	17,125
4.0	6.0	7.0	8.0	16.0	30.0	18.0	3.0	100.0
				Median: $10,200				
415	559	641	736	1,682	3,458	2,276	422	10,968
4.0	5.0	6.0	7.0	15.0	32.0	21.0	4.0	100.0
				Median: $10,970				
3,211	4,096	4,663	5,307	11,070	21,636	13,258	2,674	72,503
4.0	6.0	6.0	7.0	15.0	30.0	18.0	4.0	100.0
				Median: $10,300				

Table 6-31. Number of Households and Worker Household Income Distributions for Concord Township, Based Upon Alternative Assumptions

Assumption	Number of Households	$0–999	$1,000–1,499	$1,500–1,999	$2,000–2,499	$2,500–2,999	$3,000–3,999	$4,000–4,999	$5,000–5,999	$6,000–6,999	$7,000–7,999	$8,000–9,999	$10,000–14,999	$15,000–24,999	$25,000+
Original	16,498	1.0	1.0	1.0	2.0	2.0	5.0	5.0	6.0	7.0	7.0	14.0	28.0	17.0	4.0
1a. SIC reweight	16,595	1.0	1.0	1.0	2.0	2.0	4.0	5.0	6.0	7.0	7.0	14.0	28.0	17.0	4.0
1b. SIC reweight	16,728	1.0	1.0	1.0	2.0	2.0	4.0	5.0	6.0	7.0	7.0	14.0	28.0	17.0	4.0
2a. Low FAR	11,452	1.0	1.0	1.0	2.0	2.0	4.0	5.0	6.0	7.0	7.0	14.0	28.0	17.0	4.0
2b. High FAR	18,398	1.0	1.0	1.0	2.0	2.0	4.0	5.0	6.0	7.0	7.0	14.0	28.0	17.0	4.0
3. Districts	21,085	1.0	1.0	1.0	1.0	1.0	4.0	5.0	6.0	7.0	7.0	15.0	28.0	17.0	4.0

1a. The 1970 employment for each three-digit SIC in the four-county reference area was multiplied by the percentage change in two-digit employment between 1960 and 1970, a procedure which increases the 1970 weight of SICs which were expanding in the recent past and which decreases the 1970 weight of SICs which lost employment in the same period.

1b. The procedure in 1a. was repeated for those SICs which are typically considered to be exogenous or economic locators in conventional economic base theory, i.e., primarily SICs 19–39. The 1960–70 growth in other SICs was compared with the 1960–70 growth of the population or of particular SICs which they theoretically service. The arithmetic difference in growth rates was then used to weight the 1970 employment totals, a procedure which resulted in certain growing SICs losing some of their 1970 employment "weight," because they grew more slowly than did their base.

2a. The Floor Area Ratio matrix of the industrial and commercial districts which actually produced the lowest final floor area to land ratios were substituted for Concord Township's industrial and commercial district matrices.

2b. The same substitution as 2a, but the highest floor area ratio producing matrices were used instead.

3. A light industrial district with planned available site area of 5,300,478 sq. ft. replaced a commercial district and generated a labor force of 6,258 additional workers.

many of the workers are women. This shift from a commercial to a light industrial district also produces the only discernible shift (upward) in the income
distribution. This would seem to suggest that employment in industrial districts
generates higher household incomes than does employment in commercial
districts. As a cross check, Table 6-32 compares the percentage of total potential employment represented in industrial SICs for each town with the
estimated median incomes of worker households for each town. It is readily
apparent from Table 6-32 that the percent of total employment accounted
for by the industrial districts in a township is related to that township's median
household income. In general, the higher the proportion of industrial employment, the greater is the median household income.

Comparing Township Income with Other Income Distributions

About 45 percent of all employment reported for the four-county
suburban area in *County Business Patterns* was industrial in nature, whereas
potential industrial employment in these six townships averaged about 76
percent, ranging from Edgmont's 0.0 percent up to Thornbury's 96.7 percent.
The potential median income of worker households in the six townships was
estimated at $10,300 (ranging between $9,825 and $10,970), as compared with
the median of $10,235 estimated for the total four-county employment.[49]

In order to evaluate the income algorithm per se, the worker household income distribution for the four-county area, which was calculated
using the algorithm, was compared with the average household income distribution of that portion of U.S. SMSAs which lie outside central cities, i.e.,
areas similar to the four-county suburban area. Since the income, earnings, industry and occupational relationships which were used to estimate coefficients
for the income algorithm all came from the same *CPR* sample which provides
the noncentral city household income distribution, the latter serves as a good
bench mark for judging how reasonably our algorithm recombines these relationships to derive final household income from an estimated labor force. Table 6-33

Table 6-32. Median Worker Household Incomes and Percentage of Total Potential Employment in Industrial Districts, by Township

Township	Estimated Median Household Income	Percentage of Potential Employment in Industrial Districts
Thornbury	$10,970	96.7
Aston	$10,560	85.2
Middletown	$10,200	89.6
Edgmont	$ 9,875	0.0
Concord	$ 9,860	66.8
Birmingham	$ 9,825	41.4
All	$10,300	75.9

Table 6-33. Income Distribution and Medians for Households, by Six–Township, Four–County, and U.S. SMSA Fringe Areas

Area	Income								Median
	$0– 1,999	$2,000– 2,999	$3,000– 3,999	$4,000– 4,999	$5,000– 5,999	$6,000– 7,999	$8,000– 9,999	$10,000– 14,999	$15,000+	
	Percent of Worker Households									
Six-Township	3.0	2.5	3.7	4.4	5.6	13.7	15.3	29.8	22.0	$10,300
Four-County	3.1	2.7	3.8	4.5	5.7	13.8	14.7	29.1	22.2	$10,235
	Percent of All Households									
U.S. SMSA Fringe	6.8	4.4	4.5	4.4		11.7	13.1	27.6	22.9	$10,025

summarizes the income distributions and medians for worker households in
the six township and four-county areas, and income distributions and medians
for all households residing in suburban fringe areas of U.S. SMSAs.

   The U.S. SMSA fringe household income distribution has a slightly
lower median income and significantly greater representation of households
in the $0-$4,000 income class than does that of worker households. But this
is to be entirely expected, due to the fact that about 14 percent of U.S. households derived their income from sources other than earnings and that the
median unearned income of these households was about $3,200.[50] The U.S.
distribution also had a slightly higher percentage of households in the highest
income bracket, a finding quite consistent with the generally higher income
brackets of suburban household heads who commute from suburb to central
city. In short, it would appear that our income estimating procedures, including
the algorithm, its coefficients and basic assumptions, yield reliable estimates
of worker household incomes.

NOTES

37. Since we are interested essentially in estimating income *distributions* from
   a known profile of industrial employment, we must go beyond
   the previous attempts to project *aggregate* income derived from
   industrial sectors. For a representative overview of this latter
   approach, see John M. Mattila, "Metropolitan Income Estimation,"
   Urban Affairs Quarterly, Vol. 6., No. 2, December 1970, pp. 178–
   197.
38. U.S., Bureau of the Census, *Current Population Reports,* Series P–60, No.
   75, "Income in 1969 of Families and Persons in the United States,"
   (Washington: 1970).
39. U.S., Department of Labor, Bureau of Labor Statistics, *Employment and
   Earnings, States and Areas 1939–69,* Bulletin 1370–7 (Washington:
   1970).
40.

	U.S.: 1969			*Philadelphia SMSA: 1969*		
Manufacturing Employees	*Weekly Earnings*	*Employment*		*Weekly Earnings*	*Employment*	
		(Millions)	*(Percent)*		*(Thousands)*	*(Percent)*
Durable Goods	$145.33	11.8	58.8	$147.14	304	52.5
Nondurable Goods	119.60	8.3	41.2	125.76	276	47.5
All Manufacturing	$134.40	20.1	100.0	$136.50	580	100.0

$$134.40 \div 136.40 = 98.5 \text{ percent}$$

Sources: U.S., Dept. of Labor, Bureau of Labor Statistics, *Employment and Earnings, States and Areas 1939–69,* Bulletin 1370–7, pp. 482–3, and *Employment and Earnings,* January 1971, Vol. 17, No. 7, pp. 52 and 76.

41. The most straightforward way of adjusting the distribution is to compare
   the U.S. mean with the local mean. The percentage difference in

the means is then applied to each interval in the U.S. distribution, to "slide" the distribution up or down the intervals, where the local mean is higher or lower, respectively, than the U.S. mean.

42. In 1959, wage and salary income for the U.S. represented 70 percent of total income, and 73 percent of total income in Pennsylvania. Herman Miller, *Income Distribution in the United States,* U.S., Department of Commerce, Bureau of the Census (Washington: Government Printing Office, 1966), Table A–4.

43. See Appendix Q for a computer program of the male-female weighting procedure. Because the number of females in certain industries and occupations was so small, some distributions were missing. However, proxy distributors for occupational averages or for similar industries were substituted. The appendix also cites missing distributions and the source of their surrogates.

44. U.S., Department of Labor, Bureau of Labor Statistics, *Tomorrow's Manpower Needs,* Vol. IV, "The National Industry-Occupational Matrix and Other Manpower Data," Bulletin 1606 (Washington: February 1969). Also published in BLS Bulletin 1599, *Occupational Employment Patterns for 1960 and 1975.* See Appendix R for our version of the matrix, the occupational groups of which have been condensed to the detail found in published *CPR* earnings and income data.

45. Bureau of Labor Statistics, *Tomorrow's Manpower Needs,* Vol. IV, p. 9.

46. See Appendix S for calculations.

47. See Appendix T for earnings distributions by occupational-industry group.

48. Recall from Appendix N that the mix of final SICs within a township could vary, and the final household income as well, when a different reference area is used in the employment algorithm. Concord Township's worker household income distribution was, however, virtually the same when calculated on the basis of either four-county or Delaware County reference area employment distributions. This is a finding of some significance, given that in Concord's industrial district only about 65 percent of the allowed three-digit SICs found in the four-county reference area was also present in the Delaware County reference area; for Concord's four commercial districts, between 88 percent and 92 percent of four-county SICs were also present in Delaware County. In short, the much more limited set of SICs which were found in Delaware County produced the same household income distribution for Concord Township as the broader four-county set.

49. The four-county employment represents total jobs on all shifts which were then adjusted to labor force figures by the single job holding rate and employment rate coefficients. The resultant figures were then entered in the income algorithm to calculate the four-county income distribution.

50. Calculated from data in Table 29, U.S., Bureau of the Census, *Current Population Report,* Series P–60, No. 75.

Part III

Nonexclusionary Zoning:
Performance and Policy

Chapter Seven

Measuring Exclusion in Suburban Townships

> Frequently—one is tempted to say normally!—the political appoint-
> ees and career executives concerned do not see themselves as
> involved with, much less responsible for, the urban consequences
> of their programs and policies. . . . No one has made clear to
> them that they are simultaneously redistributing employment
> opportunities, segregating neighborhoods, or desegregating
> them. . . .[1]

Chapters 5 and 6 were essentially concerned with estimating the probable
distribution of housing costs and household income implicit within township
zoning ordinances. During the course of these complementary analyses, specu-
lation was offered from time to time about the likelihood of exclusionary
zoning in one or more of the townships. The workplace-residence standard
combined with the findings from these two chapters are sufficient to begin
systematically comparing each township's housing prices, rents and household incomes, and to thereby determine the presence and magnitude of exclusion in their zoning ordinances.

  The reader should, of course, recognize that all of the data and
quantitative relationships discussed in this chapter are potential rather than
observed; that is, they were derived from the zoning ordinances of each
township under the assumption that the townships attained the type and
amount of development which they sought. Therefore, the figures on housing
units, prices, rents, worker households and incomes taken from earlier chapters and analyzed in this chapter are no more than carefully prepared estimates
of what townships desired, despite an appearance of reality which the figures
might acquire when presented (without further caveat) throughout this
chapter in concrete terms.

  Before proceeding further, it should also be stated plainly that
exclusion *due to the effects of zoning* is what the standard should detect and

measure. Without question, many of the worker households could not possibly afford even the least expensive new construction built within the terms of nonexclusionary residential zoning. No one would suggest that the high cost of residential development is an unimportant issue, but it must be separated from the unnecessarily high cost of housing which is due primarily to unreasonable zoning practice so that the latter can be clearly and unambiguously identified. This separation must disentangle notions similar to distinctions made by housing market analysts between housing need and housing demand, whereby the former considers all forms of housing program necessary to adequately house a population within its economic means, and the latter ". . . concerns itself with what people will actually do within the framework of given income and tastes, prices, rents, construction costs and mortgage terms."[2] In short, how does residential zoning exclude households from residence in townships by requiring housing with costs which exceed the market minimum or which exceed the ability and willingness of people to pay such costs?

A Matrix of Household Income and Housing Demand

In estimating what households of given income are likely to pay for housing, so as to determine whether, and how many, households could not afford "zoned" housing costs, one might apply the housing costs actually paid by households of various income levels. An average ratio of rent to income does capture modal income-related housing demand, but it also blurs the extremely high or low ratios in various income classes which, depending upon relative magnitude, could seriously overestimate or underestimate actual zoning exclusion. To avoid the uncertainties associated with an average ratio, a matrix of housing costs (both rents and values) by income class will be used. The last such matrix covering the suburban portion of the Philadelphia SMSA was published in 1960 by the U.S. Bureau of Census. At the time this study was being written, the equivalent matrix for 1970 data was not expected to be published for at least another year, and the fourth count summary tapes, from which it might have been derived, had not yet been released. Although the matrix for 1970 clearly would be preferred, the suburban matrix of more recent vintage for another SMSA was chosen for purposes of demonstrating how the matrix might be used. New Haven's suburban matrix, derived from the 1967 Bureau of Census Special Pre-Test, was chosen to represent the matrix for the Philadelphia SMSA.[3] The New Haven matrix is a reasonably good proxy, considering that (1) the 1967 New Haven suburban income level probably corresponds closely to Philadelphia's 1970 suburban income level, and (2) the structure-tenure relationships of the 1960 occupied stock differed very little for the two SMSA suburban areas. In short, the New Haven matrix is an acceptable substitute for illustrative purposes and may, in fact, produce results very little different than those obtainable with the actual 1970 Philadelphia suburban matrix.

As published, the New Haven matrix portrays a single distribution for each household income level, which assigns households to various rent and price intervals and, quite obviously, to renter- or owner-tenure categories as well. However, before any suburban matrix is applied to a discrete set of local townships, it should be further subdivided into renter-income and owner-income matrices. Such a refinement ensures that the actual split which current township residents exhibit can be used to adjust the suburban-wide tenure split implicit for all household income categories. This, of course, assumes that moderate- and average-income households will make tenure decisions similar to those expressed in existing township housing patterns and in the current tenure choices of township households. Since the full development of township land areas is hypothetical, one cannot be sure what the choices might be. It seems reasonable to assume that if zoning were changed so that more families can afford to own rather than rent, they are likely to make tenure decisions rather similar to those of current township residents rather than to replicate the average tenure split of an entire SMSA suburban area. For example, if the matrix for an entire suburban area showed 40 percent of all households rented, but it was further known that only 30 percent of all households in a particular set of townships rented, then the number of renters one might expect from all households in each income category should be adjusted to reflect the 30 percent rental propensity prior to their being distributed among the several rent intervals. When this refinement is made to the overall New Haven matrix, two independent matrices of values and rents, by household income, result, as shown in Table 7-1. In addition, a table of revised tenure splits is also generated, which divides households at each income level into renter or owner categories, as shown in Table 7-2.

As an illustration, assume there are 10,000 households at the $10,000 to $14,999 income level. How many of them would be likely to demand owner-occupied houses priced between $20,000 and $24,999? From Table 7-2 of tenure splits, about 90 percent of households receiving between $10,000 and $14,999 are potential homeowners. Of these 9,000 or so homeowners, the matrix in Table 7-1 tells us that about 27 percent, or 2,430 households, prefer to own houses priced between $20,000 and $24,999. Similar calculations will yield a profile of preferences or demand for housing of every price and rent, given only an overall household income distribution and the information contained in Tables 7-1 and 7-2.

The two matrices in Table 7-1 are capable of translating a given township's household income distribution, by owner and renter categories, into housing requirements of various price and rent levels. But, from discussion in the introductory portion of this chapter, it is plain that exclusion can only be considered as a consequence of housing whose costs, relative to matrix

Table 7-1.   Adjusted Value and Rent Distributions of Housing by Income Level, New Haven, Connecticut, 1967

Household Income ($)	Housing Values ($)									
	<7,500	7,500-9,999	10,000-12,499	12,500-14,999	15,000-19,999	20,000-24,999	25,000-29,999	30,000-34,999	35,000-49,999	50,000 and Over
Less than 2,000	4.3	3.9	6.7	10.5	32.0	19.6	9.4	5.7	5.0	3.0
2,000-2,999	3.9	6.3	7.0	14.4	36.8	14.0	5.0	4.8	5.0	2.9
3,000-3,999	4.9	3.8	7.0	10.4	35.8	20.1	9.0	4.7	2.7	1.6
4,000-4,999	4.6	2.2	7.6	10.6	32.8	20.9	11.2	4.5	3.8	1.8
5,000-5,999	5.6	1.2	6.4	12.5	35.9	21.6	9.1	3.3	1.8	2.5
6,000-7,999	2.9	2.0	4.8	10.3	39.8	23.9	8.5	3.5	3.2	1.1
8,000-9,999	2.3	0.8	3.6	7.7	39.5	26.8	10.1	5.6	3.0	0.7
10,000-14,999	1.8	0.6	2.4	5.7	31.7	26.8	14.8	9.4	5.4	1.4
15,000-24,999	2.9	0.6	1.5	3.6	19.5	23.1	16.6	13.7	14.6	3.8
25,000 and over	4.3	0.0	0.5	1.4	5.1	8.4	10.4	14.9	31.2	23.7

Rents ($)

Household Income ($)	<30	30-39	40-49	50-59	60-79	80-99	100-119	120-149	150-199	200 and Over
Less than 2,000	1.5	3.6	3.9	3.9	11.9	20.6	15.5	21.8	14.9	2.4
2,000-2,999	1.4	1.0	3.4	1.4	11.7	25.5	16.2	24.8	13.1	1.4
3,000-3,999	2.6	0.3	2.6	2.9	11.0	24.5	22.5	19.0	11.0	3.7
4,000-4,999	3.4	0.3	1.4	0.0	6.6	22.3	20.0	30.0	13.4	2.6
5,000-5,999	0.6	0.0	0.0	2.5	7.2	17.5	24.8	30.4	15.3	1.7
6,000-7,999	1.1	0.0	1.1	1.9	5.2	17.3	24.1	30.4	17.4	1.5
8,000-9,999	1.0	0.0	0.0	1.0	4.9	15.6	24.4	28.3	21.5	3.4
10,000-14,999	1.3	0.7	0.7	1.3	5.3	9.3	20.0	27.3	26.0	8.0
15,000-24,999	1.0	0.0	0.0	0.0	2.1	13.4	16.5	21.6	27.8	17.5
25,000 and over	0.0	0.0	0.0	0.0	0.0	3.3	10.0	21.7	26.7	38.3

Table 7-2. Revised Tenure Split by Household Income Level, New Haven, Connecticut, 1967

Household Income Levels ($)	Tenure Split	
	Own (Percent)	Rent (Percent)
under 1,500	0.759	0.241
1,500–1,999	0.771	0.229
2,000–2,999	0.787	0.213
3,000–3,999	0.769	0.231
4,000–4,999	0.763	0.238
5,000–5,999	0.758	0.242
6,000–7,999	0.756	0.244
8,000–9,999	0.862	0.138
10,000–14,999	0.902	0.098
15,000–24,999	0.938	0.062
25,000 and over	0.963	0.037

income demand, are too high due to zoning. Recall that the workplace-residence standard explicitly requires communities to allow the structure type and density of houses with the lowest market prices and rents in their zoning ordinances, even for households which cannot afford them. Therefore, all housing units required whose "affordable" values and rents are below the current minimum market supply price of new construction will be allocated to the lowest possible market supply price category. That is, values of all units which the lowest income households can afford, and which are less than the $15,000 to $19,999 category in the matrix, are allocated to the $15,000 to $19,999 value category, and affordable monthly rents of all units less than $120 are allocated to the $120 to $149 rent category. By so doing, the requirements of households for housing are restricted to potential new construction prices and rents, so that zoning ordinances are held accountable only for exclusion due to zoning per se, and not to insufficient incomes. Vertical lines drawn for the two current housing supply pure frontiers on the rent and price matrices in Table 7-1 circumscribe supply areas of market exclusion, so that its effects are clearly separated from the effects of exclusionary zoning.

However, the matrices must be adjusted to avoid the unjustified appearance of exclusion due to underestimates of household ability to pay. More specifically, above-market housing costs due to zoning can only be considered as exclusionary when they screen out households which demonstrably cannot afford these costs. To illustrate, housing units of $20,000 to $24,999 value which are unavailable to families and households in the $25,000 and over income class who require such housing, as per the matrix in Table 7-1, would constitute insufficient evidence to charge the township with exclusionary zoning. There are, in short, certain rent income and rent value "cells" within each matrix which cannot be accepted in the case against exclusionary zoning. Standard rules of thumb relating annual housing carrying costs and household income are used to identify these cells. Annual carrying costs of housing, which account for less than 10 percent in the 0 to $5,000 income class, 15 percent in the $5,000 to $10,000 class, and 20 percent in the over $10,000 income classes, disclose in Table 7-1 certain nonexclusionary values for the $10,000 or higher income classes and nonexclusionary rents in the $4,000 or higher income classes. When the housing cost "sacrifice frontier" was applied to these same matrices, a steplike horizontal line separates nonsacrifice housing costs from the sacrifice or exclusionary housing costs. Only the northeast portion of each matrix (right of the market exclusion line and above the non-sacrifice exclusion line) in Table 7-1 can be considered correctly as a matrix which defines income related housing requirements consistent with the workplace-residence standard. Accordingly, the revised matrices distribute households only in those price and rent intervals which, if zoning allowed, all but the most impecunious of families can afford; to leave the matrices as they were would greatly increase exclusion due to factors other than zoning.

Estimating Housing Requirements From Household Income

The preceding section has provided a set of coefficients with which one can systematically translate the household income distributions from Chapter 6 into an array of housing requirements by tenure, prices and rents. The process of translation requires some elaboration to make clear how the methodological assumptions and the standard of workplace and residence combine. That process consists of:

1. Adjusting a township's potential household income distribution from Chapter 6, wherein the total households in the distribution are accepted when less than, or else they are set equal to, total housing units. If a township's zoning ordinance generates fewer worker households than housing units, then the number of households in the income distribution is allocated directly to tenure categories and rent and price levels by use of Tables 7-1 and 7-2. Recall, however, that the workplace-residence standard permits townships to zone for more worker households than housing units; therefore, the number of worker households must be set equal to the total number of housing units to determine the relative mix of housing requirements and supply, and the exclusion which results from that mix. The fraction

$$1 - \frac{\text{total housing units}}{\text{total worker households}}$$

is applied to each income level in the total household income distribution

to assure that a proportionate number of households at each income level
is included in the adjusted household total;

2. Dividing the number of worker households in each income class into
either renter or owner tenure on the basis of a potential tenure split, as
shown in Table 7-2;

3. Distributing the total number of renters and owners in each income class
across rent and value intervals by using the rent-income and value-income
matrices, respectively, as found in Table 7-1.

The straightforward approach and numerous calculations inherent
in this process, as in similar data manipulations, again suggest a simple computer algorithm.[4] As an illustration of that algorithm, output from the algorithm for worker households making between $8,000 and $9,999 in Aston
Township is condensed in Table 7-3 for the three translation steps, 1, 2, and
3, just outlined.

The result tabulated in step 3 is the requirement for housing, by
tenure, prices and rents, which might be expected from each township's worker-
household population. The next stage is evaluation of the housing stock, which
emerged as a principal finding of Chapter 5, in terms of these housing requirements.

Discontinuities: Housing Requirements
and the Stock of Housing

In the previous section, the requirements for housing on the part
of worker households in each township was estimated; these requirements
will now be compared with the stock of housing which was derived from the
townships' zoning ordinances in Chapter 5. The requirements for and stock of
housing units, by tenure and cost, in each township are systematically compared
and the discontinuities or differences are tabulated as shortfalls or surplus
where demand is less than or greater than the stock respectively, as shown
in Table 7-4. Shortfall is the absolute number of households which are excluded
from township residency due to housing costs, and surplus is the number of
housing units which cannot be afforded by these households. Although the
requirements-stock comparison primarily identifies shortfalls or surplus within
single-housing cost intervals, low-cost housing surpluses are allocated to higher-
cost housing requirements when higher-cost stocks are insufficient. Thus, in
Table 7-4 the 612 households in Aston Township which might require housing
of $35,000 value and over are not considered as being excluded from Aston
Township because there are sufficient surpluses of housing in the $20,000–
$34,999 price category. Shortfalls and surpluses tend to run in fairly predictable
patterns: there is always less low-income, low-cost stock than is required, i.e.,
shortfalls, and more high-cost stock than is required, i.e., surplus.

Table 7-3. Potential Housing Demand of Aston Township Households in $8,000–$9,999 Income Class

Step 1	All Households	3,361		
	All Housing Units	1,126		
	Adjusted Households	1,126		
Step 2	All Renters	$(0.138 \times 1,126) = 155^{a}$		
	All Owners	$(0.862 \times 1,126) = 971^{a}$		

Step 3	Renter Rents (\$)[a]		Owner Values (\$)[a]	
	under		under	
	120^{b}	$(0.468 \times 155) = 73$	$15,000^{b}$	$(0.143 \times 971) = 140$
	120–149	$(0.283 \times 155) = 44$	15,000–19,999	$(0.395 \times 971) = 383$
	150–199	$(0.215 \times 155) = 33$	20,000–24,999	$(p.268 \times 971) = 260$
	200+	$(0.034 \times 155) = 5$	25,000–34,999	$(0.157 \times 971) = 152$
			35,000–49,000	$(0.030 \times 971) = 29$
			50,000+	$(0.007 \times 971) = 7$

[a] Figures rounded to nearest whole number.

[b] All housing demanded below market supply price is tabulated separately to measure magnitude of extrazoning effort required to provide housing, but it will be added to lowest market supply price to determine exclusionary zoning.

Source: Output from Housing Demand Algorithm, as described in Appendix U.

While patterns in Table 7-4 do communicate the essential discontinuities, they should be indexed so that a township's performance can be reduced to one or two easily grasped dimensions which indicate and measure exclusion in its zoning ordinance. The discontinuity between housing stock and requirements can be measured in three ways: (1) shortfall of housing units by tenure type, (2) shortfall of housing units by price or rent, and (3) shortfall of housing units due to the joint effects of both tenure and prices or rents.

1. Tenure Exclusion Ratio. This measure will portray each township's overall tenure balance of stock and requirements. If the stock in each tenure category is divided by its requirements, the resultant quotient is that ratio of tenure requirements which is either excluded or in excess. Because the total stock must be either rented or owned, if one form of tenure is shown to be excluded, i.e., a ratio of less than one, the other must, perforce, be in excess, i.e., a ratio greater than one. Accordingly, this ratio is useful primarily for assessing the relative balance of tenure choice rather than as an index of outright exclusion as such.

2. Rent and Price Exclusion Index. The ratio of tenure exclusion describes the tenure characteristics of the stock alone, relative to overall requirements, but the particular prices or rents of housing within these tenure opportunities will ultimately determine how many and what proportion of households are excluded by reason of cost. It is here that the patterns of housing shortfall become useful. Looking at the stock in each tenure category separately, and dividing that stock's shortfall by its demand, yields the percentage

Table 7-4. Potential Requirements for and Stock of Housing Units in Township Zoning Ordinances, by Tenure, Rent, Price, Surplus, Shortfall, and Median Household Income, Delaware County, Pennsylvania, 1971

Owner-Occupied Housing

Price of Units ($)	Median Household Income ($)	Aston Township				Birmingham Township				Concord Township			
		Requirements	Stock	Shortfall	Surplus	Requirements	Stock	Shortfall	Surplus	Requirements	Stock	Shortfall	Surplus
15,000–19,999	9,150	2,717	0	2,717	–	964	23	941	–	3,242	62	3,180	–
20,000–24,999	10,910	1,489	4,026	–	2,537	510	23	487	–	1,717	63	1,654	–
25,000–34,999	12,660	1,286	2,417	–	1,131	436	0	436	–	1,467	667	800	–
35,000–49,999	16,365	446	0	0	-446	158	1,635	–	1,477	526	6,594	–	6,068
50,000+	18,410	166	0	0	-166	64	669	–	605	212	0	0	-212
All	10,755	6,104	6,443	2,717	3,056	2,132	2,350	1,864	2,082	7,164	7,386	5,634	5,856

Renter-Occupied Housing

Rent of Units ($)	Median Household Income ($)	Aston Township				Birmingham Township				Concord Township			
		Requirements	Stock	Shortfall	Surplus	Requirements	Stock	Shortfall	Surplus	Requirements	Stock	Shortfall	Surplus
120–149	6,275	545	0	545	–	219	49	170	–	732	310	422	–
150–199	8,040	168	0	168	–	61	98	–	37	203	630	–	427
200+	13,430	270	645	–	375	87	0	50	-37	293	67	0	-226
All	7,585	983	645	645	375	367	147	220	0	1,228	1,007	422	201
Total*		7,087	7,088	3,430	3,431	2,499	2,497	2,084	2,082	8,392	8,393	6,056	6,057

Owner-Occupied Housing

Price of Units ($)	Total	*Edgmont Township*				*Middletown Township*				*Thornbury Township*			
15,000–19,999	9,150	383	42	341	—	4,038	684	3,354	—	934	0	934	—
20,000–24,999	10,910	192	682	—	490	2,172	1,311	861	—	521	0	521	—
25,000–34,999	12,660	162	0	0	-162	1,853	2,929	—	1,076	458	0	458	—
35,000–49,999	16,365	59	1,483	—	1,424	633	4,382	—	3,749	164	1,648	—	1,484
50,000+	18,410	25	730	—	705	237	267	—	30	62	811	—	749
All	10,410	821	2,937	341	2,457	8,933	9,573	4,215	4,855	2,139	2,459	1,913	2,233

Renter-Occupied Housing

Rent of Units ($)	Total	*Edgmont Township*				*Middletown Township*				*Thornbury Township*			
120–149	6,275	98	0	98	—	846	120	726	—	180	0	180	—
150–199	8,040	25	0	25	—	252	242	10	—	56	0	56	—
200+	13,430	30	72	—	42	383	470	—	87	97	0	97	—
All	7,585	153	72	123	42	1,481	832	736	87	333	0	333	0
Total*		974	3,009	464	2,499	10,414	10,404	4,951	4,942	2,472	2,459	2,246	2,233

*Total requirements may not be equal to total stock in any one township, due to rounding. Similarly, total shortfalls and surplus may diverge slightly, due to rounding.

Table 7-5.   Measures of Exclusion* For Township Zoning Ordinances

Measure	Aston	Birmingham	Concord	Edgmont	Middletown	Thornbury
1.						
Renter	0.656	0.401	0.820	0.471	0.562	0.000
Owner	1.056	1.102	1.031	3.577	1.072	1.150
2.						
Rent	0.725	0.599	0.344	0.804	0.497	N.A.
Price	0.445	0.875	0.786	0.415	0.472	0.894
3.						
Total	0.484	0.835	0.722	0.477	0.475	0.913

*Measure 1. (a ratio) differs from 2. and 3. (indexes) in that no exclusion in 1. is signified by a value of 1.00, i.e. "balanced" tenure choice, whereas in 2. and 3. a 0.0 value signifies no exclusion and 1.0 means complete exclusion.

of households which are excluded from residential opportunities in the township. Exclusion is mild where the index value is close to zero, i.e., few are excluded, or intense when the index value is close to one.
3. General Exclusion Index. Ratio 1. and Index 2. focus on particular tenure cost factors which contribute to household exclusion. Overall perspective on total exclusion may be gained by dividing total shortfall by total requirements in each tenure and price or rent cell; this represents the proportion of all housing units which are either unaffordable or inappropriate, for reasons of tenure, to households which require housing units. No exclusion is signified by an index value of zero, and substantial exclusion is denoted by index values which approach unity.[5]

These measures allow for convenient comparison of how township zoning ordinances fared, relative to one another, and how closely they came to meeting the workplace-residence standard for nonexclusion. Looking first in Table 7–5 at the ratio of tenure balance (1), Concord Township provided rental stock equal to 82 percent of requirements, significantly higher than any of the four next best townships, which ranged from about 40 percent to 66 percent. Thornbury Township is clearly the worst, as it provided no rental stock at all for households which might require that form of tenure. No township provided less than 100 percent of potential requirements for owner-occupied units, and Edgmont provided three and one-half times as much owner-occupied stock as required. Considering that Edgmont had fewer overall requirements for housing units (due to its modest commercial and industrial employment zoning) than the potential stock provided, Edgmont could have easily increased its share of rental stock to accommodate more than 47 percent of rental demand.

Due to the formulation of the rent and price index (2.), Thornbury can have no rent index value as such, because division by zero (i.e., 333 rental requirements ÷ 0 rental stock) is mathematically undefined. But upon reflection, this interpretation is fully consistent with the index; without question, Thornbury Township's zoning ordinance does not exclude any portion of rental demand for reasons of cost. Other townships do, however, provide rental stock of such high cost or of such small magnitude that a sizable proportion of rental requirements is excluded. Edgmont's ordinance results in over 80 percent of the rental requirements being excluded, closely followed by Aston, with about 73 percent, down to a relative low of about 34 percent for Concord Township. Concord Township excluded the smallest proportion of potential renters and excludes the smallest proportion of rental requirements after costs of its available rental stock are considered. Cost exclusion in the owner-occupied stock follows a slightly different pattern. Although Thornbury continues as the worst offender, i.e., 89 percent of owner requirements are excluded, Concord is now the third worst, at 79 percent (over twice as much owner as rental exclusion in Concord), and Edgmont Township is best, excluding only about 42 percent of its owner requirements. Other than Thornbury's consistently high index of owner and renter exclusion, Middletown alone exhibits remarkably stable exclusion, i.e., about 50 percent of rental requirements and 47 percent of requirements for owner-occupied units—only slightly higher than the two lowest observations. The remaining four townships show a rather uneven balance of cost exclusion as between rental and owner requirements, with two townships having higher indices of rental than owner exclusion and the other two having higher indexes of owner exclusion. However, even the two lowest exclusion indexes of 34 percent and 42 percent are unacceptable in terms of the standard, which requires no evidence of exclusion, i.e., 0 percent.

In measuring the joint effects of rental- and owner-occupied exclusion, Index 3. captures the net effect of a township's zoning ordinance in terms of total residential exclusion. As expected, Thornbury Township was the worst: over 91 percent of all household requirements for housing was excluded by the residential stock. Birmingham and Concord followed close behind, despite the latter's low index of rental exclusion. Middletown Township shaded Edgmont Township by only a narrow margin as the mildest offender, despite the fact that the former was the most evenly balanced in tenure exclusion and the latter was least balanced.

All of the measures above evaluate exclusion on the basis of mismatched distributions of potential housing stock, by costs and tenure, and housing requirements, by household incomes and tenure, where the total stock is equal to or greater than total demand. The degree of mismatch, or discontinuities, observed makes more precise the true extent of exclusionary zoning in our sample townships.

Exclusion and Household Income

The measures developed and discussed above identify the presence and magnitude of exclusion in townships resulting from their zoning ordinances. The measures also shed some light on the factors which contribute to exclusion, particularly housing tenure and cost factors. Cost factors operate primarily to exclude lower-income households, due to shortfalls in the low-cost housing stock. In other words, low-income households doubtless bear the brunt of whatever exclusion occurs in each township. Table 7–4 contains all the information necessary to determine how worker households at several income levels fared in terms of housing shortfalls of various costs. As before, the shortfall in stock of housing units of a given price is divided by the total potential household requirements for stock of that price. The quotient is an index of household income exclusion, where income is measured by its median. Table 7–6 assembles that data in order of increasing median household incomes.

Of all the townships, Birmingham and Concord Townships did not

Table 7-6.   Exclusion of Households by Median Household Income and Township

Median Household Income	Aston	Birmingham	Concord	Edgmont	Middletown	Thornbury
$ 6,275	1.000	0.776	0.577	1.000	0.858	1.000
$ 8,040	1.000	0.000	0.000	1.000	0.040	1.000
$ 9,140	1.000	0.976	0.981	0.890	0.821	1.000
$10,910	0.000	0.535	0.963	0.000	0.397	1.000
$12,660	0.000	1.000	0.545	0.000	0.000	1.000
$13,430	0.000	0.575	0.000	1.000	0.000	1.000
$16,365	0.000	0.000	0.000	0.000	0.000	0.000
$18,410	0.000	0.000	0.000	0.000	0.000	0.000
Total	0.484	0.835	0.722	0.477	0.475	0.913

Source: Table 7-4.

exclude households with median incomes of about $8,000, primarily because of the townships' multi-family zoning. Aston excluded households in only the three lowest median-income classes and Thornbury excluded the households with six lowest median-incomes, but, predictably, no township excluded the two highest median-income household classes. One might find many other equally informative patterns, but they all communicate essentially the same information: *exclusion is concentrated in, and often confined to, the lowest income households.* It is this finding which does great violence to the workplace-residence standard which specifies comparable residential access for worker households at each income level. There is, obviously, very unequal residential access in these townships which they would have to correct to bring their zoning ordinances in compliance with the standard.

NOTES

1. Daniel P. Moynihan, *Toward A National Urban Policy* (New York: Basic Books, 1970), pp. 8–9.
2. Chester Rapkin and William G. Grigsby, *The Demand for Housing in East-wick* (Philadelphia: Institute for Urban Studies [now Institute for Environmental Studies], University of Pennsylvania, 1960), p. 3.
3. See Morton Lustig, Janet R. Pack, Kent Eklund, Joseph Hayman, Glenn Neuks, Linda Pecaites, Bonnie Towles, *Standards for Suburban Housing Mix* (Philadelphia: Fels Center of Government, University of Pennsylvania, 1971), Table 6–9, p. 223.
4. See summary of data inputs and formal computer program in Appendix U.
5. Another type of measure signifying total or general exclusion indicates the degree to which each township's total housing stock could accommodate the total number of worker households spawned by township zoning, independent of any cost or tenure considerations. Such an index is simply the number of unaccommodated households (all households minus all housing units) divided by all households. Since the standard in use throughout this volume is essentially concerned with the distributive inconsistencies or discontinuities between an equal number of households and housing units which arise from township zoning ordinances, this index would be useful for illustrative rather than analytic purposes.

Chapter Eight

Rezoning to Eliminate Exclusion

Except in a general sense, we have only sketchy information on
the many factors leading to the establishment of or change in
zoning ordinances. Analyses in the popular press have been confined primarily to supposedly "exclusionary" local land use
policies—that is, practices such as excluding multi-family uses
or maintaining requirements for large lots per single-family unit.
Even here our knowledge is nominal.[1]

The standard development in Chapter 3 has been applied to six suburban,
developing townships and all are found to depart from it in varying degrees.
Assuming that compliance with the standard is either accepted voluntarily
or that compliance becomes mandatory by force of law, what are the possible
corrective changes which townships might make in their zoning ordinances
to eliminate exclusion? Exclusion was the joint result of both residential zoning
and commercial or industrial zoning, and so it is plain that by changing the
provisions of one or the other (or both), exclusion may be eliminated. The
several factors within zoning ordinances which were discussed at considerable
length in Chapters 5 and 6 and in earlier sections of this chapter will provide
the understanding necessary to make the requisite corrections. It will prove
convenient to concentrate on a single township, so as to focus discussion on
the alternative strategies themselves rather than the several mixtures of strategy
required for all six townships. Concord Township was chosen for illustrative
purposes somewhat arbitrarily, although Concord exhibits interesting combinations of tenure and cost exclusion and the narrative of its ordinance defined
more precisely the relevant factors than did the ordinances of most other
townships. In looking at Concord Township, the "polar" strategies of corrective
residential rezoning alone, or industrial/commercial rezoning alone, will first
be discussed. Because it is very likely that individual townships might prefer

to change some of both types of uses, a general strategy for rezoning will
also be developed.

Commercial and Industrial Rezoning

Three factors inherent in zoning commercial and industrial districts
(economic districts)[2] which affect the number and relative income of worker
households are: (1) the allowed economic uses, (2) the allowed intensity of
those uses upon the site, and (3) the amount of township land devoted to
economic districts. The allowed uses determine the representation of employment in various Standard Industrial Classifications (SICs) in economic districts
so that, in theory at least, a judicious mixture of uses tends to minimize
low- and moderate-income households and thereby enables townships to meet
the standard less painfully. For example, Thornbury Township evidenced the
most extreme exclusionary practices of all the townships, but it would have
experienced even greater exclusion were it not for the fact that its allowed
SICs produced a household population with the highest median income observed among the six townships.[3] There is, then, the possibility that townships
might deliberately select SICs to yield a work force whose median household
income is maximized. The potential gain from such a strategy would appear
to be quite limited because even the best paying industries have associated with
them a sizable complement of support personnel whose occupations and pay-
checks are distributed across the lower wage and income categories.

It might be argued that Thornbury Township, in light of its consistently high score on every measure of exclusion, might have given more
than passing interest to selecting high-wage industries. For purposes of illustrat-
ing what might occur were Concord to rezone its economic districts, one can
apply Thornbury's lower percentage share of worker households earning $8,000
or less to Concord's household population. On the assumption that Concord
might similarly zone for higher incomes, as Thornbury has presumably done,
one can thereby evaluate the probable effect of Concord Township altering
its allowed uses so as to comply more fully with the performance standard.
Whereas 37.6 percent of Concord Township's households have incomes of
$8,000 or under, only 29.6 percent of Thornbury's households are in the same
income class. Therefore, about 670 fewer households at the $8,000 and
under income level would need to be accommodated by Concord's low-cost
stock, which has a current shortfall of 3,602 units.[4] Since only about 1,800
units of that shortfall can be traced to the lower half of household incomes
separated by the stock's median household income,[5] those 670 households, which Concord might avoid by pursuing commercial and industrial rezoning similar to Thornbury's zoning, reduce exclusion in the $8,000 and
lower income level by a bit more than a third.

Even if Concord were to adopt Thornbury's zoning, it is quite likely that total exclusion will remain virtually unabated, since Concord currently experiences severe housing shortfalls for households having $16,000 or less income. Since Thornbury's seemingly advantageous zoning produces an income profile with 76 percent of households making $15,000 or less, there is little chance that Concord could begin to comply with the performance standard; compliance is possible only if Concord can select (and identify!) industries which pay enough to sustain a worker household population with median incomes in excess of $15,000. Obviously, Concord cannot use this as a strategy for attaining compliance; the reality of widely distributed earnings and income associated with even highly specialized industries removes this possibility from serious consideration.

Rezoning economic districts to comply with the performance standard also can be accomplished by altering the intensity of uses upon zoned land or by changing the amount of zoned land; they are equivalent policies because their net effect is that of either reducing or enlarging the number of worker households of unchanging income distribution. Only to the degree that local property taxation is based upon considerations of the gross amount of land consumed by economic enterprises for site purposes, rather than upon capital investment in plant or some notion of capitalized revenues or profits, can Concord hope to maintain an optimal tax base, *ceteris paribus*, by lowering the allowed intensity of uses (floor to land area ratio) and enlarging the amount of land zoned for these uses.

Setting aside considerations of tax base viability, changing the number of worker households by either means must be shown to have direct effect upon the standard before it is known how effective such a change might be. The standard requires that the housing stock in townships must accommodate all worker households, up to 100 percent of the stock. Therefore, if there are currently more worker households than housing units, as is the case in Concord Township, enlarging the size of economic districts or increasing allowed intensity of uses will have no effect whatever on Concord's compliance with the performance standard. The only way Concord can move toward compliance by industrial or commercial rezoning is to lower the absolute number of potential worker households below the total number of potential housing units. Concord Township could conceivably rezone its economic districts to reduce the number of all worker households in such manner that the smallest segment of the housing stock could accommodate all of the worker households which require housing of its price or rent characteristics. In short, if households which now suffer the greatest disparity were sufficiently reduced in number to fit within the unaltered residential stock, then exclusion would perforce be eliminated. Exclusion is greatest in the $15,000 to $24,999 value category, wherein median household incomes are about $10,000.[6] Since half the currently zoned stock of 125 units in the $15,000 to $24,999 value category must accommodate households with incomes of $10,000 or less (the lower half of the $10,000 median), Concord's zoning will be in compliance only when the total number of potential households in all income classes are reduced by rezoning economic districts, so that only about 63 households have incomes of $10,000 or less.[7]

Therefore, economic district rezoning must first reduce total potential worker households to the level of current zoned housing units, a drop of 8,104 worker households, from 16,497 to 8,393. After this initial drop, 4,282 of the resulting 8,393 households would require owned housing units in the $10,000 or less income category. Since the unaltered residential zoning allows only 63 housing units to households in this income class, rezoning of economic districts would have to reduce potential worker households by another 4,219 (4,282 - 63 = 4,219) to comply with the standard for nonexclusion. All told, current economic zoning, which hypothetically generates 16,497 worker households, must be sufficiently changed to drop that total down to 124, at which point only 63 are in the $10,000 or less income class. This enormous reduction (99 percent) of worker households implies a proportionate reduction of zoned land in economic districts. Accordingly, the 38,623,384 square feet of gross district land area currently zoned for economic uses [8] would be reduced to 290,061 square feet. Since Concord, and other townships, would doubtless view the resultant loss of employment and taxable property as a form of fiscal suicide, one might safely conclude that rezoning in this manner to comply with the performance standard is highly unlikely. As a point of passing interest, were Concord to reduce its work force and worker households by applying the lowest floor to land area ratios observed in the other five townships, the 16,497 households generated by Concord's current economic zoning would drop to 5,045, of which 2,574 would receive incomes of $10,000 or less.[9]

We conclude that the mechanics of the performance standard itself, and the relative stability of earnings and incomes in various industrial categories, combine in such ways as to eliminate effectively Concord's recourse to changing its economic district zoning and thereby complying with the performance standard. It might be pointed out that Concord was "restricted" in its use of economic district rezoning only because its residential zoning was so skewed toward high-cost dwelling units. If the discontinuities were few, and only negligible exclusion was evident in Concord's original zoning, then a modest change in Concord's economic district zoning might result in compliance with the standard. But the fact remains that Concord Township saw fit to engage in residential zoning with such distorted housing cost characteristics that no acceptable change in economic zoning could right the balance. Since only modest results are possible with a dramatic altering of economic district zoning, Concord can redress its imbalance only with substantial changes in its residential zoning.

Residential Rezoning

It appears that Concord would have to engage in such drastic rezoning of its economic districts to comply with the performance standard of
nonexclusion that virtually all nonresidential tax base would disappear and with
it most of the space needs of commercial and service activities required by a
resident population. A far more sensible strategy for Concord to pursue would
be to rezone its residential districts to allow housing of the type which worker
households prefer and can afford. This is, of course, the response sought by
a workplace-residence standard which is designed primarily to allow maximum
local control over zoning, subject only to requirements of internal consistency
between worker household's income, and housing prices and rents. That requirement for internal consistency harnesses fiscal motivation of economic
district zoning to the task of providing a more realistic stock of housing opportunities in the developing portions of metropolitan areas. Concord, like
other developing townships, is currently under no such restriction and has
zoned its housing stock in such a way that highly unbalanced shortfalls and surpluses are produced, of the magnitude and direction shown in Table 8-1.

Since shortfalls are in the least expensive portions of the potential
stock, and surplus units are too costly for many worker households, Concord
could remove all exclusion by simply rezoning residential districts to multi-
family or row house densities and letting the market settle the demand patterns
for less dense, more costly housing. Concord would be unlikely (and unwise) to
pursue this course because the township would probably be so inundated with
pent-up demand for low- to moderate-cost housing that unit-land prices would
rise well above those offered elsewhere in large-lot districts, the result being
that Concord would experience only low- and moderate-cost housing development.[10] Moreover, current market forces tend to discourage disparate
price levels in adjacent residential areas, an economic fact which effectively
inhibits developers and prospective owners from building houses much more expensive than the minimum.

**Table 8-1. Potential Housing Units in Concord Township's Zoning
Ordinance by Tenure, Rent, Price, Shortfall, Surplus, and Median Household
Income, 1971**

Housing Tenure	Housing Prices and Rents	Housing Median Income	Housing Stock Shortfalls	Housing Stock Surplus
Own	$15–19,999	$ 9,150	3,180	–
Own	$20–24,999	$10,910	1,654	–
Own	$25–34,999	$12,663	800	–
Own	$35–49,999	$16,365	–	5,856
Rent	$120–149	$ 6,275	422	–
Rent	$150–199	$ 8,040	–	201
Rent	$200	$13,430	–	–

The most logical strategy would entail the rezoning of residential land so that housing densities and tenure choices are created which are consistent with the price and rent profile of household requirements. This zoning strategy would make available housing units which are not merely affordable, but which also would better match household preferences and tend to maximize the township's residential tax base. Table 8-1 indicates that 6,056 households were excluded from housing and residence in Concord Township. If residential rezoning were to alter the housing stock so that none of the 8,393 worker households were excluded, then the schedule of housing units, by price, rent and tenure, required by worker households would define the necessary stock characteristics.[11] Even though a number of residential zoning configurations can be devised which are not exclusionary, the configuration of housing requirements implied in Table 7-4 allows preferences for housing to be more fully expressed.

We shall illustrate this process by tracing housing requirements back through tenure and cost characteristics to actual zoning categories: household requirements of 1,467 owner-occupied units selling for $25,000 to $34,999, 526 owner-occupied units of $35,000 to $49,000 value, and 212 owner-occupied units priced at over $50,000 correspond to lot size districts of 20,000 sq. ft., 43,560 sq. ft., and 87,120 sq. ft., respectively. Estimating homeowner requirements is quite straightforward, since tenure splits are negligible for large-lot, single-family housing. However, the projected demand for inexpensive owner-occupied units must also account for the fact that some single-family structures will be rented, and there is the collateral consideration that a handful of units in multi-family structures will have resident owners. These complexities can be sorted in the following manner. First, worker households which require 4,959 owned units selling between $15,000 and $24,999 can be satisfied by units in multi-family structures and by single-family units on 5,000 sq. ft. lots. Total demand of 4,959 will be diminished first by 295 owner-occupied, multi-family units, the number representing 0.240 of 1,230 multi-family units which must be provided to yield the 935 required rental units with rents between $120 and $199.[12] After reducing the total need of 4959 by 935 units, the remaining 4664 owner-occupied units must then come from 5131 single-family houses, 467 of which are required by renters at rents of $200 or more.[13] Since only 293 rental units with rents over $200 are demanded, the 467 single-family rentals more than satisfy this demand. These simple calculations demonstrate how one might generate a profile of housing requirements for structure types and densities, and their residential zoning equivalents. Table 8-2 summarizes this profile for Concord Township.

Recall, however, that Concord Township originally devoted 8,032 acres of gross residential land area [14] to the potential stock of 8,393 housing units, a fact which implicitly excluded some 72 percent of worker households which, in terms of the standard, had rights of access to that stock. As demon-

Table 8–2. Requirements for Housing Units and Land in Concord Township's Residential Zoning Districts

| *Housing Unit Requirements by Type and Density* | | | | *Gross Residential District Land Area* |
Lot Size (sq. ft.)	Structure Type	Dwelling Units (Number)	Land Area per Unit (sq. ft.)	Required (sq. ft.)
3,000	Multi-family	1,230	3,750	4,612,500
5,000	Single-family	5,131	6,250	32,068,750
20,000	Single-family	1,467	23,810	34,929,270
43,560	Single-family	526	50,650	26,641,900
87,120	Single-family	212	101,300	21,475,600
		8,393		119,728,020
				(About 2,750 acres)

strated above, exclusion is avoidable by rezoning residential districts to provide a housing stock appropriate to the requirements of 8,393 households. In rezoning to house these 8,393 households, only 2,750 acres of gross residential land is actually required, leaving a surplus land area of 5,283 acres.[15] This is the result of rezoning land at a higher average residential density for an equal number of housing units. The disposition of that "surplus" land area is still subject to the standard. If Concord Township rezones it for uses other than residential or economic, the standard does not apply, since it is concerned with the effects of mixing these particular uses; that is, the standard stipulates how land is to be developed as between residential and economic purposes, not whether it is to be developed at all or how much should be put to public use. If townships wish to remain undeveloped, and do not employ exclusionary zoning in that pursuit, then their decision is not directly influenced by the standard.

If all the surplus is devoted to economic districts, then Concord remains in compliance, because its newly rezoned housing stock need only accommodate an equal number of worker households when total worker households equal or exceed zoned housing units. Under the standard, adding even more worker households cannot affect compliance or township responsibility. But, if Concord wants to devote some or all of that surplus to residential uses, the standard stipulates that Concord must ensure that each increment of housing supply will accommodate a representative mix of incomes of worker households, up to the point where additional stock increments produce housing units in excess of total worker households. Increments of supply which push the total stock of housing units beyond the total number of worker households are not subject to the standard and may be of any density, structure or cost.

To illustrate the mechanics involved and the final residential pattern which might prevail, we will assume for the moment that Concord chose to devote its entire surplus to residential use. That being the case, the first point to consider is how much of the surplus 5,283 acres must be allocated, in compliance with the standard, to remaining "unhoused" worker households. Since 8,393 of the 16,497 total potential worker households could be accommodated on 2,750 acres of land area, the remaining 8,104 households can also be housed on land area proportional to their size, i.e., $8,104 \div 8,393 = 0.966$; therefore, an additional 2,654 acres ($0.966 \times 2,750$ acres) is required to house all remaining worker households. When land required to house the remaining worker households is subtracted from the initial surplus of 5,283 acres, this yields a "discretionary" surplus of 2,629 acres unencumbered by the standard. Where Concord Township had originally accommodated only 2,337 worker households, it has now (hypothetically) rezoned its residential districts, thereby accommodating all 16,497 of its potential worker households, and has met the standard in full without rezoning any of its economic districts. The residential land remaining, Concord's discretionary surplus, will yield greater residential tax base relative to household services in large-lot development; we might therefore assume that Concord would choose to zone all the surplus for one-acre development. If so, 2,261 additional one-acre units would result, thereby bringing total housing units on one-acre lots, or larger, to 2,787, down considerably from 6,594 similar units in the existing zoning ordinance. In terms of total land area devoted to residential lots of an acre or more, our hypothetical rezoning produces 4,800 acres of expensive, taxable residential land area, a 37 percent reduction in land area from the 7,668 acres contained in Concord's current zoning.

Assessing the Need for Financial Assistance

Were Concord to rezone its residential areas in any of the ways described above, it could no longer be claimed that the township engaged in exclusionary zoning. This does not, of course, mean that all 8,393 households could afford the minimum cost housing, because the requirements matrix was designed to detect zoning exclusion, not the inadequacy of household income.[16] This deliberate separation will prove useful, however, because it is now possible to estimate public sector responsibility for subsidizing a known number of worker households, either directly or indirectly, to meet the cost of privately financed housing. The preferred method of subsidy is a topic of current controversy by housing experts and public officials.[17] Our primary purpose here is to demonstrate the dimensions of the need for housing assistance by worker households and to indicate the tenure implications of that need. Total potential worker household requirements for owner-occupied units costing $15,000 to 19,999 in Concord Township is 3,242, of which 712 represent requirements by families who would not be able to afford the full cost of homeownership. Of the 732 households requiring rental units in the $120 to $149 range, 193 could not afford market rents.[18] Therefore, even after rezoning, housing assistance would be required for about 16 percent of all renters (193 ÷ 7,164 = 0.099). [19] The approximate magnitude of assistance required may be estimated from the income distribution of these households as shown in Table 8-3.

Owners comprise the bulk of worker households which would require some measure of housing assistance, accounting for about 79 percent of all such households. The majority of households (about 53 percent) requiring assistance have incomes of less than $5,000. Two-fifths of this lowest income group are renters. All households requiring housing assistance which have incomes of $5,000 or greater are owners. These figures are based upon a total household population of 8,393 for Concord Township, but the relative magnitude of need would remain constant whatever the number of worker households happens to be.

General Zoning Strategy Model

The choices open to Concord Township in rezoning to comply with the standard make it clear that (1) only residential rezoning can create a profile of nonexclusionary housing units because household income patterns are relatively resistant to economic district rezoning, and (2) the performance standard forces townships to reexamine the overall pattern of land devoted to residential versus economic uses. That is, once Concord has rezoned its residential districts to accommodate incomes of worker households, the increased density of residential use, as a result of that rezoning, would free so much land for other uses that the entire land-use mix might well become a point of issue. In the preceding section, which discussed residential rezoning,

Table 8-3. Households Requiring Housing Assistance by Income and Tenure

Income of Households Requiring Assistance	Owners (Number)	Renters (Number)	All	
			(Number)	(Percent)
$2,000	61	46	107	12
$2,000–2,999	66	34	100	11
$3,000–3,999	76	58	134	15
$4,000–4,999	82	55	137	15
$5,000–5,999	100	0	100	11
$6,000–7,999	178	0	178	20
$8,000–9,999	149	0	149	16
$10,000–14,999	0	0	0	0
$15,000–24,999	0	0	0	0
$25,000+	0	0	0	0
All	712	193	905	100
Percent of Households	79.0	21.0	100.0	–

we assumed for illustrative purposes that Concord's extra land would be converted to high cost, residential uses so as to increase the residential tax base. As noted then, Concord could have rezoned that "extra" land in any of several combinations of residential and economic use.

To examine more fully the options available to Concord, and other townships in a similar situation, we have devised a general model of alternative zoning strategies. The model proposed here considers all possible land use configurations in which townships might zone for residential and economic purposes, any one of which is nonexclusionary, i.e., in compliance with the performance standard. That is, our model defines the full range of choices available to Concord in such a manner that worker households are not excluded from residential opportunities. However, the model does not include options for analyzing the devoting of land to public uses or the keeping of land in an undeveloped state, as long as residential or economic zoning is not used to implement either of these decisions.

The total amount of land currently slated by Concord Township for development of the type affected by the zoning standard is 8,919 acres (8,032 in residential districts, plus 887 acres in economic districts). Let us first establish the implications of zoning the 8,919 acres for the polar extremes of all economic and all residential development. If that entire amount of land were devoted exclusively to economic districts, 165,935 worker households would result. On the other hand, if that same total land area were, instead, devoted to nonexclusionary residential development, then 27,234 such households could be accommodated. These two extreme cases anchor a range of mixes, from 0 percent of total land in residential districts and 100 percent in economic districts, to 100 percent of total land in residential districts and 0 percent in economic districts; this menu of choices can be portrayed by the set of axes W and H in Table 8–4. The line A–B connects the polar extremes on each axis and contains all the mix possibilities between worker households and housing units which comply with the standard.[20] Another line (L-M) connects all points where worker households are equal in number to worker housing units, point L representing zero units of each, and point M the maximum number of each. Line L-M has several important properties, the first of which establishes an upper bound to a decision space of mixes which are fiscally "irrational" from the perspective of Concord Township. That total space, as bounded by points LMB, represents all mixes whereby more worker housing is provided than is required of Concord Township by the standard; i.e., there are more such units than worker households which need them. Second, point M on that line is rational only if Concord is absolutely sure it can attract exactly that amount of industrial and commercial employment, as point M represents the maximum, equal mix of worker housing units and worker households which will exhaust all land area, thereby eliminating any possibility for Concord Township to increase either its economic or high

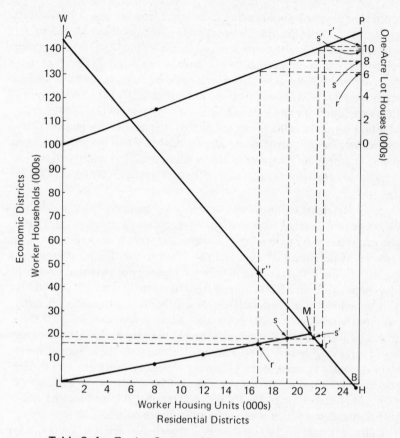

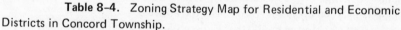

Table 8-4. Zoning Strategy Map for Residential and Economic Districts in Concord Township.

valued residential tax base. Third, the space above line *L–M,* as bounded by points *LMA,* represents zoning strategy options which yield the township a net gain in tax base.

   The situation which Concord Township faced earlier, when it was arbitrarily assumed that the township would devote the land remaining, after accommodating all worker households, to one-acre residential development, can be shown as a special case among an indeterminate number of other options on this strategy "map." Recall that Concord had rezoned to accommodate all 16,497 worker households in worker housing units, a situation depicted by point *r* on the *L–M* line. The distance between *r* and *r'* is the additional number of worker housing units which could be developed on the remaining land. It is doubtful, as postulated above, that Concord would choose to provide more worker housing than required and, therefore, we assumed that Concord would choose to zone the land for one-acre residences. Since gross residential land for all worker units averages about 14,265 sq. ft. and gross residential land for one-acre residences is 50,650 sq. ft., the numbering along axis LH would necessarily overestimate by about 255 percent the number of potential one-acre units which could be built on the extra land. Therefore, a line OP is drawn at a slope of tangent 0.283 [21] such that vertical extensions of r and r', which subtend a given number of additional worker housing units, reflect from OP on axis BP and, in turn, mark off an equivalent number of potential one-acre residences. When the unencumbered land area (segment $r-r'$) is traced in this fashion, the 2,261 additional one-acre residences are delineated on axis HP between about 6,000 and 8,000 units.

      Reversing the previous assumptions completely, what would be the result if Concord devoted the extra land to its economic districts? This, too, can be easily traced by extending a line vertically from point r to point r'' on line AB, where, by definition, all land available is put to use. The horizontal trace of point r'' to the LW axis marks off the total number of potential worker households, about 46,500 as read from the map, or some 30,000 additional worker households. Concord must decide whether it is better off with 2,261 more one-acre residences or the potential tax base represented by 30,000 additional worker households, which it probably could not get. If, for example, Concord is reasonably sure of eventually attracting only the economic development currently allowed for in its current zoning, and that one-acre residential demand will continue virtually unabated, then it is better to build up its residential tax base. Conversely, if Concord feels that it is well located and has other attractions which could reasonably assure economic development sufficient to generate 46,500 total worker households, and if it wants this type of development, then economic rezoning is the answer.

      Suppose, for example, that Concord Township has determined to its satisfaction that 19,000 worker households fairly represent the magnitude of total economic development. If some remaining land were then rezoned to increase the previous yield of 16,497 to the 19,000 worker household level, approximately how many one-acre residences could Concord also allow? Referring to Table 8-4, 19,000 is picked off on the LM axis (point s) and traced horizontally to determine the resultant housing stock (point s'). The performance standard requires the entire housing stock to accommodate worker households before any land surplus, where such surplus is indicated by points to the left of line AB, can be devoted to higher cost housing. Point s on the LM line equates 19,000 worker households with the required stock of worker housing units and is to the left of line AB; the magnitude of surplus is therefore measured by line $s-s'$. The distance remaining between s and s', as measured on the LH axis, is roughly equivalent to 1,000 one-acre residences when traced to and measured on the BP axis. Note, again, that point M is the point where conversion of surplus land to extra one-acre residences must end. At point M, all land is consumed in equating worker households and worker housing units, the condition which must be met before other kinds of housing patterns are allowed by the performance standard. After point M is reached, there are no trade-offs possible between economic development and high-cost housing.

The dynamics of this strategy model place the burden of potential overzoning for economic districts squarely on the shoulders of local townships. If Concord zones for more workers than its stock of worker housing can possibly accommodate, then the standard requires that it necessarily forego residential tax base enrichment. Even if it decides to zone economic districts in a way which allows a surplus of land for high-cost housing, Concord must be sure that it is not opting for unduly large land areas in economic districts with low potential for development at the cost of additional high-cost residences of greater development potential. The performance standard thereby allows each township to zone those uses for which it has particular locational or institutional advantages. The only restriction is that, in doing so, townships must also provide housing for their labor forces; this requirement, now lacking, is needed to correct the exclusionary propensities of developing townships.

NOTES

1. Advisory Committee to the Department of Housing and Urban Development, Urban Development, *Urban Growth and Land Development: The Land Conversion Process* (Washington: National Academy of Sciences, 1972), p. 20.
2. Economic district is a shorthand term introduced here to simplify the subsequent discussions. Although some employment is generated by the residential districts, 98 percent of Concord's potential employment originates in economic districts, a percentage similar in size to the other townships.
3. See Section C of Chapter 6.
4. Total Concord households 8,393 X 0.08 (i.e., 0.38 – 0.30 = 0.08) = 670 households with $8,000 or less income. See Township Income distributions in Section C of Chapter 6 and Table 8–4 of this chapter.
5. Of the 3,602 low-cost units in shortfall, 422 were required by households with median income of $6,275 and 3,180 by households with median income of $9,150. See Table 8–4.
6. See Table 7–5.
7. There are about 125 housing units with values between $15,000–24,999 which are now allowed, only half of which are affordable to families which make less than $10,000 per year (see Table 7–4).
8. See Section B of Chapter 6.

9. A related strategy of reducing the intensity of development to such an extent that 124 worker households are employed by fewer firms, which would occupy the amount of district land previously zoned, is even less feasible. No firm would build upon land under zoning requirements which would preserve the amount of previously zoned taxable land area in economic districts at virtually wilderness levels of density. For example, the floor space required by employers of the workers who comprise the 124 households is 85,557 sq. ft., which, when spread over 38,623,384 sq. ft. of constant land area, yields a floor to land area ratio of 0.00221. This ratio is roughly equivalent to the floor area for one single-family house occupying a 15 ½ acre site. This does not mean that even lower densities are outside the realm of economic site useage by industries, but densities sufficiently low to keep the same amount of land area employing 124 household's workers are worth mentioning only for illustrative purposes.

10. Much before large-lot zoning became an exclusionary norm, Milgram found that land zoned for intensive row house use in suburban Philadelphia sold for about $7,400 per raw acre, whereas single-family or twin-house uses commanded $2,800 per acre. Grace Milgram, *The City Expands: A Study of the Conversion of Land from Urban Use, Philadelphia 1945-62* (Washington: Department of Housing and Urban Development, Government Printing Office, 1968).

11. Household requirements, by tenure and cost, available from Table 7-4.

12. See Chapter 5 for the discussion and data on structure-tenure factors.

13. Since approximately 91 percent of low cost, single-family units are rented in the six township area, a total supply of 5,131 units is required to yield the 4,664 low cost, owned units ($4,664 = 0.909 X$, or $5,131 = 4,664 \div .909$). If the rents and prices of multi-family and small-lot, single-family housing were identical (which they are not), then the tenure-split factor of each would allow a simultaneous equation solution of both stock requirements to meet joint tenure and cost demand.

14. Total gross land area in Concord's residential districts was 349,870,770 square feet, or 8,032 acres. See Chapter 5 for further discussion of residential district land areas.

15. 349,870,770 sq. ft. – 119,728,020 sq. ft. = 230,142,750 sq. ft. = 5,283 acres.

16. The matrix was also designed to independently estimate those who could and could not afford the least expensive market housing in each tenure class. Refer to earlier discussion of the matrix, as portrayed in Table 7-1 and as used in Appendix U.

17. For a discussion of conventional federal assistance to needy households, see George von Furstenberg and Howard R. Moskof, "Federally Assisted Rental Housing Programs: Which Income Groups Have They Served or Whom Can They Be Expected to Serve?," and George von Furstenberg, "Improving the Feasibility of Home-

ownership for Lower Income Families Through Subsidized Mortgage Financing," from The President's Committee on Urban
Housing, *Technical Studies.* (Washington: Government Printing
Office, 1968) For a discussion of housing assistance through income
transfers, see William G. Grigsby, "The Housing Effects of a
Guaranteed Annual Income," Michael Stegman, ed., *Housing
and Economics: The American Dilemma* (Cambridge: MIT, 1970),
pp. 396–422.

18. Many of the 732 which can afford $150 or less for rental housing probably
require at least two-bedroom units which will cost more than
$150. This means that the magnitude of need as described in the
text is very possibly underestimated by some unknown factor.

19. These calculations are based upon figures for Concord Township which are
derived from output of the housing demand computer algorithm,
as described in Appendix U.

20. To simplify subsequent discussion, the term worker housing will apply
to the profile of housing which worker households can afford to
occupy.

21. Tangent = $\dfrac{14,265}{50,650}$ = 0.283

Chapter Nine

Policy Implications of Applying the Zoning Standard

Obviously, governmental responses can, and do, take various forms. The choices of local government are perhaps the most difficult, for at the local level development is visible and must be dealt with in fact, not in theory.[1]

The preceding chapters were devoted to developing an explicit workplace and residence standard for zoning ordinances and to testing that standard, based upon an analysis of employment and housing relationships implicit within zoning ordinances of a sample of developing townships. Such a standard, it was assumed, would be potentially useful to public policy makers in dealing with the problems and issues surrounding exclusionary zoning. However, before policy makers could be expected to consider adopting this or any other standard, a discussion of the implications of implementing this standard on a widespread basis is certainly in order.

The technical considerations which might be encountered in any serious attempt to implement the standard were anticipated and largely dealt with, to the degree possible, in the previous chapters. The reasoning which led to adopting this particular version of the workplace-residence standard, and the interpretation of that standard in measurable terms, was laid out in Chapter 3 in considerable detail. If that version were to be found deficient by decision makers, the breadth of discussion in Chapter 3 would provide a firm basis for rearranging certain elements of the standard and for reinterpreting the data required to use a revised standard. Similarly, Chapters 4, 5 and 6 were intended to establish sound general principles for making methodological assumptions, generating appropriate data, and conducting replicable analyses required when deriving the housing and employment relationships imbedded within other zoning ordinances. Caveats, alternative procedures or sources, and all-purpose computer algorithms were frequently mentioned in these same three chapters to aid any subsequent, large-scale implementation of the standard.

Apart from the technical aspects of adoption and implemention, what are the policy implications of widespread implemention which decision makers should be aware of? Since the standard does not, of itself, yield a determinate pattern of zoning uses, the actual outcomes likely to accompany its implemention are necessarily speculative. We shall, however, offer enlightened conjecture about the policy pitfalls or difficulties which might be encountered in applying the standard.

The rezoning patterns depend upon the net outcome of many townships and municipalities deciding which particular mix of housing and economic uses allowed by the standard is best suited to their individual circumstances. Thus, in a very real sense, the final result is indeterminate and may entail successive rounds of each township adjusting its zoning in response to both its perception and analysis of real world expectations, and to the other townships' zoning, all of which must comply with the standard. Even though localities are free to choose whatever mix best fits their locational specialization and meets their particular needs, the standard imposes an implicit but largely hidden rationale on local municipalities to consider the actions of other municipalities. By considering the logical consequences which this underlying rationale would tend to produce, it is then possible to estimate probable outcomes and ensuing policy implications.

In the absence of the performance standard, current zoning of all six townships potentially results in about 3.4 labor force participants for every housing unit. With the notable exception of Edgmont Township, the six townships zoned for vastly more industrial and commercial development than could reasonably be expected. By comparison, in 1970 the whole of Delaware County had a labor force of about 169,000 and about 181,000 occupied housing units, as compared with a "zoned" labor force of 121,000 in the six townships alone. On the average, townships in Delaware County have fewer workers than households, yet the six townships combined "expect" several times as many workers as housing units in their current zoning. All of the townships could not possibly realize 3.4 workers per housing unit; it is the average number of workers each developing township can reasonably expect which provides the rationale underlying its future rezoning decisions. That is, since all townships will eventually recognize that they must pay for excessive commercial and industrial zoning in the coin of housing appropriate to workers' incomes at the cost of foregone large-lot zoning, those townships which can realistically expect concentrations of economic development will continue to zone for it and those which cannot will zone for less.

To establish the range of possible behavior which townships might exhibit, when coming to grips with the performance standard, a set of detailed illustrations will be developed. As noted above, Delaware County had just less than one worker per housing unit in 1970. When the equivalent number of workers who are also household heads are related to housing units, there were

0.56 household heads in the work force for each housing unit.[2] Similarly, the average ratio of 3.4 workers per housing unit, found for all six townships, is comparable to a mix of about two working household heads per dwelling unit.

Assume now for illustrative purposes, that six *other* hypothetical townships in Delaware County know that, on average, their combined working household head to housing unit ratio will probably not depart substantially from the average ratio of the parent county. Assume further, for the sake of convenience, that these six townships all have the land area, zoning provisions, and mix strategies of Concord Township open to them. Since each is uniquely located with respect to transportation systems, adjoining residential or economic development, natural features, etc., it is quite conceivable that some would be better advised to build a nonresidential tax base and others would tend toward a high-value residential base. Attributing Concord's current zoning to the six hypothetical townships, the total number of worker housing units is 14,016 (6 × 2,336) and the number of worker households is 98,982 (6 × 16,497).

This being the yield of housing units and households under current zoning, what is the range of possible outcomes which accompany several possible mixes of economic and residential development in these hypothetical townships which rezone to meet the performance standard? None of the townships—it should be made clear—is in any way compelled by the performance standard to zone for the countywide average of 0.56 working household heads per housing unit. Those townships which, in their own view, cannot reasonably compete for economic development will tend to rezone for residential or other uses to avoid accommodating worker households for which townships are now held responsible by the workplace-residence standard, but which are unlikely ever to materialize. The question remains, how many worker housing units and worker households would result if the six hypothetical townships comply with the performance standard and arrange their zoning with an eye toward the expected countywide worker household to housing unit ratio?

Revising our assumptions for a second illustration, how many households and standard housing units would result if all six hypothetical townships (labeled *A, B, C, D, E,* and *F*) zoned in exactly the same way, so that each township produced a worker household/worker housing unit ratio, or mix, of 0.56? By using a simplified version of the zoning strategy map developed in Chapter 8 for Concord Township,[3] a line drawn from *L* through any point where 0.56 worker households equal one worker housing unit (e.g., point *x* picks off 5,600 worker households and 10,000 worker housing units), and extended to point *y* on line *AB*, will pick off the total number of worker households and standard housing units which exhausts all land zoned for housing and employment in each of the six hypothetical townships. When traced on Table 9-1, point *y* results in 12,000 worker households and 22,000 worker housing units (point *z*).

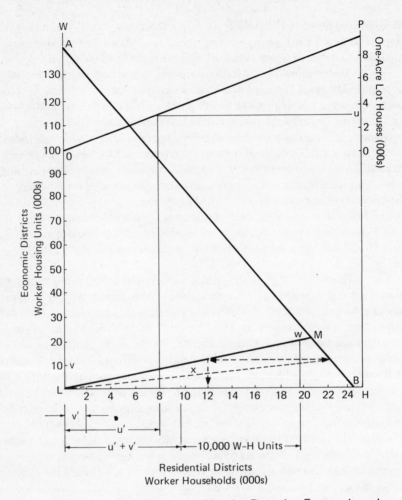

Table 9-1.   Zoning Strategy Map for Rezoning Economic and Residential Districts.

However, the performance standard stipulates that each township need only provide worker housing for its work force; therefore it is likely that rezoning would produce 12,000 worker housing units rather than 22,000, thereby freeing land for 4,000 expensive homes on large lots. Continuing our assumption that all six townships observed similar zoning practices, they might then be expected to accommodate 72,000 worker households in a stock of 72,000 worker housing units and an additional 24,000 housing units on larger lots. Compared with the housing and households in townships A through F before rezoning, i.e., under conditions similar to Concord Township's current zoning ordinance, it is quite obvious that a superior overall match between the incomes of household workers and the prices and rents of housing results.

Recognizing that industrial townships do not develop precisely with the countywide average, and that some of our six hypothetical townships may be tempted to zone more land in economic districts, how will these facts affect the resultant profile of worker households and housing units? Assume in this third illustration that townships *A*, *B* and *C* are known to be better situated with respect to economic development than the other three, and that they will therefore be justifiably tempted to zone for higher than average ratios of worker households to housing units. Accordingly, townships *D*, *E* and *F* also recognize they are not as well situated for economic development and will tend to zone for less than average ratios, to escape worker household housing obligations, thereby enlarging their high cost residential tax base. Assume further that township F decides it has virtually no economic development potential: a straight line (FO) as shown in Table 9-2, connecting a ratio of 0.0 worker households to housing units for *F*, which also passes through the group average ratio of 0.56 to 1 (point *N*), mechanically generates a linear set of ratios for the remaining townships on the assumption that the other townships have lineally related ratios and that the average ratio for all six is the observed ratio (0.56) for Delaware County.

If plotted on the zoning strategy map in the same manner that point *x* was established, these ratios determine the resultant worker households and standard housing units. From Table 9-2, Township B is seen to have a ratio of about 0.95, which yields a stock of 20,000 standard housing units and

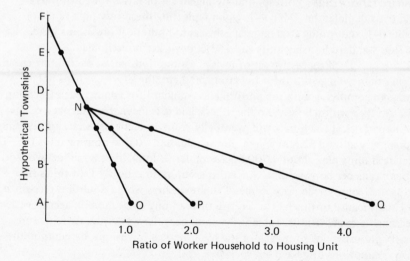

Table 9-2. Potential Ratios of Worker Households to Housing Units for Six Hypothetical Townships.

20,000 worker households when the ratio is plotted on line *A–B* of Table 9-1. Repeating the process for all six hypothetical townships, 70,900 workers' housing units and 75,100 worker households result according to these simple assumptions of relative housing and economic development specialization.

Let these assumptions for our fourth illustration be altered again to reflect the optimistic decision of townships *A, B* and *C* to overzone with respect to the countywide average ratio, but assume too that townships *D, E* and *F* continue to expect their straight-line share, as determined above. Suppose that township *A* believes, correctly or not, that it has the development potential to realize a ratio of about two worker households per housing unit, the average ratio implicit in the current zoning of the six townships as derived from the analysis in Chapters 5 and 6. Referring again to Table 9-2, a line (NP) connecting *A*'s revised ratio of 2:1 with the countywide average ratio of 0.56:1 will pick off appropriate lineal values for townships *B* and *C* (the ratios for D, E and F remain, of course, unchanged as per our assumptions). When the revised ratios for *A, B* and *C*, which represent overzoning relative to the countywide ratio, are replotted on Table 9-1, 71,400 standard housing units and 99,100 worker households result for our six hypothetical townships.

Consider, as a fifth illustration, an even more exaggerated case of overzoning in which township A zones much as Thornbury Township now does—providing for 4.45 worker households per housing unit. Assume further that townships *B* and *C* follow A's lead, but that townships *D, E* and *F* remain unchanged. Connecting point Q, the ratio of 4.45 (over eight times larger than the expected countywide average of 0.56), with point *N*, the countywide average ratio, yields a correspondingly higher set of ratios for townships *B* and *C*, as depicted on Table 9-2. Upon replotting these very high ratios on Table 9-1, the zoning strategy map, the six hypothetical townships yield 65,700 standard housing units and 152,600 worker households.

Each successive set of revised assumptions about overzoning entails higher than average ratios for the group, and are, therefore, perhaps polar cases. In complying with the performance standard for zoning, each township assesses its position relative to the others, and it is inevitable that each of the six hypothetical townships will eventually come to recognize that, jointly, they potentially allow 152,600 worker households and 70,400 housing units (65,700 standard units plus about 4,700 houses on larger lots)—that is, about two worker households per housing unit. Since this group ratio is nearly four times the expected countywide ratio, some of the townships would doubtless recognize the significance of this fact and revise their zoning to be more in accord with reasonable expectations. Table 9-3 summarizes the worker households and worker housing units for each of the hypothetical townships, based upon the five assumptions discussed above.

It is plain that any of the four illustrative mixes (including the case of dramatic overzoning for worker households relative to housing units), all

Table 9-3. Mix of Worker Housing Units and Worker Households Yielded Under Various Illustrative* Zoning Patterns for Six Hypothetical Townships

	Worker Housing Units					Worker Households				
	Illustrations									
Township	1	2	3	4	5	1	2	3	4	5
A	2,336	12,000	20,300	18,200	13,900	16,497	12,000	24,500	37,000	62,000
B	2,336	12,000	20,000	19,600	16,300	16,497	12,000	20,000	28,500	48,000
C	2,336	12,000	15,000	18,000	19,900	16,497	12,000	15,000	18,000	27,000
D	2,336	12,000	10,000	10,000	10,000	16,497	12,000	10,000	10,000	10,000
E	2,336	12,000	5,600	5,600	5,600	16,497	12,000	5,600	5,600	5,600
F	2,336	12,000	0	0	0	16,497	12,000	0	0	0
All	14,016	72,000	70,900	71,400	65,700	98,982	72,000	75,100	99,100	152,600

Summary of Assumptions for Each Illustration

1. Assume all six townships adopt Concord Township's current, exclusionary ordinance.

2. Assume all six townships zone alike, and in compliance with performance standard to yield the observed countywide mix of worker housing units and worker households.

3. Assume the six townships zone differently, and in compliance with the performance standard to yield the observed countywide average mix of housing units and worker households.

4. Assume Townships D, E and F continue as per illustration 3, but that Township A overzones workers to housing units to produce the mix observed for the six actual townships in Delaware County; and B and C follow suit.

5. Same as Illustration 4, except that Township A adopts the overzoning pattern observed in Thornbury Township.

of which comply with the performance standard for zoning, results in four to five times more worker housing than could be expected were the hypothetical townships allowed to zone as Concord now does. Note that even in cases of gross overzoning for economic development, the supply of worker housing remains fairly stable. While the performance standard does not attempt to maintain the total ratio of worker households to housing units in an overall balance, it offers townships rational incentives to maintain a greatly improved balance. Because actual development will always lag behind the total land available for development, a precise balancing is unnecessary. Put somewhat differently, it is quite likely that a potential stock of housing will be allowed that is affordable to the bulk of worker households which accompany actual levels of economic development.

Potential Impact of Rezoning to Comply
with Standard

We have reviewed in the preceding section the possible ways in which townships might rezone their land when faced with the proposed performance standard. It was seen that countywide expectations temper the propensity for individual townships to overzone for worker households, relative to housing units, but, even were gross overzoning to occur, the developing townships would still allow far more worker housing units than now obtain under existing zoning practice. Given that rezoning will produce residential and economic use mixtures which fall within the range of outcomes discussed above, what then is the potential impact: (1) upon commercial and industrial development in general, and, in particular, upon the future opportunity for worker households to find affordable housing in partially developed municipalities which already have a substantial commercial and industrial tax base, and (2) upon the housing market?

Impact on Commercial and Industrial Development.   Looking at the commercial and industrial land markets, there would appear to be a slight bias toward zoning for higher proportions of industrial, rather than commercial, worker households for any given total of worker households. This bias is derived from the generally higher household incomes of industrial district workers [4] which, of course, marginally reduce the township's responsibility for providing lower-cost housing. However, this potential source of bias may be partially or entirely offset by a number of other considerations favoring commercial development. First, many states share sales taxes with localities and earmark a proportion of the local tax yield for jurisdictions in which the sales taxes are collected. Commercial development also produces significantly higher amounts of commercial land and floor area per worker household. Based on data generated in Section B of Chapter 6, a household whose head is employed in a commercial district accounts for about 4,000 sq. ft. of taxable land

area and 1,000 sq. ft. of floor area, whereas comparable figures for a household head employed in industrial districts are 1,300 sq. ft. and 500 sq. ft.,
respectively. There is also a good chance that a township could attract at least
enough commercial development to service its resident population, but the
chances of that same township attracting industrial development which has no
functional relationship to the township's residential sections per se might very
well be nil. Finally, there may be a greater measure of environmental risk
associated with industrial rather than commercial development, despite the
performance standards imposed upon industrial development by contemporary
zoning practice. On balance, it is impossible to know how these several considerations interact in any given circumstance and so it is probably best to
accept current mixes of commercial and industrial development as indicative
of future mixes. Consequently, there is no firm basis from which a relative
shortage of land for either commercial or industrial land uses might be predicted.

There is another set of issues about commercial and industrial uses
in townships which are already partially developed. Recall that the performance
standard would allow townships which are substantially undeveloped to concentrate upon economic development and to zone for more worker households
than total housing units, if these townships forego high-cost residential development. What then are the effects of applying the performance standard to
partially developed townships which presently have inventories of, and zone
exclusively for, both high-cost residential development and economic development? This situation is depicted on Table 9–1 by points *u, v,* and *w.* Point *u*
measures an existing stock of 3,000 housing units standing on one-acre lots in
residential districts which consume land equivalent to about 8,000 worker
housing units, as marked by point *u'* on axis LB. This partially developed township also has existing economic development, which produces about 10,000
worker households, as shown by point *v,* and which consumes land equal to
v' as measured on axis *LB.* The sum of *u'* and *v'* consumes land equivalent in
size to that which would accommodate about 10,000 worker housing units.

Assume the performance standard is now applied to this township's
zoning ordinance. Since only a very small fraction of worker households can
afford the houses on one-acre lots, much of the remaining undeveloped land
currently zoned exclusively for one-acre lots or for commercial and industrial
land must be rezoned for housing to accommodate the 10,000 worker households who currently work in the township. A revised zoning code which allowed
sufficient worker housing for all current worker households would consume an
additional portion of total district land equal to 10,000 units on the *LB* axis.
When added to the land already devoted to expensive residential development
and economic development, the sum of all land committed to development
which complies with the performance standard is equivalent to a little less than
20,000 worker housing units, as shown by point *w* on line *LM.* The township
may, of course, zone the remaining land for worker households and residential

units which these households can afford on a one-for-one basis (about 1,000 of each), or the township can zone for large lots and still comply with the performance standard.

Assume now that considerably more economic development than that implied by the 1,000 or so additional worker households would have occurred in the absence of the performance standard. What are the indirect effects? First, the economic development which might otherwise have taken place in the township will have to locate elsewhere. Undeveloped townships with balanced zoning plans, or other partially developed areas, including the central city, with balanced housing stocks, would stand to gain this increment of tax base. However, there is no reason to believe that the distribution of the region's tax base will improve markedly or that the fiscal needs of poor suburban municipalities and the central cities will be met. At minimum, there would be a slight redistribution of fiscal resources to localities which house families of workers.

Impact on the Housing Market.   The housing market will also be affected by the performance standard, but the impact may be considerably greater. As noted in the discussion of potential rezoning behavior, over four times more housing which workers can afford would be allowed than is zoned for now. If private construction were to build new units at market prices for middle-income families and for low- to moderate-income families under subsidy programs, these families would release a large number of occupied units, which would significantly stimulate the housing filtering process. Depending upon the volume and price range of new housing construction, considerable improvement in the filtering process could well result, thereby releasing a chain of owned and rented units to lower-income families. If new construction is confined to the private market, expanded housing choice and residential opportunities are substantially improved, but primarily for those families which can afford market prices or for those few fortunate enough to find filtered, existing housing in fiscally sound communities. Low- and moderate-income families might also find a larger, but still insufficient, stock of newly constructed housing opportunities if nonprofit sponsors or public agencies build housing of the appropriate structural and density characteristics which are allowed by the performance standard. Obviously, the performance standard only removes zoning impediments to low-cost housing types: the private and public housing industries must respond to realize the potential created by the performance standard, a potential which does not exist under present zoning practice.

Subversive Strategies and Policy Response

The range of possible outcomes and impacts expected when townships must comply with the performance standard are, of course, predicted on townships actually complying. However, it is not at all inconceivable that certain municipalities might try to subvert the intent of the performance standard, while only appearing to comply with its provisions. Three broad types of subversion might be envisioned: statutory zoning, whose written provisions comply with the performance standard, but which contain implicit elements which effectively deny the possibility of apartments or of high density, moderate-cost housing; the systematic transfer of the burden for exclusion to other development controls; and the geographic isolation of lower-cost housing and families to discourage or punish prospective residents by purposely denying equal access to public goods and services within the municipality.

Statutory Compliance and Effective Evasion.   Zoning which complies with the performance standard in all surface aspects could, for example, allow high-density, low-cost housing in virtually undevelopable portions of the township, thereby effectively denying housing opportunities and access. The most obvious way for developing townships to evade housing responsibilities is to allow low-cost housing only in such areas as swampland, adjacent to noxious industries, in aircraft flight zones, or on quarries.[5]
Partially developed suburbs might also be tempted to rezone economically viable areas of existing commercial and industrial development for low-cost housing, and then overlook the enforcement of nonconforming use provisions of its zoning ordinance to perpetuate the existing use *and* to comply with a surface interpretation of the performance standard. Judicial vigilance would then be required to enforce the intent of the performance standard, particularly in instances when the intent to evade is transparent. There is a real danger of calcifying the performance standard if its provisions are specified in sufficient detail to deal precisely with anticipated situations such as these and, consequently, of then being unable to respond effectively to other unforeseen situations. Even so, it is quite possible to apply the performance standard, as currently formulated, separately to undeveloped portions of townships covered by zoning and to the actual characteristics of developed portions, regardless of their zoning. All the foregoing analysis in earlier chapters proceeded on the assumption that zoning of already developed areas corresponded very closely with the actual development; where the two are at variance, the actual development should be assessed. By applying it in this manner, the standard would weigh past development and potential development on the same scale, thereby assuring more realistic treatment, but it would also eliminate the opportunity for evasion by townships which might rezone existing development into nonconforming uses merely to comply with a performance standard for zoning per se.

Shift Exclusionary Function to Other Municipal Controls.   Faced with the prospect of having to comply with the intent of the performance standard for zoning, townships might seriously consider transferring most of the exclusionary burden from zoning ordinances to other local developments controls. Based upon the experience of Levitt and Sons, Inc., "many of the major codes [i.e., building, plumbing, fire codes] now in use (FHA, BOCA, etc.) . . . are not major stumbling blocks," but rather "it is in the area of zoning that the greatest dollar savings in house construction can be obtained."[6] The fact that other development codes are now relatively unimportant, due to the effectiveness of exclusionary zoning on housing costs, may change in the future once zoning becomes subject to the performance standard. Requirements might be added, for example, to building codes, which would increase the construction or development costs of housing to such a degree that only middle- or upper-income families could afford the least costly dwelling type allowed by zoning. This would be a risky avenue for a township to take because housing costs would increase in roughly proportional terms, putting the township's premium housing at a competitive disadvantage as a consequence.[7] Of equal, or perhaps greater, risk is the chance that such a move might be construed by the courts as a not so subtle circumvention, particularly in light of the sweeping decision rendered in the *Southern Burlington County NAACP* v. *Township of Mount Laurel* case. Though the plaintiffs specifically sought injunctive relief from an obviously exclusionary zoning ordinance, the court granted relief and then went beyond by requiring the Township of Mount Laurel to: analyze the housing needs of residents, present and future workers; determine all low- and moderate-income housing required and plan the means to provide it; and describe all the factors which might bar the implementation of providing the housing, including alternative plans and municipal actions, and the reasons why the alternative plans were not adopted.[8] Although the decision is now under appeal and may not be sustained in its entirety, the willingness of the courts to examine all factors related to exclusionary practices will give pause to those who might otherwise be tempted to develop a parallel set of exclusionary development codes.

Compliance with Internal Isolation. Finally, a township which cannot otherwise avoid accommodating families in low- or moderate-cost housing might, as a last resort, try systematically to isolate the lower-cost residential districts in patterns which enable the township to selectively provide lower levels of municipal services, thereby cutting municipal service costs or discouraging low-cost housing development, or both.[9] If townships are able successfully to deprive low-cost residential areas of equal access to libraries, recreational facilities, fire protection, and other essential public facilities due to the location of low-cost residential areas within the township, then some of the benefits of residing in fiscally healthy townships will be reduced, even though low-cost housing opportunities per se may have improved. The performance standard for zoning cannot, of course, guard against an internal barrier to access, but, again, the courts have shown keen interest in precisely this problem. "In *Hawkins* v. *Shaw,* 437 Fed. 2d. 1286 (5th Circ. 1971) the Court declared that a municipality cannot discriminate in the use of municipal services and said that a town could be compelled to submit a plan for the equitable distribution of such services."[10]

All things considered, it would seem that townships have little chance of avoiding the mix of housing costs and family incomes required by the standard. If basic institutional changes in zoning, taxation or metropolitan government were to occur in the future, then obviously the performance standard would have to be revised accordingly or perhaps dropped entirely as a superfluous stricture. Until such basic alterations are made in the fabric of local governance, the performance standard for zoning surely deserves serious consideration as an attractive measure to curtail the worst abuses associated with exclusionary zoning of municipalities.

NOTES

1. Task Force on Land Use and Urban Growth, *The Use of Land: A Citizens' Policy Guide to Urban Growth,* A Task Force Report Sponsored by the Rockefeller Brothers Fund (New York: Thomas A. Crowell, 1973), prepublication copy, p. 56.
2. The potential six township labor force expected from current zoning patterns was estimated as 121,276 and its working household head population as 72,503 (about 60 percent of the labor force). When Delaware County's labor force of 168,698 is reduced by 40 percent and divided by the county stock of housing units, 0.56 working household heads per housing unit results ($168,698 \times 0.60 = 100,880 \div 180,669 = 0.56$).
3. The range of choices which were open to Concord Township with respect to zoning for worker households and worker housing units are assumed to be those open to townships A through F. See Table 9-1.
4. Refer again to Section C of Chapter 6, which discusses the effects of altering the industrial-commercial mix upon household income.
5. After being required to zone for apartments by the Pennsylvania Supreme Court in *Girsch Appeal,* 437 Pa. 237, 263 A.2d 395, 1 E.R.1140 (1970), Nether Providence Township (also in Delaware County) zoned an existing quarry for apartments. Noted by Ann L. Strong, Professor of City Planning, University of Pennsylvania in the *Evening Bulletin* (Philadelphia: November 27, 1970), p. 45, in Edward F. Mannino, "Land Use Planning and The Political Process," *The Shingle,* April 1971, p. 90 (Philadelphia: The Philadelphia Bar Association, 1971).
6. Levitt and Sons, Inc., "Levitt's Comments," report of the President's Committee on Urban Housing, *Technical Studies* (Washington: Government Printing Office, 1968), Vol. II, p. 70.

7. "A major difference between zoning and building codes is that uniformity
    applies in the former only to specific districts; whereas in the latter
    the ordinances apply to the community as a whole. The producer
    or consumer who finds that a zoning ordinance requires him to
    develop or purchase more land than he wishes has the opportunity
    of moving either to a less restricted zone or, within a particular
    zone, to areas where land costs are lower. But building codes
    involving costly features cannot as easily be avoided. The only
    escape is either to move to another area where production of new
    housing is less constrained, to economize on other features of
    the home, or not to build at all." Leland S. Burns and Frank G.
    Mittelback, "Efficiency in the Housing Industry," report of the
    President's Committee on Urban Housing, *Technical Studies*
    (Washington: Government Printing Office, 1968), Vol. II, pp.
    97–98.
8. Summarized from *Southern Burlington County NAACP* v. *Township of
    Mount Laurel,* 117 N.J. Super 11 (Sup. Ct. 1971), opinion written
    by Martino, A.J.S.C.
9. In addition to the generally shoddy workmanship found in housing recently
    built under the HUD Section 235 subsidy program, that program
    has also been instrumental in effectively separating a newly con-
    structed, low-income housing development from essential public
    services in one southern city. See John Herbers, "Outlying Housing
    for Blacks in Columbia, S.C. Assailed: Program Said to Create
    Isolated Shanty Towns," *New York Times,* March 25, 1972.
10. *Southern Burling County NAACP* v. *Township of Mount Laurel,* (N.J.),
    p. 21.

Appendixes

Appendix A

Township Selection Criteria and Townships Selected

The broad, general set of criteria for the sample mentioned in the preceding text were narrowed to these considerations: (1) the actual change in population from 1960 to 1970; (2) the projected change in population density, 1960-1985; (3) the projected change in population 1960-1985, and (4) the actual 1960 population density relative to the 1985 projection. Whereas Delaware County grew by 8.5 percent between 1960 and 1970, the average population growth for the rapidly developing townships in the sample was 25.0 percent, the lowest being 14.4 percent. These townships are Aston, Concord, Middletown and Thornbury. Two additional rural and more slowly developing townships, Birmingham and Edgmont, which averaged only about 6 percent growth, were also added to the latter group to represent townships with very high development potential on the extreme fringe of the urbanizing area.

The second criterion for classifying the townships was based upon the projected rate of increase in population density. Population density projections for 1985 are based upon population projections developed by the Delaware Valley Regional Planning Commission.* The rapidly developing areas were expected to go from 915 to 2,009 persons per square mile, an increase of 128 percent. The 1985 population projections developed by the Delaware Valley Regional Planning Commission in 1967 are based upon data collection superdistricts, two of which included the townships of interest. The superdistricts which correspond to the rapidly developing townships are 323 and 424. Projected 1960-1985 population increases for these superdistricts are 91.3 percent and 460.8 percent. The expected population growth in the superdistricts ranges from about two to ten times the increase expected for all of Delaware County.

With respect to the 1960 density relative to 1985 expected density

*Delaware Valley Regional Planning Commission, *1985 Regional Projections for the Delaware Valley: Plan Report No. 1* (Philadelphia: Delaware Valley Regional Planning Commission, 1967).

Table A-1. Classification Data for Developing Townships

	Area (sq. mi.)	Population			Population Growth (Percent)		Population Density (Persons per sq. mi.)				
Rapidly Developing		1960	1970	1985	1960–1970	1960–1985	1960	$\frac{1960^*}{1985\ SD}$	1970	$\frac{1970^*}{1985\ SD}$	1985
Aston	5.90	10,595	13,704	—	23.9	—	1,796	0.86	2,323	1.11	—
Concord	13.78	3,149	4,592	—	45.8	—	228	0.11	333	0.16	—
Middletown	13.43	11,256	12,878	—	14.4	—	838	0.40	959	0.46	—
Thornbury	9.16	2,035	2,652	—	30.3	—	222	0.11	290	0.14	—
Total	42.27	27,035	33,826	—	25.0	—	636	0.30	800	0.38	—
Super District 323	33.90	52,175	—	99,824	—	91.3	1,539	0.52	—	—	2,945
Super District 424	29.40	5,793	—	32,486	—	460.8	197	0.18	—	—	1,105
Super District 323 and 324	63.30	57,969	—	132,310	—	128.2	915	0.44	—	—	2,090
Slowly Developing											
Birmingham	8.84	1,093	1,281	—	17.2	—	124	0.11	145	0.13	—
Edgmont	9.74	1,404	1,368	—	-2.6	—	144	0.13	140	0.13	—
Total	18.58	2,497	2,649	—	6.1	—	134	0.12	142	0.13	—
Super District 424	29.40	5,793	—	32,486	—	460.8	197	0.18	—	—	1,105
Delaware County	184.43	553,154	600,035	801,197	8.5	44.8	2,999	0.69	3,253	0.75	4,344

*The denominator is the population density of super districts which correspond most closely to the township groupings. Rapidly Developing Townships = SD 323 and 424; Slowly Developing Townships = SD 424.

Sources: Bureau of Statistics, Department of Internal Affairs, Commonwealth of Pennsylvania, Pennsylvania Statistical Abstract, 1969 (Harrisburg, Pennsylvania: 1970); Delaware Valley Regional Planning Commission, 1985 Regional Projections for the Delaware Valley: Plan Report No. 1. (Philadelphia: Delaware Valley Regional Planning Commission, 1967), tabulations from 1970 Census, first count summary tapes.

(persons per square mile), by 1970 the county had reached 69 percent of its 1985 projected density while the developing superdistricts have attained only 52 percent and 18 percent of their 1985 projected densities. These data are collected in Table A-1.

In summary, townships appropriate for the study were chosen on the basis of development completion and potential. Criteria for classification of townships as slowly or rapidly developing were based upon 1960–1970 population growth; 1985 growth projections; 1960–1985 density per square mile ratios; and degree of change in those ratios from 1960 to 1985. As might be expected, the rapidly developing townships are nearer the eastern border of the county, adjacent to the City of Philadelphia, while the slowly developing areas are further west.

Appendix B

Apartments in Commercial Zoning Districts

Because some zoning ordinances allow both commercial and multi-family residential uses in the same district, one must rely upon actual development patterns in commercial districts to assess the potential for apartment housing. Consequently, it proved necessary to supplement zoning ordinance data by examining the records of the Delaware County Assessor's Office so that estimates of apartment development in commercial districts could be made. The task itself was somewhat complicated because in business or commercial districts (1) dwellings already present at the time of passage of the ordinance may be allowed to remain as nonconforming uses; (2) apartments may be allowed above commercial establishments; (3) rooming or boardinghouses may be permitted, and (4) apartments or dwelling units not connected with other commercial enterprise may be allowed.[1] The general provisions section of the ordinance may contain height requirements or open space stipulations. Commercial districts may contain the only areas of lower-cost housing in a given township. Of the six developing townships under study, four permit multi-family housing in business districts; three of four permit multi-family housing only in business districts.

Collecting information on residential uses in commercial districts presented considerable difficulties. First, many of the existing residences in these districts are nonconforming uses. It is unclear whether these should be included in any study of potential residential capacity. On the one hand, the uses may eventually disappear; on the other hand, given the durable nature of housing, they will be present for an appreciable period in the future.

A second complicating feature is the existence of apartments above commercial uses. It is difficult to assess the extent to which this type of mixed

---

1. In the present context, hotels and motels are not considered as housing for the community. Our present interest lies in housing of a nontransient nature. Mobile home districts are considered residential, as most occupants remain for more than a purely transient period.

Table B-1. Ratio of Apartments to Total Use District Areas*

Zone	Area in Apartment Use (Acres)	Area of Zone (Acres)	Apartment Total (Percent)
Aston			
R (A, B, C)	0.82	2,719.33	0.03
B Business	8.69	237.17	3.66
LI	0.13	847.06	0.02
	3.23	3,803.56	
Middletown			
R (1, 1A, 2, 3, 4, 4a)	5.95	7,934.92	0.07
A-1 (Apartments)	61.00	61.00	100.00
B	0.74	88.33	0.84
	67.69	8,084.25	
Concord			
R (1, 2, 2D, 3)	11.06	7,968.36	0.14
R-A (Garden Apartments)	0.00	44.84	0.00
R-AH High Rise Commercial (C1, C2, C2A, C3)	2.87	499.57	0.57
	13.93	8,531.51	
Thornbury			
No Apartments			
Birmingham			
R (1, 2)	0.00	4,927.92	0.00
Business	3.47	357.98	0.97
Edgmont			
R (A, B, C)	108.46	3,650.80	2.97

*Apartment acreage includes one-unit apartments, such as those on second floors of houses. In many cases it was impossible to determine from the tax assessor's records how many units an "apartment" contains.

Source: Delaware County Tax Assessor's Records

use in a common structure exists by looking through the county assessor's records. And the records, presently, give no indication of the future quantity of similar housing units. Development of a realistic capacity figure for this type of housing is virtually impossible.

A third difficulty in analyzing residential uses in commercial districts lies in discovering the number of such uses in existence. If residential uses are permitted in commercial districts, the allocation of land area between residential and commercial uses must be determined, as it will have a bearing on potential housing units and employment. Since no specific land area within mixed commercial districts is reserved for residential use, no map measurement of residential land area can be made. It was therefore necessary to compile the records of individual residential properties in commercial districts, making use of the county tax assessor's records. This task involved the rather tedious process of locating the address given on the individual property record, and scanning the zoning map to determine if the property was located in a commercial district. The procedure was facilitated in the present case by (1) the semirural character of the townships under study, and the fact that one of the townships had no apartments, and (2) the convenience gained by the assessor's office having separated apartment records from those of other properties. A complication was caused by the absence of street address numbers on the zoning maps. Nevertheless, by considering the type of property (an apartment above a store would probably find itself in a commercial district), and with the assessor's aid in locating the addresses on the map, the extent of apartment development in the commercial districts was determined.

The next step involved summing the land area taken up by the apartments in commercial districts and dividing by total area of the commercial district to determine the percentage of commercially zoned land in residential use. The percentages, shown in Table B-1, are rough indicators rather than precise figures upon which to base housing estimates. The imprecision is caused by the inclusion of apartments above stores and by the difficulty of determining how much of the area given on the tax assessor's records for apartments was actually devoted to residential, as opposed to commercial, use. In any case, the highest ratio of apartment to commercial land use in any of the townships was 3.6 percent; the ratio was less than 1 percent in three out of the five townships containing apartments. Thus, even though developing municipalities occasionally allow apartments in their commercial areas, only a miniscule proportion of these areas are likely to be devoted to apartments.

Appendix C

Estimating Rents for Multi-Family Structures from First Count Census Rent Distributions in Enumeration Districts Eds, 1970

EDs which had 15 or more units with cash rents were examined in the initial sample. For each ED, the number of single-family units having reported values were subtracted from all single-family units. The remaining "unvalued" units are assumed to be rented single-family houses. These rented single-family units were then compared with all cash rental units in the ED and the percentage of single-family rentals calculated. EDs were then grouped according to this percentage in 0–20, 20–30, 30–40, 40–50, 50–60, 60–70, 70–80 and 80–100 categories, as shown in Table C-1 at the end of this appendix.

Rent distributions of all units in EDs by rented single-family percentage categories were then calculated, the results of which are shown below.

Rented* Single-family Unit as Per- cent of All Cash Rent Units	All	Cash Rent Intervals ($)								Median Rent ($)
		40	40–60	60–80	80–100	100–120	120–150	150–200	200	
0–20	2,108	11	7	13	48	137	704	1,031	157	157
20–30	395	5	1	3	6	58	140	163	19	127
30–40	704	25	12	71	110	123	176	141	46	122
40–50	179	9	3	13	28	10	31	37	48	146
50–60	178	18	5	51	15	36	44	5	4	100
60–70	62	4	3	6	13	15	6	12	3	106
70–80	90	5	5	10	12	13	11	26	8	120
80–100+	1,151	86	67	124	178	178	165	235	118	113

*Rented units are assumed to be those single-family units which lack reported values.

In this array of rent distributions, the 0–20 percent category most closely represents multi-family simply by definition. However, before making it the final choice, one final check ought to be considered. That is, since all EDs are designed by the Census to have approximately the same total number of

205

housing units, those EDs which have high proportions of multi-family to all rental housing (or low percentages of single-family to all rental housing) also ought to have overall higher proportions of total rental units, due to tendencies for concentration of rental units in multi-family structures. To aid in determining whether or not this relationship exists, the diagram below was prepared.

A line connecting the mean number of units per ED at the mid-point of each percentage category is highest at the 0–20 percent category and falls dramatically as the percentage of single-family units increases, a relationship which fully supports the choice of the 0–20 percent category as representing multi-family rentals.

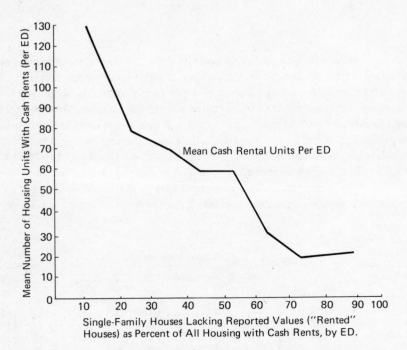

Mean Number of Rented Housing Units by Percent of All Rental Units in Single-Family Houses for Selected EDs in Delaware County, Pennsylvania, 1970.

Table C-1. Distribution of Rents of Mixed Multi- and Single-Family Units, for Block Groups, by Percent of Cash Rental Units to Nonowned Single-Family Units in Delaware County Census Tracts and Enumeration Districts, 1970

Census Tract and Block Group		Percent Cash Rental Units	Rents ($)								
			<40	40–59	60–79	80–99	100–119	120–149	150–199	200–299	All
Percent Cash Rental Units—0 to 20 Percent											
4099.03	3	13	1	1	4	3	11	54	69	60	203
4099.02	9	13	1	0	1	3	7	24	60	1	97
4093.00	3	13	1	0	0	6	15	59	34	0	115
4093.00	1	19	0	3	2	15	17	34	18	4	93
4087.00	4	19	0	0	1	2	2	3	85	16	109
4085.00	1	18	1	0	3	9	8	69	114	4	210
4083.00	1	16	2	3	0	2	6	18	67	1	96
4081.01	4	19	1	0	0	0	4	29	4	3	41
4081.01	1	17	0	0	0	0	22	73	9	0	107
4069.03	1	14	0	0	0	2	2	65	72	4	145
4078.01	3	12	1	0	0	1	17	32	11	1	63
4078.03	3	11	1	0	0	2	2	38	107	3	153
4078.05	1	10	1	0	0	3	6	26	48	40	133
4078.05	4	07	1	0	0	0	14	123	301	18	457
4081.03	4	05	0	0	2	0	4	57	32	2	97
4094.00	3	09	0	0	0	0	4			2	
All			11	7	13	48	137	704	1031	157	2119
			0.01	0.00	0.01	0.02	0.06	0.33	0.49	0.08	1.00
Percent Cash Rental Units—20 to 30 Percent											
4062.02	3	27	0	0	0	0	0	29	35	0	64
4080.01	1	21	1	0	2	1	10	55	20	1	91
4081.03	1	29	1	0	0	0	0	2	44	4	51
4085.00	2	23	0	1	0	1	3	2	57	11	75
4099.03	2	26	3	0	1	4	45	52	7	3	115
All			5	1	3	6	58	140	163	19	396
			0.01	0.00	0.01	0.02	0.15	0.35	0.41	0.05	1.00

(continued)

Table C–1 continued

Census Tract and Block Group	Percent Cash Rental Units	Rents ($)								
		<40	40–59	60–79	80–99	100–119	120–149	150–199	200–299	All
Percent Cash Rental Units—30 to 40 Percent										
4078.03	7	34	1	1	2	1	1	3	58	3	70
4078.04	7	38	1	0	2	1	0	7	24	2	37
4081.02	1	33	3	4	10	13	41	41	7	1	120
4086.00	2	39	7	1	6	13	24	37	8	0	96
4087.00	5	30	2	1	14	17	12	20	5	1	77
4090.00	2	39	1	2	5	14	10	15	9	1	57
4090.00	3	40	3	0	7	15	19	10	3	1	58
4091.00	4	35	2	1	23	30	4	5	3	1	69
4092.00	3	38	5	2	2	6	7	33	3	0	58
4099.02	1	38	0	0	0		5	5	21	36	71
All			25	12	71	110	123	176	141	46	713
			0.04	0.02	0.10	0.16	0.17	0.25	0.20	0.07	1.00
Percent Cash Rental Units—40 to 50 Percent										
4069.02	3	41	0	2	1	7	5	27	27	1	70
4078.02	2	40	1	0	1	1	0	2	8	47	60
4086.00	3	47	8	1	11	20	5	2	2	0	49
All			9	3	13	28	10	31	37	48	179
			0.05	0.02	0.07	0.16	0.06	0.17	0.21	0.27	1.00
Percent Cash Rental Units—50 to 60 Percent										
4069.04	0220	58	4	5	46	6	4	0	0	0	65
4087.00	3	56	8	0	3	4	15	29	3	4	66
4091.00	3	50	6	0	2	5	17	15	2	0	47
All			18	5	51	15	36	44	5	4	178
			0.10	0.03	0.29	0.08	0.20	0.25	0.03	0.03	1.00

Percent Cash Rental Units—60 to 70 Percent

Tract	%	C1 (0.06)	C2 (0.05)	C3 (0.10)	C4 (0.21)	C5 (0.24)	C6 (0.10)	C7 (0.19)	C8 (0.05)	Total
4088.00	67	0	2	2	9	9	0	8	1	31
4090.00	69	4	1	4	4	6	6	4	2	32
All		4	3	6	13	15	6	12	3	63
		0.06	0.05	0.10	0.21	0.24	0.10	0.19	0.05	1.00

Percent Cash Rental Units—70 to 80 Percent

Tract	%	C1	C2	C3	C4	C5	C6	C7	C8	Total
4078.02	77	0	2	0	1	1	0	16	5	30
4080.01	79	0	1	5	6	7	2	1	1	29
4085.00	71	0	0	2	3	3	0	2	0	14
4092.00	75	4	1	3	1	0	6	1	0	16
4094.00	78	0	1	0	0	2	0	3	2	18
4095.00	78	1	0	0	1	0	3	3	0	9
All		5	5	10	12	13	11	26	8	106
		0.05	0.05	0.10	0.12	0.13	0.11	0.26	0.08	1.00

Percent Cash Rental Units—80 to 100 Percent

Tract	Code	%	C1	C2	C3	C4	C5	C6	C7	C8	Total
4099.04	0201	80	4	1	0	2	7	0	0	1	15
4100.00	0203	100	0	2	0	0	6	3	3	0	15
4100.00	0204	100	5	4	2	2	1	3	5	1	23
4072.01	0209	100	9	2	7	1	1	1	0	3	22
4072.02	0210	100	1	4	4	6	6	2	2	1	28
4072.02	0210	100	5	5	7	6	10	2	5	4	41
4101.00	0212	100	7	7	4	2	9	8	14	5	59
4103.01	0214	100	1	1	3	12	5	8	2	7	22
4103.01	0215	100	3	2	6	6	14	11	5	2	48
4103.02	0216	100	0	0	2	2	6	5	5	4	29
4062.01	2	82	0	4	4	0	3	5	1	3	16
4062.02	1	100	2	3	3	3	4	1	5	0	17
4062.02	2	100	1	0	0	9	0	1	2	1	13
4069.02	1	100	1	1	1	5	4	6	7	5	30
4069.02	2	100	0	5	5	3	5	10	3	7	29
4069.04	2	100	1	7	7	4	1	0	10	7	44
4071.02	2	100	1	7	7	7	7	3	0	2	28

(continued)

Table C-1 continued

Census Tract and Block Group		Percent Cash Rental Units	Rents ($)								All
			<40	40–59	60–79	80–99	100–119	120–149	150–199	200–299	
4072.01	1	100	2	1	2	2	4	3	6	2	24
4072.02	1	100	3	11	2	3	1	3	4	0	30
4078.01	1	100	0	1	0	0	0	0	2	2	5
4078.01	2	86	2	0	0	1	1	2	22	2	28
4078.01	4	100	1	0	0	0	0	0	14	5	21
4078.02	4	90	1	2	0	3	1	5	7	1	20
4078.02	5	100	2	0	1	0	0	1	0	18	20
4078.03	1	100	0	0	0	0	0	0	5	8	16
4078.03	2	100	0	0	0	0	0	7	3	2	12
4078.03	4	100	0	0	2	0	0	0	6	0	12
4078.03	6	100	7	0	2	5	5	5	6	1	31
4078.04	1	100	0	0	0	0	0	0	4	0	5
4078.04	3	100	0	0	0	1	2	1	6	2	12
4078.04	5	100	1	0	0	0	0	0	6	1	7
4078.04	6	100	0	1	1	0	0	0	3	0	5
4078.05	2	100	0	0	0	1	0	1	9	3	15
4078.05	3	80	1	0	0	2	2	4	9	3	20
4080.01	2	100	1	0	1	0	0	0	3	7	11
4080.02	1	100	0	0	1	2	0	0	3	2	8
4080.02	9	100	—	—	—	—	—	—	—	—	51
4081.01	3	100	0	1	5	6	7	2	1	1	26
4081.02	2	100	1	1	0	1	2	4	1	3	13
4081.02	4	100	1	0	0	0	0	0	0	4	5
4082.00	1	80	3	2	26	37	23	8	4	1	105
4083.00	3	100	1	0	2	0	0	4	4	3	15
4085.00	3	100	0	0	0	1	0	3	1	0	5
4086.00	4	100	0	0	0	0	4	1	7	5	17
4087.00	2	100	0	0	1	0	0	0	1	1	5
4088.00	2	85	8	0	9	17	9	7	3	0	53

4088.00	3	84	1	0	3	6	5	6	2	2	25
4090.00	1	100	0	0	0	0	2	0	6	2	10
4091.00	1	100	1	0	0	0	3	1	2	0	9
4091.00	2	100	0	0	0	0	0	2	1	2	5
4091.00	5	100	3	1	2	3	1	8	3	1	22
4092.00	1	100	0	0	0	0	2	1	1	4	8
4092.00	5	100	3	0	1	5	2	1	3	0	15
4095.00	1	100	0	0	0	3	3	7	5	0	18
4095.00	4	100	1	0	0	0	0	0	3	5	9
4095.00	5	100	0	0	1	0	0	0	5	3	9
4099.02	2	90	1	2	1	3	8	7	3	4	29
4099.02	9	100	1	1	1	5	2	2	5	3	20
All			86	67	124	178	178	165	235	118	1,198
			0.07	0.06	0.10	0.14	0.14	0.14	0.20	0.10	1.00

Appendix D

Converting Economic Activities Allowed by Zoning Ordinances into Equivalent SICs

After accepting the SIC as a system of economic activities, there remains the task of converting the allowed uses to SICs. Where the code has a list of specifically prohibited activities, those activities are tagged with an SIC and removed from a master list of all possible SICs, the remainder constituting a residual list of allowed SICs. Where the code lists only certain permitted activities, those activities are tagged with the appropriate SIC. If the list of allowed SICs contains a provision for similar activities which are allowed if they, too, meet performance standards, two approaches are possible. First, a complete listing is made of all specifically allowed activities in all districts which specify similar performance criteria; activities on the composite list which are missing in the individual districts, that only specify performance criterias, are assumed to be "allowed." The other approach is to include SICs which manufacture similar products or are known to use similar technology and production processes and which probably meet the performance standards. The latter approach is a bit arbitrary since there are no readily available criteria for similar products or processes.

We have elected to use the first alternative. Light industrial districts in four townships were used to create: (1) a composite of those SICs which they had in common (actually a rather limited list); (2) a composite of all SICs found in one or more townships; and (3) a composite based on all SICs, but with selected omission of those SICs which were obviously incompatible with the type of district, e.g., agriculture in a manufacturing district. The last composite was chosen to represent the allowed uses in the two districts which stipulated only "light industrial" use. Table D-1 gives the results of this procedure.

In their desire to attract clean, relatively nuisance-free industries, all townships in the group specifically allow for research and development (R and D) laboratories and for office buildings. Unfortunately, not all R and D establishments are given a SIC and no office buildings are identified with a SIC. Both provide for activities which are carried on in conjunction with certain SIC

Table D-1.   Light Industry SICs by Township

Allowed SICs in Four Townships with "Light Industrial" Districts			
Aston	*Birmingham*	*Concord*	*Thornbury*
2000	2000 (excluding: 2010)	2000	2000 (excluding: 2011, 2094)
2100	2100	2100	—
2200	2210–2240	2200	—
2300	2300	2300	2390
2440/2490	2440/2490	2440/2490	—
2500	2500	2500	—
2640/2660	2640/2650	2640/2660	2600 (excluding: 2630)
2700	2700	2700	—
2830/2844	2830/2844	2830/2844	2821/2830/2840
3000	3000	3000	—
3100 (excluding: 3110, 3120)	3100	3100 (excluding: 3110, 3120)	—
3200	3200	3200	—
3400	3400	3400	—
3570	3570–3590	3570–3590	—
3600	3600	—	3600
3800	3800	3800	3800
3900	3900	3900	3900
4100	—	4100	—
4200	4220	4200	4220
4710/4720	—	4710/4720	—
4800	—	4800	—
4900	—	4900	—
—	5000	5049/5070/5082 5086/5095	—
—	—	5252	—
—	—	5320	—
—	—	5800	—
—	—	5960/5990	—
—	7210	7210	—
7391/7392	7391/7392	7391/7392	7391/7392
7397/7399	7397/7399	7397/7399	7397/7399
7520/7530	7530	7530	7530
7690	7690	7640/7690	7690
8920	8920	8920	8900
9100	9100	—	9100
9200	9200	—	9200
9300	9300	—	9300

*SICs present in three or more township districts, or SICs allowed in two districts which clearly involve production activities compatible with light, nonnuisance industries (e.g. 4800—communications, 4900—electric, gas, sanitary utilities, 7210—laundry and dry cleaning facilities).

Composites for Use in "Light Industry" Districts where SICs Are Not Specified		
All SICs Represented	*All SICs in Common*	*Selected SICs** ·
2000	2000 (excluding: 2010, 2094)	2000 (excluding: 2010, 2094)
2100	–	2100
2200	–	2200
2300	2390	2300
2440/2490	–	2440/2490
2500	–	2500
2600 (excluding: 2630)	2640/2650	2640/2660
2700	–	2700
2821/2830/2840	2830/2844	2830/2840
3000	–	3000
3100	–	3100
3200	–	3200
3400	–	3400
3570–3590	–	3570–3590
3600	–	3600
3800	3800	3800
3900	3900	3900
4100	–	4100
4200	4220	4200
4710/4720	–	4710/4720
4800	–	4800
4900	–	4900
5000	–	–
5252	–	–
5320	–	–
5800	–	–
5960/5990	–	–
7210	–	7210
7391/7392	7391/7392	7391/7392
7397/7399	7397/7399	7397/7399
7520/7530	7530	7530
7640/7690	7690	7690
8900	8920	8920
9100	–	9100
9200	–	9200
9300	–	9300

Table D-2. SIC Equivalents of CAO and A Establishments

Central Administration Office and Auxiliaries	*"Equivalent" Standard Industrial Classifications*	
1. Central or Administrative offices	8110	(Legal Services)
	8930	(Accounting, Auditing, and Bookkeeping)
	7391	(Business Consulting Services)
2. Sales Office	5320	(Mail Order Houses)
	5350	(Direct Selling Organizations)
3. Trading Stamp Centers	7396	(Trading Stamp Services)
4. Research and Development	7391	(Research and Development Laboratories)
	7397	(Commercial Testing Laboratories)
	8921	(Nonprofit Research Agencies)
5. Warehousing and Storage	4225	(General Warehousing and Storage)
	4226	(Special Warehousing and Storage)
6. Automobile Parking	7520	(Parking Lots and Structures)
7. Repairs and Maintenance of Vehicles, Equipment, and Related	7538	(General Auto Repair Shops)
	7690	(Miscellaneous Repair Shops)

Sources: U.S., Department of Commerce, *Standard Industrial Classification Manual* (Washington: Government Printing Office, 1967), Appendices A and B, pp. 585–603; U.S., Department of Commerce, *1967 Enterprise Statistics: Central Administrative Offices and Auxiliaries* (Washington: Government Printing Office, 1971), ES 67 (P)-1.

industries, and are lumped in with parking, power plant, warehousing, repair shops and other supporting activities under the catchall definition of Central Administrative Office and Auxiliary (CAO and A). All the CAO and A activities have been differentiated and tagged with an equivalent SIC code of activities with similar economic characteristics, as shown in Table D-2. Even though CAO and A employment is not identified with industry group numbers in the SIC code, it is necessary to assign an SIC number simply to apply the many statistical estimates of important industrial characteristics already coded in terms of SIC.

The SIC itself refers to actual products of processes associated with economic enterprises, varying from a two- to four-digit code depending upon the detail with which those products or processes are described. For this reason, a zoning ordinance which describes the activities which it allows (or prohibits) in varying degrees of specificity will necessarily be translated in terms of an appropriately detailed SIC code. Thus, the language used in Birmingham Township's light industrial district (see Light Industrial Composite, Table D-1) will allow only SIC 2844 (toilet preparation), of all possible 2800 activities (chemical and allied products), yet permits all four-digit SICs associated with the first two digits "30" (rubber and plastic products). To simplify the coding of activities, two- and three-digit entries are rounded out to the fourth digit place with zeros, the implication being that all possible digits in the third and fourth place represent allowed activities. For reasons discussed in the text pertaining to the limited availability of employment and land use data for four-digit detailed codes, a table of allowed uses within each district was generated which lists all allowed uses in not more than three-digit detail, i.e., 2800, or 2840, but not 2844.

Deriving Floor Area Ratios from Township Zoning Ordinances

```
      REAL*8 DUMMY (10)
      CHARACTER*1 STAR (16,10) /160*' '/
      DIMENSION X (16,10), CHAY(8), ELL (9)
10    DO 11 I=1, 16
      DO 11 J=1, 10
      X(I,J)=0.
      STAR (I,J)=' '
11    CONTINUE
20    READ (5, 1, END = 100) IDI, CHAY, A, Y, ID2, ELL
 1    FORMAT (A4, 2X, 8F4.2, 8X, 2F4.2/A4, 2X, 9F4.2)
      IF (ID1.EQ.ID2) GO TO 30
      READ(5,2) DUMMY
 2    FORMAT (10A8)
      GO TO 20
30    DO 40 I=1,8
      DO 40 1F=1,10
      X(I,IF) =Y/(1.IF+CHAY(I)+ ELL(9))
      IF((X(I,IF)/IF).LT.A) GO TO 40
      X(I,IF) = A*IF
      STAR (I,IF) = '*'
40    CONTINUE
      DO 50 IF = 1,10
      X(9,IF) = Y/(1./IF+ELL(1)+CHAY(4))
      IF ((X(9,IF)/IF).LT.A) GO TO 41
      X(9,IF)=A*IF
      STAR (9,IF)='*'
41    X(10,IF)=Y/(1./IF+ELL(2)+CHAY(3))
      IF ((X(10,IF)/IF).LT.A) GO TO 42
      X(10,IF) = A*IF
      STAR (10,IF)= '*'
```

```
42   X(11,IF)=Y/(1./IF+ELL(3) + CHAY (2))
     IF((X(11,IF)/IF).LT.A) GO TO 43
     X(11,IF) = A*IF
     STAR (11,IF)='*'
43   X(12,IF) = Y/(1./IF+ELL(4) + CHAY(5))
     IF((X(12,IF)/IF).LT.A) GO TO 44
     X(12,IF)=A*IF
     STAR (12,IF)='*'
44   X(13,IF)=Y/(1./IF+ELL(5)+CHAY(8))
     IF((X(13,IF)/IF).LT.A) GO TO 45
     X(13,IF)=A*IF
     STAR (13,IF)='*'
45   X(14,IF)=Y/(1./IF+ELL(6)+CHAY(4))
     IF((X(14,IF)/IF) .LTA) GO TO 46
     X(14,IF)=A*IF
     STAR (14,IF)='*'
46   X(15,IF)=Y/1.IF+ELL(7)+CHAY(5))
     IF((X(15,IF)/IF) .LT.A) GO TO 47
     X(15,IF)=A*IF
     STAR(15,IF)='*'
47   X(16,IF)=Y/(1./IF+ELL(8)+CHAY(2))
     IF((X(16,IF)/IF).LT.A) GO TO 50
     X(16,IF)=A*IF
     STAR(16,IF)='*'
50   CONTINUE
     WRITE(6,3)ID1
 3   FORMAT('1',40X,'DISTRICT',A4/36X,'FAC'/'FL',7X,'1',7X,'2',7X,
     1'3',7X,'4',7X,'5',7X,'6',7X,'7',7X,'8',7X,'9',6X,'10',6X,'11'
     26X,'12',6X,'13',6X,'14',6X,'15',6X,'16')
     DO 75 IF=1,10
75   WRITE(6,4) IF,(X(I,IF),STAR(I,IF),I=1,16)
 4   FORMAT(' ',I2,1X,16(F7.2,A1))
     GO TO 10
100  STOP
     END


     /GO
```

Sample Floor Area Ratio Matrices for Districts 21 and 22

		Floor Area–Parking Class (16)															
	Floors (1–10)	1	2	3	4	5	6	7	8	9	10	11	12	13	14	15	16
District 21	1	0.20	0.20	0.20	0.20	0.20	0.20	0.20	0.20	0.20	0.20	0.20	0.20	0.20	0.20	0.20	0.20
	2	0.22	0.22	0.22	0.22	0.22	0.22	0.22	0.22	0.22	0.22	0.22	0.22	0.22	0.22	0.22	0.22
	3	0.23	0.23	0.23	0.23	0.23	0.23	0.23	0.23	0.23	0.23	0.23	0.23	0.23	0.23	0.23	0.23
	4	0.24	0.24	0.24	0.24	0.24	0.24	0.24	0.24	0.24	0.24	0.24	0.24	0.24	0.24	0.24	0.24
	5	0.24	0.24	0.24	0.24	0.24	0.24	0.24	0.24	0.24	0.24	0.24	0.24	0.24	0.24	0.24	0.24
	6	0.24	0.24	0.24	0.24	0.24	0.24	0.24	0.24	0.24	0.24	0.24	0.24	0.24	0.24	0.24	0.24
	7	0.24	0.24	0.24	0.24	0.24	0.24	0.24	0.24	0.24	0.24	0.24	0.24	0.24	0.24	0.24	0.24
	8	0.24	0.24	0.24	0.24	0.24	0.24	0.24	0.24	0.24	0.24	0.24	0.24	0.24	0.24	0.24	0.24
	9	0.24	0.24	0.24	0.24	0.24	0.24	0.24	0.24	0.24	0.24	0.24	0.24	0.24	0.24	0.24	0.24
	10	0.24	0.24	0.24	0.24	0.24	0.24	0.24	0.24	0.24	0.24	0.24	0.24	0.24	0.24	0.24	0.24
District 22	1	0.22	0.30	0.30	0.30	0.30	0.30	0.30	0.30	0.30	0.30	0.30	0.30	0.30	0.30	0.30	0.30
	2	0.28	0.40	0.53	0.60	0.60	0.60	0.60	0.60	0.60	0.53	0.40	0.60	0.60	0.60	0.60	0.40
	3	0.30	0.45	0.62	0.83	0.90	0.90	0.90	0.90	0.83	0.62	0.45	0.90	0.90	0.83	0.90	0.45
	4	0.31	0.48	0.68	0.94	1.18	1.20	1.20	1.20	0.94	0.68	0.48	1.18	1.20	0.94	1.18	0.48
	5	0.32	0.50	0.72	1.02	1.30	1.50	1.50	1.50	1.02	0.72	0.50	1.30	1.50	1.02	1.30	0.50
	6	0.33	0.51	0.75	1.08	1.41	1.68	1.80	1.80	1.08	0.75	0.51	1.41	1.80	1.08	1.41	0.51
	7	0.33	0.53	0.78	1.13	1.49	1.80	2.10	2.10	1.13	0.78	0.53	1.49	2.10	1.13	1.49	0.53
	8	0.33	0.53	0.79	1.17	1.56	1.90	2.26	2.40	1.17	0.79	0.53	1.56	2.40	1.17	1.56	0.53
	9	0.34	0.54	0.81	1.20	1.62	1.99	2.39	2.70	1.20	0.81	0.54	1.62	2.70	1.20	1.62	0.54
	10	0.34	0.55	0.82	1.22	1.67	2.07	2.50	3.00	1.22	0.82	0.55	1.67	3.00	1.22	1.67	0.55

Note: The floor area–parking class is the floor area class developed for employee (k) parking, classes 1–8, and the adjustments for customer (j) parking, classes 9–16.

Floor Area Ratio Matrices (Height Constrained) for Districts 21 and 22

HEIGHT CONSTRAINED FARs

Floor Area – Parking Class

Districts	Number of Floors	1	2	3	4	5	6	7	8	9	10	11	12	13	14	15	16
21	1	0.20	0.20	0.20	0.20	0.20	0.20	0.20	0.20	0.20	0.20	0.20	0.20	0.20	0.20	0.20	0.20
21	2	0.22	0.22	0.22	0.22	0.22	0.22	0.22	0.22	0.22	0.22	0.22	0.22	0.22	0.22	0.22	0.22
21	3	0.23	0.23	0.23	0.23	0.23	0.23	0.23	0.23	0.23	0.23	0.23	0.23	0.23	0.23	0.23	0.23
21	4	0.24	0.24	0.24	0.24	0.24	0.24	0.24	0.24	0.24	0.24	0.24	0.24	0.24	0.24	0.24	0.24
21	5	0.24	0.24	0.24	0.24	0.24	0.24	0.24	0.24	0.24	0.24	0.24	0.24	0.24	0.24	0.24	0.24
21	6	0.24	0.24	0.24	0.24	0.24	0.24	0.24	0.24	0.24	0.24	0.24	0.24	0.24	0.24	0.24	0.24
21	7	0.24	0.24	0.24	0.24	0.24	0.24	0.24	0.24	0.24	0.24	0.24	0.24	0.24	0.24	0.24	0.24
21	8	0.24	0.24	0.24	0.24	0.24	0.24	0.24	0.24	0.24	0.24	0.24	0.24	0.24	0.24	0.24	0.24
21	9	0.24	0.24	0.24	0.24	0.24	0.24	0.24	0.24	0.24	0.24	0.24	0.24	0.24	0.24	0.24	0.24
21	10	0.24	0.24	0.24	0.24	0.24	0.24	0.24	0.24	0.24	0.24	0.24	0.24	0.24	0.24	0.24	0.24
22	1	0.22	0.30	0.30	0.30	0.30	0.30	0.30	0.30	0.30	0.30	0.30	0.30	0.30	0.30	0.30	0.30
22	2	0.28	0.40	0.53	0.60	0.60	0.60	0.60	0.60	0.60	0.53	0.40	0.60	0.60	0.60	0.60	0.40
22	3	0.28	0.40	0.53	0.60	0.60	0.60	0.60	0.60	0.60	0.53	0.40	0.60	0.60	0.60	0.60	0.40
22	4	0.28	0.40	0.53	0.60	0.60	0.60	0.60	0.60	0.60	0.53	0.40	0.60	0.60	0.60	0.60	0.40
22	5	0.28	0.40	0.53	0.60	0.60	0.60	0.60	0.60	0.60	0.53	0.40	0.60	0.60	0.60	0.60	0.40
22	6	0.28	0.40	0.53	0.60	0.60	0.60	0.60	0.60	0.60	0.53	0.40	0.60	0.60	0.60	0.60	0.40
22	7	0.28	0.40	0.53	0.60	0.60	0.60	0.60	0.60	0.60	0.53	0.40	0.60	0.60	0.60	0.60	0.40
22	8	0.28	0.40	0.53	0.60	0.60	0.60	0.60	0.60	0.60	0.53	0.40	0.60	0.60	0.60	0.60	0.40
22	9	0.28	0.40	0.53	0.60	0.60	0.60	0.60	0.60	0.60	0.53	0.40	0.60	0.60	0.60	0.60	0.40
22	10	0.28	0.40	0.53	0.60	0.60	0.60	0.60	0.60	0.60	0.53	0.40	0.60	0.60	0.60	0.60	0.40

Appendix F

Estimating Values for *A* and *B* from Township Zoning Ordinances

Of the 36 possible values for both *A* and *B*, 11 had to be independently estimated for use in the algorithm. The easiest to estimate were values of *B* missing from six commercial-business districts. In these six districts, there was no hint of any restriction, unlike the case in district 41 where the maximum was clearly stated in percentage terms, or in districts 31, 32, 33 and 34 where the maximum was calculable from landscaping requirements of parking areas.* The six districts for which no maximums were specified were given an arbitrary value of 1.00 which is in accordance with observed practice and is quite logical, given that other districts which did control total site development allowed up to 95 percent (average 84 percent) of the site to be developed.

Only two industrial districts lacked values for *B*. The five districts which did specify values for *B* averaged about 0.67 over a range from 0.60 to 0.75; they also had *A* values averaging 0.36 over a wider range of 0.25 with the ratios of *B* to *A* spanning an equally broad range of 1.5 : 1 to 3.0 : 1 (with a mean ratio of about 1.9:1). In other words, there was no simple relationship among the values of *B*, or the values of associated *A*s, or the ratio of *B*s to *A*s. However, even though the extreme ratios of *B* to *A* varied by a factor of two, their mean ratio of 1.9:1 was very close to the 2:1 ratios associated with the other three districts. This being the most frequently observed relationship, it was used to

*In these last four districts, the code requires that at least 10 percent of land used for parking be devoted to open or landscaped areas. Therefore, the formula

$$B = 1.00 - 0.10 \left(\frac{1 - A}{1.10} \right)$$

applies the 10 percent landscaping requirement of the smallest possible parking area where it is assumed that users of land prefer building uses to parking when they are free to choose between them.

generate "reasonable" estimates of *B* by doubling the known *A* values of 0.25 and 0.40 in the districts for which *B* is not specified.

In comparison with unstated values of *B* in eight districts, only three (among the same eight) lacked values for *A*. Two of the three districts were in one township and all three were commercial-business districts. The districts with known *A* values averaged about 0.319 over a wide range from 0.20 up to 0.55; of this group, districts with the lowest and highest *A* values had similar *B*s of 0.92 and 0.95. In other words, the districts with equally high values of *B* had such widely differing *A*s that, in effect, the average value of observed *A*s is probably as good an estimate as can be expected. Rounding off the 0.319 to 0.30 for the sake of convenience yields an average estimate, shorn only of specious accuracy, which is used as a proxy for similar districts. Because two of the three districts lacking an *A* value are designated "shopping center" or "planned business" district, it was decided that 0.25 be used instead of 0.30 because: (1) it was the value actually stipulated by another district of similar "shopping center" type of business use; and (2) it was reasonably close to the average for all business-commercial uses. The remaining "conventional" business district was given 0.30 as its "*A*" value.

Appendix G

Procedures Used in Calculating Township Parking Standards

In developing the constant parking proportion (k), it was decided to work first with employee parking. Data are available on the number of employees per 100 sq. ft. of floor area for specific industries. It is inconvenient, however, to use employees per 100 sq. ft. floor area for each industry in the computations. Therefore, a simple group of eight floor area classes (FAC) was developed, and each SIC industry permitted in the townships was assigned to the appropriate class: for example, an SIC with 225 square feet per employee would be in class 2 in the table below. The procedure seems to insert an added step in the computation, but it saves computer programming and operating time in the end, with but negligible loss of precision.

Floor Area Classes (FAC)

Class	(Square feet per worker)	
	Range	Mean
1	0–199	150
2	200–299	250
3	300–499	400
4	500–799	650
5	800–1099	950
6	1100–1499	1300
7	1500–2199	1850
8	2200+	2700

The k factor is computed by dividing the required square feet of parking per employee by the square feet of floor area per employee. The case of ordinance ambiguity encountered earlier when determining equivalent SICs and estimating unspecified values of B and A occurs here as well, because the zoning provisions for some districts do not clearly specify what parking requirements should apply, e.g., the use of such terms as "suitable" or "adequate" parking. Therefore, the parking requirements which were specified for similar districts in nearby townships were employed as "proxy" requirements.

Seven manufacturing districts required parking for employees only unless an individual firm was likely to generate unusual customer parking demands which would entail supplemental parking facilities. Of the seven, five specified the number of spaces relative to employees and the remaining two districts required the parking to be "adequate." Three districts specified one parking space per main shift employee, one district specified three parking spaces per four main shift employees, and the remaining district specified two parking spaces per three main shift employees. The two districts which required that parking be "adequate" were assigned the 3:4 ratio.

As to parking space size, four of the same five districts specified the size of each parking space to be 200 sq. ft. for automobile storage, plus "maneuvering space"; no less than 300 sq. ft. was the minimum space (including maneuvering) allowed by two of the four. A fifth district stated the standard as 350 sq. ft. as minimum parking space. The 300 sq. ft. standard was used for the two remaining townships which stipulated no quantitative standard.

Appendix H

Parking Space Requirements for Customers, by District

	Districts	
Use Type	*31, 33, 34*	*41*
Tourist or Boarding Home	1.5 sp./room	1 sp./room
Hotel, Motel, Inn	1.5 sp./room	1 sp./2 bedrooms
Theater, Church, Auditorium	1 sp./60 sq. ft.	1 sp./10 seats
Restaurant	1 sp./50 sq. ft.	1 sp./50 sq. ft.
Hospital		1 sp./750 sq. ft.
Bowling Alley	3 sp./alley	
Club	1 sp./150 sq. ft.	
Office Building		1 sp./500 sq. ft. in excess of 1,000 sq. ft.
Telephone Office		1 sp./2,000 sq. ft.
Service Station or Garage	1 sp./200 sq. ft.	1 sp./500 sq. ft. service area
Retail Store	1 sp./100 sq. ft.	1 sp./750 sq. ft.
Wholesale or Industrial Building	1 sp./1,000 sq. ft.	1 sp./1,000 sq. ft.
Building, not specified above	1 sp./1,000 sq. ft.	

Appendix I

The Calculation of j Values and their Relationship to k Values in the Floor Area Ratio Algorithm

All of the four districts for which j values must be calculated require customer parking space of undefined size (assumed to be 300 sq. ft.) to be provided for x sq. ft. of floor space or for some particular activity which could be related to a given amount of floor space. The parking space per square feet of floor area specifically required in one district for a particular category was used for that same activity in another district when the requirement could not be computed easily in the second district; for example, one parking space per 60 sq. ft. of floor area was required for theaters in one ordinance, and was then applied to another ordinance requiring one parking space per 10 seats. In the case of hotels and motels, all the districts required parking spaces in relation to the number of square feet attributable to a hotel or motel unit, and related that to the parking space. In making that calculation, we relied upon the advice of Douglas McGerity, Office of the Director of Project Development, Holiday Inns, Inc. (Nashville, Tennessee), who stated in a telephone conversation (October 1971) that the average room built by his organization was 27' by 12', or 324 sq. ft., and that, on average, each room required an additional 100 sq. ft. for backup services such as lobbies, restaurants, plant, office space, etc. Mr. McGerity further noted that the architectural firm which designs most Holiday Inns also designs hotel-motel developments for other chains, all of which generally conform to Holiday Inn space usage standards. Thus, each unit of about 425 sq. ft. can be related to the required amount of parking space. The following table summarizes the j values implicit in the specific customer parking requirements of the four districts for each of eight categories.

j and k Values by District and FAC

FAC	Districts 31, 33, 34		District 41	
	j	k	j	k
9	0.33	0.49	0.33	0.47
10	3.00	0.68	0.40	0.75
11	6.00	0.98	6.00	1.20
12	1.06	0.39	0.71	0.32
13	1.50	0.25	0.60	0.11
14	5.00	0.49	5.00	0.47
15	0.33	0.39	0.40	0.32
16	0.33	0.98	0.60	0.23

Thus, in the four districts for which particular js are specified, there are sixteen possible Floor Area Classes (FACs), the first eight FACs with k values only and the second group of eight FACs with summed values of j and k. By so doing, the FAR algorithm can be used for districts which lack j-type requirements simply because FACs 9–16 contain k values only, i.e., $j + k = k$ when $j = 0$. The computer program in Appendix E describes the computation routine more fully.

Appendix J

Converting Central Administrative Office and Auxiliary Employment to Equivalent SIC Employment

Our allocation of central administrative office and auxiliary employment to SIC industries is based on a Bureau of the Census report which gives the percentage distribution of five kinds of CAO and A in each of six industry groups.*

Table J–1.   U.S. Percentage Distribution of *CAO* and *A* Employment by Major Industry Group, 1967

CAO and A	Min- ing	Construc- tion	Manu- factur- ing	Whole- sale	Retail	Services	All
Central Administra- tive Office	84.5	79.8	69.8	79.2	59.6	64.8	69.0
Research, Development and Testing Laboratories	9.3	–	23.6	0.5	0.1	–	14.2
Warehousing	1.1	–	1.8	14.0	30.8	4.4	9.8
Trading Stamp Redemption Centers	–	–	–	–	–	23.0	0.8
Other	5.1	20.2	4.8	6.2	9.6	7.7	6.2
All	100.0	100.0	100.0	100.0	100.0	100.0	100.0

*U.S., Bureau of the Census, *1967 Enterprise Statistics: Central Administrative Offices and Auxiliaries,* ES 67 (P)–1 (Washington: Government Printing Office, n.d.).

The total reference area employment shown in *County Business Patterns* for *CAO* and *A*s, by industry group, is then multiplied by the appropriate national industry distribution and summed for each kind of *CAO* and *A*. This approach will yield useful results as long as the SIC composition of each major industry group in local areas is roughly comparable to that of the U.S. If the SIC composition of major industries is very different locally, then SIC distributions in Table 2, pages 6–11 (1967 *Enterprise Statistics,* ES 67 (P)-1) should be used to weight the industry distribution according to the SIC composition of local industry groups. When this procedure is carried out for total *CAO* and *A* employment in Delaware County and Philadelphia's four suburban counties (Pennsylvania), employment in each kind of *CAO* and *A* is estimated as shown in table J–2.

Table J–2.   County Employment in Types of *CAO* and *A*, 1969

	Delaware County Employees	Four-County Employees
Central Administrative Offices	3,705	10,509
Research, Development and Testing Laboratories	762	2,163
Warehousing and Storage	526	1,493
Trading Stamp Centers	43	122
Other–Sales Office	64	183
Other–Automobile Parking	199	564
Other–Repair of Vehicles, Equipment, Related	70	198
All	5,369	15,232

Since each of these *CAO* and *A*s was tagged with an equivalent SIC in Appendix D, their employees are now easily added to the equivalent SIC employment currently listed in *County Business Patterns* totals, the employment total of each *CAO* and *A* type being divided proportionately among several equivalent SICs on the basis of existing SIC employment totals (Table J–3).

The important point of this exercise is not to find the most precise, representative estimate of *CAO* and *A* employment in SIC terms, but rather, to sort out and roughly estimate the size of the vastly different classes of *CAO* and *A* which lie submerged in a *CBP* total. The number of *CAO* and *A* employees is substantial; "equivalent" SIC employment was 3.27 times *CBP* reported employment for the same SICs in Delaware County and 2.12 times the reported employment for the four suburban counties.

Table J–3. *CAO* and *A* Employment in "Equivalent" SICs, 1969

	Delaware County			Four Counties		
SICs	*CBP Existing*	*CAO and A Equivalent*	*Total*	*CBP Existing*	*CAO and A Equivalent*	*Total*
739 (2)	484	2,486	2,970	2,444	7,052	9,496
811	–	293	293	–	830	830
893	111	926	1,037	575	2,627	3,202
739 (1) (7)	90	555	645	310	1,576	1,886
892	–	207	207	–	587	587
422	–	526	526	102	1,493	1,595
739 (6)	–	43	43	–	122	122
535	144	64	208	549	183	732
752	–	199	199	–	564	564
753	597	47	644	2,341	133	2,474
769	214	23	237	850	65	915
All	1,640	5,369	7,009	7,171	15,232	22,403

Appendix K

Deriving Mean Number of Floors, by SIC Three-Digit Industries

The average floor area per worker and the mean number of floors are both derived from the Ide study, but it is somewhat more difficult to elicit building height for three-digit SICs than floor area per worker, for a number of reasons.

First, where floor space per worker was calculated from a base of 28,779 establishments (which ensured broad coverage of detailed SICs), the mean number of floors was calculated from a sample base of 3,182 establishments, with consequent loss of three-digit detail.[*] In addition, the mean number of floors published in the report was calculated only for eight broad industry groups, which necessitated access to the raw data for staff computation of two- and three-digit SICs. The raw data also proved to be somewhat troublesome because establishments were coded in the URA–BPR land use system, which is based upon, but not identical with, the SIC system.[**] Further, a table published in the Ide report, which cross-tabulated the average number of employees by the average number of stories, indicated that 29 establishments with 10.0 or more stories had nine or fewer employees, an average of less than one person per floor.[***] From this it was inferred that at least some 1.0-story establishments had probably been miscoded as 10.0 stories.

All of these difficulties were handled at the same time by the following procedure. A card deck of all 3,182 establishments was duplicated from the original Ide deck. The deck was systematically re-sorted to arrange the URA-

---

[*]Edward Ide and Associates, *Estimating Land and Floor Area Implicit in Employment Projections: How Land and Floor Area Usage Rates Vary by Industry and Site Variable*, 2 Vols. (Washington: U.S., Federal Highway Administration, 1970), pp. 11–13 and Table B–25, p. B–26.

[**]Ibid., pp. 11–12. See also U.S., Urban Renewal Administration and Bureau of Public Roads, *Standard Land Use Coding Manual* (Washington: Government Printing Office, January 1965), pp. 3–24.

[***]Ide, *Estimating Land and Floor Area*, Table B–39, p. B–80.

BPR uses in SIC serial order, the sorting itself accomplished by use of an SIC/ URA–BPR "equivalence" table designed and assembled by the staff for this purpose. Several sortings and deck print-outs were required to clean up all the SIC categories at the two- and three-digit level. A final print-out was then made according to two- and three-digit SICs.

Knowing the general pattern of number of square feet per employee by SIC, all derived SICs on the print-out with 10.0 or more stories were scanned in terms of the total recorded floor space and number of employees. Where there was general agreement, it was assumed that the number of employees recorded was likely to be correct. Thirty-eight establishments with 10 or more stories and 25 or fewer employees were found to have highly suspicious values for the recorded number of stories. Twenty-one of these had 1,000 square feet or less floor area with 10 or more stories, a condition which would, at best, imply a building 10 feet by 10 feet. The remaining 17 had between 1,000 and 3,000 square feet of floor area also with 10 or more stories, yielding, at best, a similarly implausible building 15 by 20 feet. The cards for these 38 establishments were then pulled from the deck and the value recorded for mean number of floors was divided by 10.0 to correct for obvious miscodings. Once the cards were replaced in the deck, the mean number of stories was calculated for all establishments comprising each three-digit SIC.

Appendix L

Ratio of Main Shift to Total Workers, and Mean Number of Floors, by SIC Three-Digit Industries

SIC	Main Shift ÷ Total Workers	Mean Number of Floors	SIC	Main Shift ÷ Total Workers	Mean Number of Floors
140	1.00	1.131	279	1.00	2.000
160	1.00	1.073	281	0.75	1.567
170	0.99	1.414	282	0.72	1.375
192	0.88	1.000	284	0.97	2.100
201	0.91	1.400	285	0.94	2.500
202	0.86	1.864	289	0.82	1.375
203	0.99	1.792	291	0.83	3.750
204	0.82	1.700	295	0.78	1.000
205	0.59	1.719	301	0.65	1.667
207	0.69	3.000	302	0.71	1.500
208	0.92	1.686	307	0.60	1.400
209	0.81	1.679	311	0.72	2.667
221	0.69	2.125	314	1.00	1.700
225	0.88	2.120	315	0.86	2.500
228	0.47	1.000	321	0.72	1.433
229	0.75	1.500	325	0.82	1.111
231	0.98	2.262	326	1.00	1.667
238	0.96	2.167	327	1.00	1.045
241	1.00	1.250	328	1.00	1.500
242	1.00	1.000	329	0.70	1.500
243	0.97	1.292	331	0.83	1.125
244	1.00	1.000	332	0.89	1.462
251	1.00	2.357	333	0.47	1.000
252	1.00	1.000	334	0.81	1.500
253	0.90	1.125	335	0.56	1.000
263	0.69	1.000	336	0.88	1.540
264	0.76	1.500	339	0.79	1.425
265	0.66	1.125	341	0.38	2.000
271	0.83	2.313	342	0.94	1.143
272	1.00	1.650	344	0.90	1.700
273	0.90	2.000	345	0.91	1.100
275	0.97	1.500	346	0.81	1.333
278	1.00	1.500	347	0.89	1.800

(continued)

237

Appendix L continued

SIC	Main Shift ÷ Total Workers	Mean Number of Floors	SIC	Main Shift ÷ Total Workers	Mean Number of Floors
348	0.95	1.667	531	0.87	3.139
349	0.85	1.353	533	0.67	1.250
352	0.85	1.100	534	1.00	1.000
353	0.75	1.150	539	0.87	1.206
354	0.96	1.000	541	0.84	1.245
355	0.86	1.182	542	0.63	1.143
356	0.81	1.083	545	0.74	1.000
359	0.93	1.333	546	1.00	1.000
361	0.88	1.200	549	0.75	1.000
364	0.77	1.143	551	0.99	1.208
367	0.74	1.222	553	0.94	1.288
369	0.87	2.000	554	0.74	1.000
371	0.81	1.214	559	0.88	1.071
373	0.75	1.000	561	0.95	1.813
375	0.89	1.000	562	0.77	2.250
381	1.00	1.500	563	0.92	1.600
382	0.97	1.333	565	1.00	2.333
384	1.00	2.333	566	1.00	1.620
391	1.00	1.500	569	0.76	2.000
399	1.00	1.167	571	1.00	1.769
401	0.80	1.750	572	0.96	1.807
404	0.87	1.250	573	0.95	1.000
411	0.66	1.500	581	0.70	1.490
412	0.53	1.500	591	0.69	1.483
413	0.71	1.400	592	0.79	1.000
414	0.73	1.000	593	1.00	2.000
421	0.87	1.267	594	0.90	1.300
422	0.86	2.300	595	0.81	1.333
440	0.90	1.500	596	1.00	1.333
450	0.50	2.000	597	1.00	1.600
471	0.91	1.000	598	1.00	1.667
472	0.84	1.000	599	0.92	1.295
478	0.93	1.063	601	0.96	4.086
481	0.89	4.750	611	1.00	1.765
483	0.82	5.000	631	1.00	3.100
491	1.00	8.500	641	1.00	1.377
492	1.00	5.833	651	1.00	1.000
501	1.00	1.233	653	1.00	1.233
502	1.00	3.667	654	1.00	1.000
503	1.00	2.000	655	1.00	1.333
504	0.91	1.471	656	1.00	1.500
505	0.95	1.667	661	1.00	1.557
506	1.00	1.182	721	0.95	1.218
507	1.00	2.286	722	1.00	2.333
508	0.98	1.268	723	0.95	1.662
509	0.96	1.682	724	1.00	1.000
521	0.99	1.214	726	1.00	2.500
522	1.00	1.000	729	0.80	1.000
523	1.00	1.000	731	1.00	2.400
524	1.00	1.500	733	1.00	2.000
525	0.87	1.344	734	0.89	1.167

SIC	Main Shift ÷ Total Workers	Mean Number of Floors	SIC	Main Shift ÷ Total Workers	Mean Number of Floors
735	1.00	2.500	810	1.00	2.047
736	1.00	1.333	821	0.98	1.771
739	0.90	1.475	822	0.99	3.209
752	0.69	1.000	824	0.94	1.275
753	0.97	1.161	861	1.00	4.000
754	1.00	1.000	863	0.94	2.000
762	0.94	2.000	864	0.93	5.167
769	1.00	1.200	866	0.90	1.806
780	0.42	2.750	891	0.98	2.431
801	1.00	1.286	893	0.95	1.769
802	1.00	1.500	901	0.96	5.964
806	0.63	4.844	902	0.55	1.643
807	1.00	1.333	903	0.62	1.333
809	0.80	1.750	905	0.88	2.500

Source: Edward Ide and Associates, *Estimating Land and Floor Area Implicit in Employment Projections: How Land and Floor Area Usage Rates Vary by Industry and Site Variable,* 2 Vols. (Washington: U.S., Federal Highway Administration, 1970).

Appendix M

Employment Algorithm Coefficients in Coding Sheet Form

Employment Algorithm Coefficients in Coding Sheet Form

SIC	Reference Area Employment	Floor Area Per Worker (sq. ft.)	Mean Number of Floors	Ratio Main Shift to Total Workers	Single Job Holding Rate	Employment Rate	Floor Area Class k^*	Floor Area Class $k+j^{**}$
1420	828	200	1.13	1.00	100.0	97.2	2	
1440	144	328	1.13	1.00	100.0	97.2	3	
1500	6,751	189	1.13	1.00	96.4	94.0	1	
1610	1,928	146	1.07	1.00	96.4	94.0	1	
1620	2,274	70	1.07	1.00	96.4	94.0	1	
1710	3,249	349	1.41	0.99	96.4	94.0	3	
1720	1,323	1,135	1.41	0.99	96.4	94.0	6	
1730	1,840	1,757	1.41	0.99	96.4	94.0	7	
1740	2,944	100	1.41	0.99	96.4	94.0	1	
1750	1,607	90	1.41	0.99	96.4	94.0	1	
1760	842	207	1.41	0.99	96.4	94.0	2	
1770	667	416	1.41	0.99	96.4	94.0	3	
1790	3,083	336	1.41	0.99	96.4	94.0	3	
1900	750	206	1.13	0.87	98.7	96.2	3	
2010	1,462	516	1.40	0.91	98.5	95.5	4	
2020	1,996	332	1.86	0.86	98.5	95.5	3	
2030	3,065	761	1.79	0.99	98.5	95.5	4	
2040	379	1,134	1.70	0.82	98.5	95.5	6	
2050	2,480	425	1.72	0.59	98.5	95.5	3	
2070	816	641	3.00	0.69	98.5	95.5	4	
2080	635	899	1.69	0.92	98.5	95.5	5	
2090	494	573	1.68	0.81	98.5	95.5	4	
2140	175	282	1.00	1.00	98.5	97.5	2	
2220	175	576	1.89	0.78	98.5	98.5	4	
2230	456	218	1.89	0.78	98.5	98.5	2	
2240	121	315	1.89	0.78	98.5	98.5	3	
2250	4,097	464	2.12	0.88	98.5	98.5	3	
2260	385	500	1.89	0.78	98.5	98.5	4	
2270	952	291	1.89	0.78	98.5	98.5	2	
2280	972	317	1.00	0.47	98.5	98.5	3	

2290	952	391	1.50	0.75	98.5	98.5	3
2310	1,555	1,001	2.26	0.98	98.5	94.1	5
2320	2,453	191	2.17	0.98	98.5	94.1	1
2330	2,411	471	2.17	0.98	98.5	94.1	3
2340	440	135	2.17	0.98	98.5	94.1	1
2360	337	471	2.17	0.98	98.5	94.1	3
2380	676	528	2.17	0.96	98.5	94.1	4
2390	610	632	2.17	0.98	98.5	94.1	4
2430	373	862	1.29	0.97	98.7	96.2	5
2490	156	779	1.17	0.99	98.7	96.2	4
2510	901	652	2.36	1.00	98.7	96.2	4
2520	965	807	1.00	1.00	98.7	96.2	5
2540	987	301	1.71	0.97	98.7	96.2	3
2620	1,700	355	1.37	0.67	98.5	97.5	3
2630	560	508	1.00	0.69	98.5	97.5	4
2640	5,011	561	1.50	0.76	98.5	97.5	4
2650	3,352	726	1.13	0.66	98.5	97.5	1
2710	1,958	195	2.31	0.83	98.5	97.5	3
2720	1,811	307	1.65	1.00	98.5	97.5	3
2730	418	483	2.00	0.90	98.5	97.5	5
2750	2,190	456	1.50	0.97	98.5	97.5	4
2760	1,123	935	1.90	0.93	98.5	97.5	3
2780	350	753	1.50	1.00	98.5	97.5	4
2790	477	360	2.00	1.00	98.5	97.5	4
2810	1,972	685	1.57	0.75	98.5	97.5	3
2820	2,944	414	1.38	0.72	98.5	97.5	3
2840	5,824	352	1.65	0.80	98.5	97.5	5
2850	1,154	1,062	2.10	0.97	98.5	97.5	5
2870	259	865	2.50	0.94	98.5	97.5	7
2890	702	1,622	1.65	0.80	98.5	97.5	4
	920	778	1.38	0.82	98.5	97.5	

*For employee parking only
**For employee and customer parking

(continued)

Appendix M continued

SIC	Reference Area Employment	Floor Area Per Worker (sq. ft.)	Mean Number of Floors	Ratio Main Shift to Total Workers	Single Job Holding Rate	Employment Rate	Floor Area Class k^*	$k + j^{**}$
2910	1,400	2,020	3.75	0.83	98.5	97.5	7	
2950	130	539	1.00	0.78	98.5	97.5	4	
2990	409	501	2.38	0.83	98.5	97.5	4	
3010	4,879	811	1.67	0.65	98.5	97.5	5	
3020	175	442	1.50	0.71	98.5	97.5	3	
3060	1,940	442	1.50	0.71	98.5	97.5	3	
3070	3,951	336	1.40	0.60	98.5	97.5	3	
3170	150	1,200	2.28	0.90	98.5	97.5	6	
3220	377	577	1.28	0.84	98.7	96.2	4	
3230	654	97	1.28	0.84	98.7	96.2	1	
3250	1,997	903	1.11	0.82	98.7	96.2	5	
3270	1,672	639	1.05	1.00	98.7	96.2	4	
3290	1,929	736	1.50	0.70	98.7	96.2	4	
3310	12,481	240	1.13	0.83	98.7	97.8	2	
3320	905	362	1.42	0.89	98.7	97.8	3	
3340	550	312	1.50	0.81	98.7	97.8	3	
3350	1,847	436	1.00	0.56	98.7	97.8	3	
3360	1,448	360	1.54	0.88	98.7	97.8	3	
3390	1,015	212	1.43	0.79	98.7	97.8	2	
3410	585	699	2.00	0.38	98.7	96.8	4	
3420	374	441	1.43	0.94	98.7	96.8	3	
3430	240	532	1.47	0.86	98.7	96.8	4	
3440	5,846	470	1.70	0.90	98.7	96.8	3	
3450	4,357	363	1.10	0.91	98.7	96.8	3	
3460	415	512	1.33	0.91	98.7	96.8	4	
3470	501	473	1.80	0.89	98.7	96.8	3	
3480	1,766	724	1.67	0.95	98.7	96.8	4	
3490	2,626	355	1.35	0.85	98.7	96.8	3	
3510	9,300	269	1.18	0.85	98.7	97.8	2	
3520	430	757	1.10	0.85	98.7	97.8	4	

3530	2,262	573	1.15	0.75	98.7	97.8	4
3540	2,180	216	1.00	0.96	98.7	97.8	2
3550	3,861	881	1.82	0.86	98.7	97.8	5
3560	3,701	344	1.08	0.81	98.7	97.8	3
3570	1,714	238	1.18	0.85	98.7	97.8	2
3580	2,074	497	1.18	0.85	98.7	97.8	3
3590	2,913	169	1.33	0.93	98.7	97.8	1
3610	1,161	266	1.20	0.88	98.7	97.0	2
3620	3,046	334	1.30	0.81	98.7	97.0	2
3640	2,278	302	1.14	0.77	98.7	97.0	3
3650	702	344	1.30	0.81	98.7	97.0	3
3660	7,199	175	1.30	0.81	98.7	97.0	3
3670	3,378	189	1.22	0.74	98.7	97.0	1
3690	7,506	466	2.00	0.87	98.7	97.0	1
3710	5,315	511	1.21	0.81	98.7	97.0	3
3720	22,374	293	1.16	0.82	98.7	96.7	4
3730	4,494	205	1.00	0.75	98.7	96.7	2
3790	260	408	1.16	0.82	98.7	96.7	2
3810	336	209	1.50	1.00	98.7	96.2	3
3820	7,776	177	1.33	0.97	98.7	96.2	2
3830	113	315	1.92	0.96	98.7	96.2	1
3840	960	371	2.33	1.00	98.7	96.2	3
3860	175	408	1.92	0.96	98.7	96.2	3
3940	371	452	1.56	0.98	98.7	96.2	3
3960	750	314	1.56	0.98	98.7	96.2	3
3990	1,528	530	1.17	1.00	98.7	96.2	4
4110	847	298	1.50	0.66	96.1	97.0	2
4120	1,196	157	1.50	0.53	96.1	97.0	2
4150	706	280	1.36	0.67	96.1	97.0	1
4210	6,803	422	1.27	0.87	96.1	97.0	2
4220	102	3,257	2.30	0.86	96.1	97.0	3
4420	700	135	1.50	0.90	96.1	97.0	8
4530	375	809	2.00	0.50	96.1	97.0	1
4720	187	780	1.00	0.84	96.1	97.0	5
4810	3,244	172	4.75	0.89	96.1	98.5	4
4830	133	184	5.00	0.82	96.1	98.5	1

(continued)

Appendix M continued

SIC	Reference Area Employment	Floor Area Per Worker (sq. ft.)	Mean Number of Floors	Ratio Main Shift to Total Workers	Single Job Holding Rate	Employment Rate	Floor Area Class k^*	$k+j^{**}$
4890	113	177	4.63	0.85	96.1	98.5	1	
4910	1,090	344	8.50	1.00	96.1	97.0	3	
4920	169	296	5.83	1.00	96.1	97.0	2	
4930	8,516	341	6.36	1.00	96.1	97.0	3	
4940	523	251	6.36	1.00	96.1	97.0	2	
4950	140	251	6.36	1.00	96.1	97.0	2	
5010	3,009	1,311	1.23	1.00	97.1	95.9	9	6
5020	1,730	513	3.67	1.00	97.1	95.9	9	4
5030	469	593	2.00	1.00	97.1	95.9	9	4
5040	3,535	567	1.47	0.91	97.1	95.9	9	4
5050	82	414	1.67	0.95	97.1	95.9	9	3
5060	1,941	808	1.18	1.00	97.1	95.9	9	5
5070	1,290	851	2.29	1.00	97.1	95.9	9	5
5080	4,841	561	1.27	0.98	97.1	95.9	9	4
5090	8,352	870	1.68	0.96	97.1	95.9	9	5
5210	1,407	2,212	1.21	0.99	93.5	95.9	10	8
5230	278	666	1.00	1.00	93.5	95.9	10	4
5250	1,042	1,445	1.34	0.87	93.5	95.9	10	6
5310	14,627	231	3.14	0.87	93.5	95.9	10	2
5320	489	231	3.14	0.87	93.5	95.9	10	2
5330	4,075	532	1.25	0.67	93.5	95.9	10	4
5340	397	1,035	1.00	1.00	93.5	95.9	10	5
5350	654	850	2.28	0.87	93.5	95.9	10	5
5390	1,057	1,035	1.21	0.87	92.5	95.9	10	5
5410	13,763	464	1.25	0.84	93.5	95.9	10	3
5420	556	507	1.14	0.63	93.5	95.9	10	4
5430	38	525	1.27	0.83	93.5	95.9	10	4
5440	253	366	1.27	0.83	93.5	95.9	10	3
5460	1,278	481	1.00	1.00	93.5	95.9	10	3
5490	46	314	1.00	0.75	93.5	95.9	10	3

5510	7,806	579	1.21	0.99	93.5	95.9	10	4
5520	237	389	1.14	0.90	93.5	95.9	10	3
5530	912	784	1.29	0.94	93.5	95.9	10	4
5540	5,145	406	1.00	0.74	93.5	95.9	10	3
5590	233	382	1.07	0.88	93.5	95.9	10	3
5610	1,065	512	1.81	0.95	93.5	95.9	10	4
5620	2,690	425	2.25	0.77	93.5	95.9	10	3
5630	460	1,744	1.60	0.92	93.5	95.9	10	7
5640	189	677	1.97	0.90	93.5	95.9	10	4
5650	839	610	2.33	1.00	93.5	95.9	10	4
5660	1,081	512	1.62	1.00	93.5	95.9	10	4
5710	2,504	1,211	1.77	1.00	93.5	95.9	10	6
5720	733	613	1.81	0.96	93.5	95.9	10	4
5730	715	503	1.00	0.95	93.5	95.9	10	4
5800	21,503	270	1.49	0.70	93.5	95.9	11	2
5910	3,673	266	1.48	0.69	93.5	95.9	10	2
5920	142	288	1.00	0.79	93.5	95.9	10	2
5930	156	679	2.00	1.00	93.5	95.9	10	4
5940	548	1,214	1.30	0.90	93.5	95.9	10	6
5950	380	803	1.33	0.81	93.5	95.9	10	5
5960	893	793	1.33	1.00	93.5	95.9	10	4
5970	535	347	1.60	1.00	93.5	95.9	10	3
5980	2,193	424	1.67	1.00	93.5	95.9	10	3
5990	2,353	437	1.30	0.92	93.5	95.9	10	3
6020	3,355	100	4.09	0.96	96.1	97.9	1	
6030	105	100	4.09	0.96	96.1	97.9	1	
6120	1,009	100	1.69	1.00	96.1	97.9	1	
6140	1,069	214	1.69	1.00	96.1	97.9	2	
6150	190	214	1.69	1.00	96.1	97.9	2	
6210	147	176	2.28	1.00	96.1	97.9	1	
6310	1,758	149	3.10	1.00	96.1	97.9	1	
6320	266	149	3.88	1.00	96.1	97.9	1	
6330	2,734	149	3.88	1.00	96.1	97.9	1	
6400	1,333	149	1.44	1.00	96.1	97.9	1	
6510	2,782	165	1.00	1.00	96.1	97.9	1	
6530	803	138	1.23	1.00	96.1	97.9	1	

(continued)

Appendix M continued

SIC	Reference Area Employment	Floor Area Per Worker (sq. ft.)	Mean Number of Floors	Ratio Main Shift to Total Workers	Single Job Holding Rate	Employment Rate	Floor Area Class k*	k + j**
6550	688	58	1.33	1.00	96.1	97.9	1	
6560	546	1,242	1.50	1.00	96.1	97.9	6	
6600	471	187	1.56	1.00	96.1	97.9	1	
6790	131	156	2.28	1.00	96.1	97.9	1	
7010	2,722	875	1.00	1.00	90.8	95.3	12	5
7020	770	650	1.00	1.00	90.8	95.3	4	
7030	84	83	1.00	1.00	90.8	95.3	1	
7210	3,011	259	1.22	0.95	90.8	95.3	2	
7220	153	349	2.33	1.00	90.8	95.3	3	
7230	2,468	238	1.66	0.95	90.8	95.3	2	
7240	598	275	1.00	1.00	90.8	95.3	2	
7250	51	300	1.43	0.95	90.8	95.3	3	
7260	246	1,446	2.50	1.00	90.8	95.3	6	
7270	391	259	1.22	0.95	90.8	95.3	2	
7290	47	282	1.00	0.80	90.8	95.3	2	
7310	200	178	2.40	1.00	91.5	95.3	1	
7330	502	130	2.00	1.00	91.5	95.3	1	
7340	2,114	1,500	1.17	0.89	91.5	95.3	7	
7360	256	275	1.33	1.00	91.5	95.3	2	
7390	16,032	305	1.47	0.90	91.5	95.3	16	3
7510	403	839	1.13	0.95	91.5	95.3	13	5
7520	564	597	1.00	0.69	91.5	95.3	13	4
7530	2,474	560	1.61	0.97	91.5	95.3	13	4
7540	944	5,000	1.00	1.00	91.5	95.3	13	8
7620	550	344	2.00	0.94	91.5	95.3	3	
7640	124	270	1.61	0.98	91.5	95.3	2	
7690	915	215	1.20	1.00	91.5	95.3	2	
7810	98	340	2.75	0.42	90.8	95.3	3	
7830	837	681	2.75	0.42	90.8	95.3	14	4
7920	257	871	1.00	1.00	90.8	95.3	5	

7930	673	1,421	1.00	1.00	90.8	95.3	6		
7940	2,936	433	1.00	1.00	90.8	95.3	3		
8010	2,671	317	1.29	1.00	95.0	97.7	16	3	
8020	1,452	269	1.50	1.00	95.0	97.7	16	2	
8030	130	283	2.13	0.87	95.0	97.7	16	2	
8060	17,502	202	4.84	0.63	95.0	97.7	15	2	
8070	256	132	1.33	1.00	95.0	97.7	1		
8090	4,884	417	1.75	0.80	95.0	97.7	3	2	
8110	830	212	2.05	1.00	95.0	97.7	16		
8210	7,989	697	1.77	0.98	96.1	95.3	4		
8220	4,799	697	3.21	0.99	96.1	95.3	4		
8230	296	697	1.83	0.98	96.1	95.3	4		
8240	210	697	1.28	0.94	96.1	95.3	4		
8290	104	697	1.83	0.98	96.1	95.3	4		
8410	210	2,000	1.00	2.00	90.8	95.3	7		
8610	150	200	4.00	1.00	90.8	95.3	2		
8630	789	600	2.00	0.94	90.8	95.3	4		
8640	1,788	918	5.17	0.93	90.8	95.3	5		
8650	35	918	2.64	0.92	90.8	95.3	5		
8660	2,924	860	1.81	0.90	90.8	95.3	5		
8670	722	860	2.64	0.92	90.8	95.3	5		
8690	267	860	2.64	0.92	90.8	95.3	5		
8910	3,041	373	2.43	0.98	95.0	97.7	16		
8920	587	200	2.16	0.97	95.0	97.7	16	3	
8930	2,627	217	1.77	0.95	95.0	97.7	16	2	
8990	204	750	2.16	0.97	95.0	97.7	16	2	
9100	6,557	197	5.96	0.96	99.5	98.2	16		
9200	10,931	183	1.64	0.55	95.7	98.2	16	4	

Appendix N

Reference Area and Employment Statistics

In order to compute potential employment in the developing communities, it was necessary to determine the proportions of permitted work activities. As described in the text, the four Pennsylvania suburban counties of the Philadelphia SMSA were used as the reference area for this purpose. Other choices were possible of course: Delaware County (which contains all of the municipalities in the study), the SMSA, the state, the nation. Without again defending the four-county choice, it is useful to see how much the results have been affected by that choice. We have, therefore, compared the labor force computed with the four-county reference base with a labor force using Delaware County as reference base. Table N-1 presents the comparison.

On the whole, the Delaware County reference base produces a slightly larger labor force than the four-county base. The Delaware County base yields higher figures in manufacturing industries, and lower figures in commercial industries; the manufacturing differences are relatively larger. A glance at the last column in Table N-1 suggests that we should expect smaller differences in commercial activities because Delaware County includes almost as many of the permitted commercial SICs as does the four-county area; by contrast, Delaware County has less than 60 percent as many of the permitted manufacturing SICs.

Although it is clear that labor force estimates differ when different "pools" of industries are used as the reference base, it is not clear which reference base is best. Theoretically, the best reference area would be one so like the townships under study that all industries found in the reference area might reasonably have located in the townships during their hypothetical growth period. If the reference area is too large, it will include locations with economic assets or liabilities substantially different from those of the townships under study. If the area is too small, it may exclude quite acceptable industries because it cannot accommodate the full range of industries willing to locate there or because the element of chance is more likely to play tricks with the industrial composition of a small area than with a large one. On the whole, the larger reference area seemed a safer choice.

Table N-1.   Township Main Shift Jobs, Total Jobs, Total Workers, and Total Labor Force, based on Two Reference Areas

Districts	Four-County Area				Ratio: Delaware County Area / Four-County Area			
	Main Shift	Total Jobs	Total Workers	Labor Force	Main Shift	Total Jobs	Total Workers	Labor Force
Manufacturing								
13	22,614	27,235	26,736	27,654	1.025	1.024	1.023	1.018
22	3,328	3,950	3,878	4,005	1.090	1.074	1.071	1.051
35	15,626	18,448	17,793	18,448	1.060	1.056	1.051	1.004
53	10,750	12,740	12,399	12,805	1.020	1.011	1.005	1.004
54	9,194	10,780	10,559	10,951	1.054	1.056	1.052	1.053
62	12,375	14,973	14,761	15,283	0.902	0.915	0.915	0.914
All	73,887	88,126	86,126	89,146	1.018	1.017	1.014	1.012
Commercial								
11	3,811	4,628	4,347	4,509	0.985	0.979	0.977	0.978
12	203	279	262	272	0.978	0.975	0.973	0.971
21	5,600	6,782	6,369	6,605	0.987	0.982	0.980	0.981
31	3,406	4,115	3,872	4,000	0.989	0.983	0.979	0.981
32	4,197	5,259	4,925	5,104	0.994	0.989	0.986	0.987
33	840	1,010	950	981	0.987	0.983	0.979	0.982
34	1,598	1,897	1,780	1,852	0.999	1.008	1.004	1.005
41	1,511	1,830	1,718	1,782	1.002	0.997	0.995	0.996
51	1,412	1,710	1,606	1,666	0.987	0.982	0.980	0.981
52	918	1,112	1,044	1,083	0.987	0.981	0.980	0.981
61	442	536	503	522	0.986	0.970	0.978	0.979
All	23,965	29,158	27,376	28,380	0.990	0.961	0.983	0.984
Total	97,852	117,284	113,502	117,526	1.011	1.003	1.006	1.005

Appendix O

Computer Program for Employment Algorithm and Sample Estimate of Employment for District 62

```
0001        DIMENSION IS(300),EMP4C(300),EMPDC(300),FTWRK(300),FLRM(300),
           1JB(300),JOB(300),EMPRAT(300),FLAREA(300),AREA(20)
0002        DIMENSION ISD(300),D1(300),D2(300),D3(300),D4(300),D5(300),
           1D6(300),D7(300),ID8(300)
0003        INTEGER FLAREA,DIST(20)
0004        REAL JB,JOB
0005   101  FORMAT(2X,I2   ,2X,F9.0)
0006        READ(5,101)(DIST(I),AREA(I),I=1,18)
0007        DO 2 N=1,251
0008        READ(5,104)IS(N),EMP4C(N),EMPDC(N),FTWRK(N),FLRM(N),JB(N),
           1JOB(N),EMPRAT(N),FLAREA(N)
0009   2    CONTINUE
0010   104  FORMAT(6X,I4,1X,F6.0,1X,2F6.0,3X,F3.2,1X,F3.2,1X,F4.3,1X,F3.3,1X,
           1I2)
0011        DO 1 K=1,18
0012        DO 3 I=1,251
0013        ISD(I)=IS(I)
0014        D1(I)=EMP4C(I)
0015        D2(I)=EMPDC(I)
0016        D3(I)=FTWRK(I)
0017        D4(I)=FLRM(I)
0018        D5(I)=JB(I)
0019        D6(I)=JOB(I)
0020        D7(I)=EMPRAT(I)
0021        ID8(I)=FLAREA(I)
0022   3    CONTINUE
0023        CALL EMP(ISD,D1,D2,D3, D4, D5, D6, D7,ID8,DIST,AREA)
0024   1    CONTINUE
0025        END
```

Part B
Base Data Applied to Districts

```
0001        SUBROUTINE EMP(IS,EMP4C,EMPDC,FTWRK,FLRM,JB,JOB,EMPRAT, FLAREA,
           1DIST,AREA)
0002        DIMENSION AREA(20),DIST(20),ISIC(200),FLOOR(20),FCL(16,10),
           1IS(300),FLA1(200),FLA2(200),FTWRK(300),EMP4C(300),EMPDC(300),
           2FLRM(300),FLAREA(300)
```

(continued)

253

Appendix O, Part B continued

```
0003       DIMENSION SICF1(200),SICF2(200),PCENT1(200),PCENT2(200)
0004       INTEGER FLAREA,DIST
0005       REAL LAND1(200),LAND2(200),COEF(200),JOBM1,JOBM2,JOB1,JOB2,JB,JOB
0006       DIMENSION JOBM1(200),JOBM2(200),JOB1(200),JOB2(200),WRK1(200),
           2WRK2(200),TOTAL1(200),TOTAL2(200),JB(300),JOB(300),EMPRAT(300)
0007       SUM1=0.
0008       SUM2=0.
0009       SUM3=0.
0010       SUM4=0.
0011       SUM5=0.
0012       SUM6=0.
0013       SUM7=0.
0014       SUM8=0.
0015       SUM9=0.
0016       SUM10=0.
0017       SUM11=0.
0018       SUM12=0.
0019       SUM13=0.
0020       SUM14=0.
0021   102 FORMAT(6X,I4)
0022   103 FORMAT(2X,F4.2,14F5.2,F4.2)
0023       READ(5,1000)NR,NN
0024  1000 FORMAT(9X,I3/9X,I2)
0025   119 FORMAT(' DISTRICT '  ,I4,4X,'AREA=',F12.0)
0026       WRITE(6,119) DIST(NN),AREA(NN)
0027       READ(5,102) (ISIC(I)  ,I=1,NR)
0028       READ(5,103)((FCL(I,K),I=1,16),K=1,10)
0029       N=0
0030       DO3 IKJ=1,251
0031       N=N+1
0032       IT1=IS(IKJ)/100
0033       DO 1 I=1,NR
0034       IT2=ISIC(I)/100
0035       IF(IS(IKJ).EQ.ISIC(I)) GO TO 2
0036       IF(IT1.EQ.IT2) GO TO 2
0037     1 CONTINUE
0038       N=N-1
0039       GO TO 3
0040     2 IS(N)=IS(IKJ)
0041       EMP4C(N)=EMP4C(IKJ)
0042       EMPDC(N)=EMPDC(IKJ)
0043       FTWRK(N)=FTWRK(IKJ)
0044       FLRM(N)=FLRM(IKJ)
0045       JB(N)=JB(IKJ)
0046       JOB(N)=JOB(IKJ)
0047       EMPRAT(N)=EMPRAT(IKJ)
0048       FLAREA(N)=FLAREA(IKJ)
0049       IF(EMP4C(N).EQ.0.) WRITE(6,113)IS(N)
0050       IF(EMPDC(N).EQ.0.) WRITE(6,114)IS(N)
0051   113 FORMAT(' 4 COUNTY EMP. MISSING',I6)
0052   114 FORMAT(' DEL.CO. EMP.MISSING',I6)
0053       FLA1(N)=EMP4C(N)*FTWRK(N)
0054       FLA2(N)=EMPDC(N)*FTWRK(N)
0055       IFL=FLRM(N)
0056       TEMP=FLRM(N)-IFL
0057       IFLR=FLAREA(N)
```

```
0058          IF(TEMP.EQ.0.) GO TO 4
0059          IFL1=IFL+1
0060          COEF(N)=TEMP*(FCL(IFLR   ,IFL1)-FCL(IFLR   ,IFL))+FCL(IFLR   ,IFL)
0061          GO TO 5
0062     4    COEF(N)=FCL(IFLR   ,IFL)
0063     5    CONTINUE
0064          LAND1(N)=FLA1(N)/COEF(N)
0065          LAND2(N)=FLA2(N)/COEF(N)
0066     3    CONTINUE
0067     7    SUML1=0.
0068          SUML2=0.
0069          DO 6 I=1,N
0070          SUML1=SUML1+LAND1(I)
0071          SUML2=SUML2+LAND2(I)
0072     6    CONTINUE
0073   112    FORMAT(1X,2F20.0)
0074   110    FORMAT(   ' SIC MISSING',I5)
0075          DO 9 I=1,NR
0076          DO 10 K=1,N
0077          IF(ISIC(I).EQ.IS(K)) GO TO 9
0078    10    CONTINUE
0079          WRITE(6,110)ISIC(I)
0080     9    CONTINUE
0081          DO 8 I=1,N
0082          PCENT2(I)=0.
0083          SICL2=0.
0084          SICF2(I)=0.
0085          JOBM2(I)=0.
0086          JOB2(I)=0.
0087          WRK2(I)=0.
0088          TOTAL2(I)=0.
0089          PCENT1(I)=LAND1(I)*100.0/SUML1
0090          SICL1=PCENT1(I)*AREA(MN)/100
0091          SICF1(I)=SICL1*COEF(I)
0092          SUM13=SUM13+SICF1(I)/SICL1
0093          JOBM1(I)=SICF1(I)/FTWRK(I)
0094          JOB1(I)=JOBM1(I)/JB(I)
0095          WRK1(I)=JOB1(I)*JOB(I)
0096          TOTAL1(I)=WRK1(I)/EMPRAT(I)
0097          PCENT2(I)=LAND2(I)*100.0/SUML2
0098          IF(PCENT2(I).EQ.0.) GO TO 13
0099          SICL2=PCENT2(I)*AREA(NN)/100.
0100          SICF2(I)=SICL2*COEF(I)
0101          SUM14=SUM14+SICF2(I)/SICL2
0102          JOBM2(I)=SICF2(I)/FTWRK(I)
0103          JOB2(I)=JOBM2(I)/JB(I)
0104          WRK2(I)=JOB2(I)*JOB(I)
0105          TOTAL2(I)=WRK2(I)/EMPRAT(I)
0106    13    CONTINUE
0107          SUM1=SUM1+SICL1
0108          SUM2=SUM2+SICL2
0109          SUM3=SUM3+SICF1(I)
0110          SUM4=SUM4+SICF2(I)
0111          WRITE(7,118)IS(I),WRK1(I),WRK2(I),TOTAL1(I),TOTAL2(I),NN
0112   118    FORMAT(I5,4F9.0,37X,I2)
```

(continued)

Appendix O, Part B continued

```
0113        WRITE(6,111)IS(I),
           1COEF(I),PCENT1(I),PCENT2(I),SICL1,SICL2,SICF1(I),SICF2(I),
           2       JOBM1(I),JOBM2(I),JOB1(I),JOB2(I),WRK1(I),WRK2(I),
           3TOTAL1(I),TOTAL2(I)
0114    111 FORMAT(I5,F5.2,2F5.2,12F9.1)
0115      8 CONTINUE

0116        DO 11 I=1,N
0117        SUM5=SUM5+JOBM1(I)
0118        SUM6=SUM6+JOBM2(I)
0119        SUM7=SUM7+JOB1(I)
0120        SUM8=SUM8+JOB2(I)
0121        SUM9=SUM9+WRK1(I)
0122        SUM10=SUM10+WRK2(I)
0123        SUM11=SUM11+TOTAL1(I)
0124        SUM12=SUM12+TOTAL2(I)
0125     11 CONTINUE
0126        DO 12 I=1,N
0127        JOBM1(I)=JOBM1(I)*100.0/SUM5
0128        SICF1(I)=SICF1(I)*100.0/SUM3
0129        SICF2(I)=SICF2(I)*100.0/SUM4
0130        JOBM2(I)=JOBM2(I)*100.0/SUM6
0131        JOB1(I)=JOB1(I)*100.0/SUM7
0132        JOB2(I)=JOB2(I)*100.0/SUM8
0133        WRK1(I)=WRK1(I)*100.0/SUM9
0134        WRK2(I)=WRK2(I)*100.0/SUM10
0135        TOTAL1(I)=TOTAL1(I)*100.0/SUM11
0136        TOTAL2(I)=TOTAL2(I)*100.0/SUM12
0137     12 CONTINUE
0138        WRITE(6,116)
0139    116 FORMAT(/////)
0140        WRITE(6,115)(IS(I),PCENT1(I),PCENT2(I),SICF1(I),SICF2(I),
           1            JOBM1(I),JOBM2(I),JOB1(I),JOB2(I),WRK1(I),
           2WRK2(I),TOTAL1(I),TOTAL2(I),I=1,N)
0141    115 FORMAT(I5,5X,2F5.2,18X,10F9.2)
0142    117 FORMAT (1X,14F9.1)
0143        WRITE(6,116)
0144        WRITE(6,117)SUM1,SUM2,SUM3,SUM4,SUM5,SUM6,SUM7,SUM8,SUM9,SUM10,
           1SUM11,SUM12,SUM13,SUM14
0145        RETURN
0146        END
```

Print-out of Employment Estimate for District 62 (based on the four-county reference area)

SIC	FAR	Percent Land Allocated	Sq. Ft. Land Area	Sq. Ft. Floor Area	Main Shift Jobs	Total Jobs	Workers	Labor Force
2010	0.35	2.33	327,323	114,563	222	244	240	252
2020	0.46	1.54	216,418	110,634	303	353	347	364
2030	0.45	5.65	791,534	354,211	466	470	463	485
2040	0.42	1.10	153,571	65,268	58	70	69	72
2050	0.43	2.66	372,237	160,062	377	638	629	658
2070	0.75	0.76	105,909	79,432	124	180	177	185
2080	0.42	1.46	205,189	86,692	96	105	103	108
2090	0.42	0.73	102,348	42,986	75	93	91	96
2310	0.56	2.98	418,373	236,380	236	241	237	252
2320	0.35	1.44	201,331	71,150	373	380	374	398
2330	0.54	2.27	317,882	172,451	366	374	368	391
2340	0.35	0.18	25,525	9,021	67	68	67	71
2360	0.54	0.32	44,432	24,105	51	52	51	55
2380	0.54	0.71	99,914	54,204	103	107	105	112
2390	0.54	0.77	107,918	58,546	93	95	93	99
2620	0.34	1.91	267,586	91,648	258	385	380	389
2630	0.25	1.23	172,806	43,202	85	123	121	125
2640	0.38	8.12	1,138,422	426,908	761	1,001	986	1,102
2650	0.28	9.33	1,308,187	369,563	509	771	760	779
2810	0.39	3.73	522,643	205,137	300	399	393	403
2820	0.34	3.83	536,496	185,091	447	621	612	627
2830	0.41	5.38	754,723	311,323	884	1,106	1,089	1,117
2840	0.52	2.53	354,502	186,113	175	181	178	183
2850	0.63	0.39	54,436	34,022	39	42	41	42
2870	0.41	2.99	419,190	172,916	107	133	131	135
2890	0.34	2.25	315,062	108,696	140	170	168	172
3610	0.30	1.12	156,329	46,899	176	200	198	204
3620	0.32	3.39	475,379	154,498	463	571	564	581
3640	0.28	2.61	366,575	104,474	346	449	443	457

(continued)

Print-out continued

SIC	FAR	Percent Land Allocated	Sq. Ft. Land Area	Sq. Ft. Floor Area	Main Shift Jobs	Total Jobs	Workers	Labor Force
3650	0.32	0.80	112,839	36,673	107	132	130	134
3660	0.28	4.87	683,281	191,319	1,093	1,350	1,332	1,373
3670	0.27	2.54	356,451	96,955	513	693	684	705
3690	0.50	7.58	1,062,360	531,180	1,140	1,310	1,293	1,333
3810	0.38	0.20	28,438	10,664	51	51	50	52
3820	0.28	5.27	738,568	209,015	1,181	1,217	1,202	1,249
3830	0.48	0.08	11,262	5,406	17	18	18	18
3840	0.58	0.66	92,853	54,087	146	146	144	150
3860	0.48	0.16	22,589	10,843	27	28	27	28
3940	0.39	0.47	65,297	25,466	56	58	57	59
3960	0.39	0.65	91,701	35,763	114	116	115	119
3990	0.29	3.00	420,456	122,983	232	232	229	238
Total			14,018,303	5,400,531	12,375	14,973	14,761	15,283

The computer program produced figures based upon the Delaware County reference area as well as the four-county reference area.

Corrected Computer Program and Resultant Figures

P–1
Corrected Computer Program Employment by SIC by District
Base Data

```
0001          DIMENSION IS (300), EMP4C(300),EMPDC(300), FT
            1 WRK(300),FLRM(300),JB(300),JOB(300),EMPRAT(300),
            2 FLAREA(300),AREA(20)
0002          DIMENSION ISD(300),D1(300),D2(300),D3(300),
            2 D4(300),D5(3)),D6(300),D7(300),ID8(300)
0003          INTEGER FLAREA, DIST(20)
0004          REAL JB,JOB
0005      101 FORMAT(2X,I2,2X,F9.0)
0006          READ(5,101)(DIST(I),AREA(I),I=1,18)
0007          DO 2 N-1,251
0008          READ(5,104)IS(N),EMP4C(N),EMPDC(N),FTWRK(N)
            1 FLRM(N),JB(N),JOB(N),EMPRAT(N),FLAREA(N)
*0009         EMP4C(N)=EMP4C(N)*JB(N)
*0010         EMPDC(N)=EMPDC(N)*JB(N)
0011        2 CONTINUE
0012      104 FORMAT(6X,L4,1X,F6.0,1X,2F6.0,3X,F3.2,1X,
            1 F3.2,1X,F4.3,1X,F3.3,1X,I2)
0013          DO 1 K=1,18
0014          DO 3 I=1,251
0015          ISD(I)=IS(I)
0016          D1(I)=EMP4C(I)
0017          D2(I)=EMPDC(I)
```

*Lines added to correct the program. The change inserts "main shift job" between total jobs and floor area in the four-county reference area.

(continued)

P-1 continued

```
0018        D3(I)=FTWRK(I)
0019        D4(L)=FLRM(I)
0020        D5(I)–JB(I)
0021        D6(I)=JOB(I)
0022        D7(I)=EMPRAT(I)
0023        ID8(I)=FLAREA(I)
0024      3 CONTINUE
0025        CALL EMP(ISD, D1,D2,D3,D4,D5,D6,D7,ID8,DIST,AREA)
0026      1 CONTINUE
0027        END
```

P–2
Corrected Data

Districts	Main Shift Jobs	Total Jobs	Total Workers	Labor Force
Manufacturing				
13	22,529	26,615	26,023	26,842
22	3,312	3,847	3,776	3,902
35	15,568	17,963	17,323	17,971
53	10,751	12,476	12,129	12,533
54	9,227	10,529	10,310	10,706
62	12,560	14,919	14,709	15,241
All	73,947	86,250	84,270	87,195
Commercial				
11	3,638	4,268	4,007	4,159
12	220	258	242	251
21	5,338	6,246	5,864	6,086
31	3,263	3,795	3,567	3,689
32	4,030	4,872	4,556	4,730
33	805	932	876	906
34	1,540	1,769	1,660	1,728
41	1,493	1,747	1,640	1,702
51	1,346	1,575	1,478	1,534
52	875	1,024	961	998
61	422	494	463	481
All	22,970	26,980	25,314	26,264
Total	96,917	113,230	109,584	113,459

P–3

Corrected (A) and Uncorrected (B) Household Income by Township

	$0–1,999	$2,000–2,999	$3,000–3,999	$4,000–4,999	$5,000–5,999	$6,000–7,999	$8,000–9,999	$10,000–14,999	$15,000–24,999	$25,000+	All	$\left(\dfrac{A-B}{B}\right) \times 100$
Aston												
A	445	439	675	850	1,144	2,919	3,361	6,609	3,992	717	21,151	
–B	427	421	649	818	1,108	2,834	3,623	6,439	3,901	699	20,559	
	18	18	26	32	36	85	98	170	91	18	592	2.8 percent
Birmingham												
A	244	187	259	298	354	811	812	1,578	994	252	5,789	
–B	235	176	247	281	334	757	759	1,482	932	244	5,447	
	9	11	12	17	20	54	53	96	62	8	342	5.9 percent
Concord												
A	624	521	744	847	1,006	2,316	2,359	4,552	2,831	697	16,497	
–B	602	504	721	819	979	2,262	2,322	4,480	2,752	673	16,114	
	22	17	23	28	27	54	37	72	79	24	383	2.3 percent
Edgmont												
A	90	43	49	57	61	135	119	232	146	41	973	
–B	89	41	48	54	59	127	111	218	136	40	923	
	1	2	1	3	2	8	8	14	10	1	50	5.1 percent
Middletown												
A	457	418	614	744	972	2,412	2,737	5,207	3,019	545	17,125	
–B	452	413	602	727	951	2,349	2,661	5,079	2,965	539	16,738	
	5	5	12	17	21	63	76	128	54	6	387	2.3 percent
Thornbury												
A	239	211	329	415	559	1,377	1,682	3,458	2,276	422	10,968	
–B	236	209	326	412	557	1,377	1,680	3,465	2,287	422	10,971	
	3	2	3	3	2	0	2	–7	–11	0	–3	–

(continued)

P–3 continued

	$0–1,999	$2,000–2,999	$3,000–3,999	$4,000–4,999	$5,000–5,999	$6,000–7,999	$8,000–9,999	$10,000–14,999	$15,000–24,999	$25,000+	All	$\left(\frac{A-B}{B}\right) \times 100$
All												
A	2,099	1,819	2,670	3,211	4,096	9,970	11,070	21,636	13,258	2,674	72,503	
–B	2,041	1,764	2,593	3,111	3,988	9,706	10,796	21,163	12,973	2,617	70,752	
	58	55	77	100	108	264	274	473	285	57	1,751	2.4 percent

P–4

Corrected (A) and Uncorrected (B) Percentage Distribution of Household Income by Township

	$0–1,999	$2,000–2,999	$3,000–3,999	$4,000–4,999	$5,000–5,999	$6,000–7,999	$8,000–9,999	$10,000–14,999	$15,000–24,999	$25,000+	Total
Aston											
A	2.1	2.1	3.2	4.0	5.4	13.8	15.9	31.3	18.9	3.4	100
B	2.0	2.1	3.2	4.0	5.4	13.8	15.9	31.3	19.0	3.4	100
Birmingham											
A	4.2	3.2	4.5	5.2	6.1	14.0	14.0	27.3	17.2	4.4	100
B	4.3	3.2	4.5	5.2	6.1	13.9	13.9	27.2	17.1	4.5	100
Concord											
A	3.8	3.2	4.5	5.1	6.1	14.0	14.3	27.6	17.2	4.2	100
B	3.7	3.2	4.5	5.1	6.1	14.0	14.4	27.8	17.1	4.2	100
Edgmont											
A	9.3	4.4	5.0	5.9	6.3	13.9	12.2	23.8	15.0	4.2	100
B	9.6	4.7	5.2	5.9	6.4	13.7	12.0	23.6	14.7	4.3	100
Middletown											
A	2.7	2.4	3.6	4.3	5.7	14.0	16.0	30.4	17.6	3.2	100
B	2.8	2.5	3.6	4.3	5.7	14.0	15.9	30.3	17.7	3.2	100
Thornbury											
A	2.2	1.9	3.0	3.8	5.1	12.5	15.3	31.5	20.7	3.8	100
B	2.2	1.9	3.0	3.8	5.1	12.5	15.3	31.6	20.8	3.8	100

(Columns may not add to totals because of rounding.)

Appendix Q

Program for Weighting Two Sets (Male-Female) of Earnings Distributions

```
001          DIMENSION EARN(2,11,4),PCENT(2,11,15,4),EMEAN(3,11,4),
             1ERNNR(11,15,4),SUMERN(4),ERGDST(11,15,4),OCCSUM(4)
002     100  FORMAT(4X,I2,3X,14F4.3,F7.0,F6.0)
003          DO 1 II=1,11
004          READ(5,100)((IND,               (PCENT(I,II,J,K),J=1,14),
             1EMEAN(I,II,K),EARN(I,II,K),K=1,4),I=1,2)
005          SUM=0.
006          DO 3 K=1,4
007          DO 3 J=1,14
008       3  ERNNR(II,J,K)=PCENT(1,II,J,K)*EARN(1, II,K)+PCENT(2,II,J,K)*
             1EARN(2,II,K)
009          DO 4 I=1,4
010          EMEAN(3,II,I)=EARN(1,II,I)+EARN(2II,I)
011          EMEAN(3,II,I)=(EARN(1,II,I)/EMEAN(3,II,I))*EMEAN(1,II,I)+
             1(EARN(2,II,I)/EMEAN(3,II,I))*EMEAN(2,II,I)
012       4  SUMERN(I)=0.
013          DO 6 J=1,14
014          DO 6 K=1,14
015       6  ERGDST(II,J,K)=ERNNR(II,J,K)/(EARN(1,II,K)+EARN(2,II,K))
016          DO 7 I=1,4
017       7  SUM=SUM+EARN(1,II,I)+EARN(2 II,I)
018          DO 8 K=1,4
019       8  OCCSUM(K)=(EARN(1,II,K)+EARN(2,II,K))/SUM
020     110  FORMAT(1HO)
021          WRITE(6,112)IND
022          WRITE(6,114)((ERNNR(II,J,K),J=1,14),K=1,4)
023     114  FORMAT(1X,14F9.2)
024          WRITE(6,110)
025          WRITE(6,111)((ERGDST(II,J,K),J=1,14),EMEAN(3,II,K),K-1,4)
026          WRITE(6,110)
027          WRITE(6,111)(OCCSUM(K),K=1,4)
028          WRITE(6,110)
029          WRITE(7,113)(IND,K,(ERGDST(II,J,K),J=1,14),EMEAN(3,II,K),K=1,4)
030     113  FORMAT(I2,I1,14F5.2,F7.0)
031       1  CONTINUE
032          DO 10 II=1,2
```

(continued)

Appendix Q continued

```
033          DO 10 K=1,11
034          DO 10 J=1,4
035          SUM=0.
036          DO 11 I=1,14
037     11   SUM=SUM+PCENT(II,K,I,J)
038          IF(SUM.GT.0.99.AND.SUM.LT.1.01.) GO TO 10
039          WRITE(6,115)II,K,J,I,SUM
040    115   FORMAT(4I6,F12.3)
041     10   CONTINUE
042    111   FORMAT(1X,15F8.2)
043    112   FORMAT(' INDUSTRY',I4)
044          END
```

Occupational Coefficients by Three
Three-Digit SIC; U.S., 1975

SIC	Managers and Professionals	Clerical and Sales	Craftsmen and Operatives	Service, Laborers, Agricultural Workers	Industrial
0110	2.23	0.98	4.20	92.59	12
0120	2.23	0.98	4.20	92.59	12
0130	2.23	0.98	4.20	92.59	12
0140	2.23	0.98	4.20	92.59	12
0190	2.23	0.98	4.20	92.59	12
0710[a]	2.23	0.98	4.20	92.59	12
0720[a]	2.23	0.98	4.20	92.59	12
0730[a]	2.23	0.98	4.20	92.59	12
0740[a]	2.23	0.98	4.20	92.59	12
0810	56.22	10.41	15.54	17.83	12
0820	56.22	10.41	15.54	17.83	12
0840	56.22	10.41	15.54	17.83	12
0850	56.22	10.41	15.54	17.83	12
0860	56.22	10.41	15.54	17.83	12
0910	12.74	4.47	10.60	72.20	12
0980	12.74	4.47	10.60	72.20	12
1010	12.43	6.50	78.17	2.92	12
1020	12.43	6.50	78.17	2.92	12
1030	12.43	6.50	78.17	2.92	12
1040	12.43	6.50	78.17	2.92	12
1050	12.43	6.50	78.17	2.92	12
1060	12.43	6.50	78.17	2.92	12
1080	12.43	6.50	78.17	2.92	12
1090	12.43	6.50	78.17	2.92	12
1110	7.78	4.94	86.38	0.90	12
1210	7.78	4.94	86.38	0.90	12
1310	31.26	16.08	51.77	0.88	12
1320	31.26	16.08	51.77	0.88	12
1380	31.26	16.08	51.77	0.88	12
1410	16.47	8.66	73.07	1.79	12

[a] SICs 0100–0700 were assigned coefficients from Agriculture.

(continued)

Appendix R continued

SIC	Managers and Professionals	Clerical and Sales	Craftsmen and Operatives	Service, Laborers, Agricultural Workers	Industrial
1420	16.47	8.66	73.07	1.79	12
1440	16.47	8.66	73.07	1.79	12
1450	16.47	8.66	73.07	1.79	12
1470	16.47	8.66	73.07	1.79	12
1480	16.47	8.66	73.07	1.79	12
1490	16.47	8.66	73.07	1.79	12
1510[b]	28.49	6.42	60.74	14.35	1
1610[b]	28.49	6.42	60.74	14.35	1
1620[b]	28.49	6.42	60.74	14.35	1
1710[b]	28.49	6.42	60.74	14.35	1
1720[b]	28.49	6.42	60.74	14.35	1
1730[b]	28.49	6.42	60.74	14.35	1
1740[b]	28.49	6.42	60.74	14.35	1
1750[b]	28.49	6.42	60.74	14.35	1
1760[b]	28.49	6.42	60.74	14.35	1
1770[b]	28.49	6.42	60.74	14.35	1
1780[b]	28.49	6.42	60.74	14.35	1
1790[b]	28.49	6.42	60.74	14.35	1
1910[c]	19.57	13.82	60.53	6.07	2
1920[c]	19.57	13.82	60.53	6.07	2
1930[c]	19.57	13.82	60.53	6.07	2
1940[c]	19.57	13.82	60.53	6.07	2
1950[c]	19.57	13.82	60.53	6.07	2
1960[c]	19.57	13.82	60.53	6.07	2
1990[c]	19.57	13.82	60.53	6.07	2
2010	10.72	15.43	65.34	8.45	3
2020	13.51	20.58	61.86	4.15	3
2030	11.53	16.29	62.63	9.64	3
2040	19.36	16.88	53.56	10.21	3
2050	6.09	16.88	71.56	5.47	3
2060	15.08	20.60	54.99	9.34	3
2070	15.08	20.60	54.99	9.34	3
2080	13.98	16.72	59.68	9.61	3
2090	15.08	20.60	54.99	9.34	3
2110	10.22	15.89	63.30	10.60	3
2120	10.22	15.89	63.30	10.60	3
2130	10.22	15.89	63.30	10.60	3
2140	10.22	15.89	63.30	10.60	3
2210	6.98	10.32	77.64	5.06	3
2220	6.98	10.32	77.64	5.06	3
2230	6.98	10.32	77.64	5.06	3
2240	6.98	10.32	77.64	5.06	3
2250	6.98	10.32	77.64	5.06	3
2260	6.98	10.32	77.64	5.06	3
2270	6.98	10.32	77.64	5.06	3
2280	6.98	10.32	77.64	5.06	3
2290	6.98	10.32	77.64	5.06	3
2310	5.21	10.17	82.76	1.88	3

[b]SICs 1500–1700 were assigned coefficients from Contract Construction.
[c]SIC 1900 was assigned coefficients from Durable Manufacturing.

SIC	Managers and Professionals	Clerical and Sales	Craftsmen and Operatives	Service, Laborers, Agricultural Workers	Industrial
2320	5.21	10.17	82.76	1.88	3
2330	5.21	10.17	82.76	1.88	3
2340	5.21	10.17	82.76	1.88	3
2350	5.21	10.17	82.76	1.88	3
2360	5.21	10.17	82.76	1.88	3
2370	5.21	10.17	82.76	1.88	3
2380	5.21	10.17	82.76	1.88	3
2390	5.21	10.17	82.76	1.88	3
2410	11.04	1.30	28.88	58.78	2
2420	9.23	8.68	63.29	27.09	2
2430	9.23	8.68	63.29	27.09	2
2440	9.23	8.68	63.29	27.09	2
2490	9.23	8.68	63.29	27.09	2
2510	9.55	13.57	71.97	4.91	2
2520	9.55	13.57	71.97	4.91	2
2530	9.55	13.57	71.97	4.91	2
2540	9.55	13.57	71.97	4.91	2
2590	9.55	13.57	71.97	4.91	2
2610	13.96	11.62	67.36	7.07	3
2620	13.96	11.62	67.36	7.07	3
2630	13.96	11.62	67.36	7.07	3
2640	11.66	18.06	66.27	4.05	3
2650	10.40	15.42	68.58	5.60	3
2660	11.66	18.06	66.27	4.05	3
2710	20.37	38.46	38.78	2.41	3
2720	20.37	38.46	38.78	2.41	3
2730	20.37	38.46	38.78	2.41	3
2740	20.37	38.46	38.78	2.41	3
2750	20.37	38.46	38.78	2.41	3
2760	20.37	38.46	38.78	2.41	3
2770	20.37	38.46	38.78	2.41	3
2780	20.37	38.46	38.78	2.41	3
2790	20.37	38.46	38.78	2.41	3
2810	31.22	16.60	48.43	3.75	3
2820	22.96	7.33	64.94	4.77	3
2830	44.25	22.68	28.82	4.25	3
2840	31.22	16.60	48.43	3.75	3
2850	30.54	27.16	35.77	6.53	3
2860	30.54	27.16	35.77	6.53	3
2870	31.22	16.60	48.43	3.75	3
2890	31.22	16.60	48.43	3.75	3
2910	34.82	19.40	42.07	3.72	3
2950	16.21	27.18	46.18	10.42	3
2990	16.21	27.18	46.18	10.42	3
3010	12.31	14.89	65.75	7.05	3
3020	12.31	14.89	65.75	7.05	3
3030	12.31	14.89	65.75	7.05	3
3060	12.31	14.89	65.75	7.05	3
3070	13.40	16.68	65.75	4.17	3

(continued)

Appendix R continued

SIC	Managers and Professionals	Clerical and Sales	Craftsmen and Operatives	Service, Laborers, Agricultural Workers	Industrial
3110	11.54	8.75	67.19	12.53	3
3120	4.45	12.86	79.49	3.20	3
3130	4.45	12.86	79.49	3.20	3
3140	8.67	13.19	74.04	4.10	3
3150	4.45	12.86	79.49	3.20	3
3160	4.45	12.86	79.49	3.20	3
3170	4.45	12.86	79.49	3.20	3
3190	5.91	12.72	77.41	3.96	3
3210	14.66	13.95	61.39	9.99	2
3220	13.22	11.38	68.16	7.23	2
3230	14.66	13.95	61.39	9.99	2
3240	14.66	13.95	61.39	9.99	2
3250	11.65	12.42	50.90	25.04	2
3260	10.10	13.40	69.48	7.03	2
3270	17.33	14.81	57.47	10.79	2
3280	12.05	16.77	62.24	3.14	2
3290	12.05	16.77	62.24	3.14	2
3310	9.50	12.03	61.93	16.54	2
3320	10.64	12.18	65.28	11.89	2
3330	13.33	13.69	65.99	6.98	2
3340	10.64	12.18	65.28	11.89	2
3350	10.64	12.18	65.28	11.89	2
3360	10.64	12.18	65.28	11.89	2
3390	9.70	10.86	70.09	9.35	2
3410	19.79	15.46	60.10	4.65	2
3420	19.79	15.46	60.10	4.65	2
3430	19.79	15.46	60.10	4.65	2
3440	19.79	15.46	60.10	4.65	2
3450	19.79	15.46	60.10	4.65	2
3460	19.79	15.46	60.10	4.65	2
3470	19.79	15.46	60.10	4.65	2
3480	19.79	15.46	60.10	4.65	2
3490	19.79	15.46	60.10	4.65	2
3510	22.53	14.91	59.48	3.08	2
3520	18.32	15.79	61.53	4.36	2
3530	18.32	15.79	61.53	4.36	2
3540	18.32	15.79	61.53	4.36	2
3550	18.32	15.79	61.53	4.36	2
3560	18.32	15.79	61.53	4.36	2
3570	36.22	17.90	44.76	1.20	2
3580	18.32	15.79	61.53	4.36	2
3590	20.68	14.33	61.72	3.28	2
3610	28.16	13.82	55.27	2.75	2
3620	28.16	13.82	55.27	2.75	2
3630	28.16	13.82	55.27	2.75	2
3640	28.16	13.82	55.27	2.75	2
3650	28.16	13.82	55.27	2.75	2
3660	28.16	13.82	55.27	2.75	2
3670	28.16	13.82	55.27	2.75	2
3690	28.16	13.82	55.27	2.75	2
3710	13.39	9.72	71.32	5.57	2

SIC	Managers and Professionals	Clerical and Sales	Craftsmen and Operatives	Service, Laborers, Agricultural Workers	Industrial
3720	32.00	16.35	49.53	2.12	2
3730	13.38	9.07	71.46	6.08	2
3740	13.07	12.85	67.55	6.53	2
3750	19.38	11.97	64.04	4.61	2
3790	19.38	11.97	64.04	4.61	2
3810	32.64	17.39	47.89	2.09	2
3820	32.64	17.39	47.89	2.09	2
3830	32.64	17.39	47.89	2.09	2
3840	32.64	17.39	47.89	2.09	2
3850	32.64	17.39	47.89	2.09	2
3860	32.64	17.39	47.89	2.09	2
3870	13.14	17.87	67.41	1.58	2
3910	12.65	18.35	65.53	3.47	2
3930	12.65	18.35	65.53	3.47	2
3940	12.65	18.35	65.53	3.47	2
3950	12.65	18.35	65.53	3.47	2
3960	12.65	18.35	65.53	3.47	2
3990	12.65	18.35	65.53	3.47	2
4010	14.22	20.26	53.43	12.09	4
4020	14.22	20.26	53.43	12.09	4
4040	14.22	20.26	53.43	12.09	4
4110	5.50	9.54	78.60	6.36	4
4120	5.34	10.58	83.64	0.44	4
4130	5.50	9.54	78.60	6.36	4
4140	5.50	9.54	78.60	6.36	4
4150	5.50	9.54	78.60	6.36	4
4170	5.50	9.54	78.60	6.36	4
4210	8.38	15.66	65.64	3.04	4
4220	19.03	24.65	37.84	25.78	4
4230	19.03	24.65	37.84	25.78	4
4410	25.65	16.73	22.54	35.09	4
4420	25.65	16.73	22.54	35.09	4
4430	25.65	16.73	22.54	35.09	4
4440	25.65	16.73	22.54	35.09	4
4450	25.65	16.73	22.54	35.09	4
4460	25.65	16.73	22.54	35.09	4
4510	21.26	33.35	29.08	16.30	4
4520	21.26	33.35	29.08	16.30	4
4580	21.26	33.35	29.08	16.30	4
4610[d]	17.47	20.26	58.46	3.82	4
4710	16.72	63.73	8.58	10.97	4
4720	16.72	63.73	8.58	10.97	4
4730	16.72	63.73	8.58	10.97	4
4740	16.72	63.73	8.58	10.97	4
4780	16.72	63.73	8.58	10.97	4
4810	12.97	52.00	32.24	2.79	4
4820	14.96	59.32	24.05	1.66	4

[d]SIC 4610 was assigned coefficients from SIC 4600.

(continued)

Appendix R continued

SIC	Managers and Professionals	Clerical and Sales	Craftsmen and Operatives	Service, Laborers, Agricultural Workers	Industrial
4830	70.22	21.74	5.70	2.34	4
4890	16.84	31.40	41.00	10.76	4
4910	14.32	16.94	51.22	17.51	4
4920	14.32	16.94	51.22	17.51	4
4930	14.32	16.94	51.22	17.51	4
4940	16.22	23.92	49.90	9.95	4
4950	4.51	3.35	50.01	42.13	4
4960	14.32	16.94	51.22	17.51	4
4970	16.22	23.92	49.90	9.95	4
5010	29.72	50.12	16.61	3.55	5
5020	23.80	54.55	17.41	4.25	5
5030	27.77	56.76	13.28	2.19	5
5040	16.12	30.79	44.38	8.70	5
5050	24.18	35.33	30.64	9.85	5
5060	28.20	54.83	13.21	3.75	5
5070	28.20	54.83	13.21	3.75	5
5080	27.22	44.86	25.06	2.84	5
5090	24.18	35.33	30.64	9.85	5
5210	23.69	33.57	35.42	7.32	6
5220	23.69	33.57	35.42	7.32	6
5230	23.69	33.57	35.42	7.32	6
5240	23.69	33.57	35.42	7.32	6
5250	23.69	33.57	35.42	7.32	6
5310	16.59	67.18	8.48	7.75	6
5320	16.59	67.18	8.48	7.75	6
5330	16.59	67.18	8.48	7.75	6
5340	16.59	67.18	8.58	7.75	6
5350	16.59	67.18	8.58	7.75	6
5390	16.59	67.18	8.58	7.75	6
5410	21.10	47.45	19.92	11.53	6
5420	21.10	47.45	19.92	11.53	6
5430	21.10	47.45	19.92	11.53	6
5440	21.10	47.45	19.92	11.53	6
5450	21.10	47.45	19.92	11.53	6
5460	21.10	47.45	19.92	11.53	6
5490	21.10	47.45	19.92	11.53	6
5510	22.93	30.12	39.74	7.21	6
5520	22.93	30.12	39.74	7.21	6
5530	22.93	30.12	39.74	7.21	6
5540	25.17	3.94	68.54	2.35	6
5590	22.93	30.12	39.74	7.21	6
5610	22.07	62.13	10.87	4.93	6
5620	22.07	62.13	10.87	4.93	6
5630	22.07	62.13	10.87	4.93	6
5640	22.07	62.13	10.87	4.93	6
5650	22.07	62.13	10.87	4.93	6
5660	22.07	62.13	10.87	4.93	6
5670	22.07	62.13	10.87	4.93	6
5680	22.07	62.13	10.87	4.93	6
5690	22.07	62.13	10.87	4.93	6
5710	21.53	42.68	31.76	4.03	6

SIC	Managers and Professionals	Clerical and Sales	Craftsmen and Operatives	Service, Laborers, Agricultural Workers	Industrial
5720	21.53	42.68	31.76	4.03	6
5730	21.53	42.68	31.76	4.03	6
5810	18.16	5.95	2.42	73.46	6
5910	29.16	50.03	6.10	14.70	6
5920	24.99	49.79	21.06	4.16	6
5930	24.99	49.79	21.06	4.16	6
5940	24.99	49.79	21.06	4.16	6
5950	24.99	49.79	21.06	4.16	6
6510	27.66	51.09	5.30	15.96	7
6530	27.66	51.09	5.30	15.96	7
6540	27.66	51.09	5.30	15.96	7
6550	27.66	51.09	5.30	15.96	7
6560	27.66	51.09	5.30	15.96	7
6610	28.62	63.33	2.02	6.02	7
6710	28.62	63.33	2.02	6.02	7
6720	28.62	63.33	2.02	6.02	7
6730	28.62	63.33	2.02	6.02	7
6790	28.62	63.33	2.02	6.02	7
7010	22.21	11.02	6.55	60.23	8
7020	22.21	11.02	6.55	60.23	8
7030	22.21	11.02	6.55	60.23	8
7040	22.21	11.02	6.55	60.23	8
7210	15.41	17.76	63.92	2.90	8
7220	24.99	49.79	21.06	4.16	8
7230	24.99	49.79	21.06	4.16	8
7240	24.99	49.79	21.06	4.16	8
7250	24.99	49.79	21.06	4.16	8
7260	24.99	49.79	21.06	4.16	8
7270	24.99	49.79	21.06	4.16	8
7290	24.99	49.79	21.06	4.16	8
7310	49.85	41.54	6.96	1.65	9
7320	32.40	32.02	18.53	17.06	9
7330	32.40	32.02	18.53	17.06	9
7340	32.40	32.02	18.53	17.06	9
5960	24.99	49.79	21.06	4.16	6
5970	24.99	49.79	21.06	4.16	6
5980	24.99	49.79	21.06	4.16	6
5990	24.99	49.79	21.06	4.16	6
6010	36.19	57.50	1.31	5.00	7
6020	36.19	57.50	1.31	5.00	7
6030	36.19	57.50	1.31	5.00	7
6040	36.19	57.50	1.31	5.00	7
6050	36.19	57.50	1.31	5.00	7
6110	36.19	57.50	1.31	5.00	7
6120	36.19	57.50	1.31	5.00	7
6130	36.19	57.50	1.31	5.00	7
6140	36.19	57.50	1.31	5.00	7
6150	36.19	57.50	1.31	5.00	7
6160	36.19	57.50	1.31	5.00	7

(continued)

Appendix R continued

SIC	Managers and Professionals	Clerical and Sales	Craftsmen and Operatives	Service, Laborers, Agricultural Workers	Industrial
6210	38.23	58.90	1.27	1.60	7
6220	38.23	58.90	1.27	1.60	7
6230	38.23	58.90	1.27	1.60	7
6280	38.23	58.90	1.27	1.60	7
6310	18.51	78.94	0.92	1.62	7
6320	18.51	78.94	0.92	1.62	7
6330	18.51	78.94	0.92	1.62	7
6350	18.51	78.94	0.92	1.62	7
6360	18.51	78.94	0.92	1.62	7
6390	18.51	78.94	0.92	1.62	7
6410	18.51	78.94	0.92	1.62	7
7350	32.40	32.02	18.53	17.06	9
7360	32.40	32.02	18.53	17.06	9
7390	32.40	32.02	18.53	17.06	9
7510	16.76	7.75	68.06	7.43	9
7520	16.76	7.75	68.06	7.43	9
7530	16.76	7.75	68.06	7.43	9
7540	16.76	7.75	68.06	7.43	9
7620	13.51	7.60	75.91	2.97	9
7630	13.51	7.60	75.91	2.97	9
7640	13.51	7.60	75.91	2.97	9
7690	13.51	7.60	75.91	2.97	9
7810	46.83	20.83	15.02	17.33	13
7820	46.83	20.83	15.02	17.33	13
7830	46.83	20.83	15.02	17.33	13
7910	31.41	9.18	8.21	51.19	13
7920	31.41	9.18	8.21	51.19	13
7930	31.41	9.18	8.21	51.19	13
7940	31.41	9.18	8.21	51.19	13
8010	46.44	25.34	2.16	26.06	10
8020	46.44	25.34	2.16	26.06	10
8030	46.44	25.34	2.16	26.06	10
8040	46.44	25.34	2.16	26.06	10
8060	37.41	11.45	2.86	46.28	10
8070	46.44	25.34	2.16	26.06	10
8090	46.44	25.34	2.16	26.06	10
8110	55.37	43.74	0.10	0.79	10
8210	64.20	15.28	4.30	16.22	10
8220	64.20	15.28	4.30	16.22	10
8230	64.20	15.28	4.30	16.22	10
8240	64.20	15.28	4.30	16.22	10
8290	64.20	15.28	4.30	16.22	10
8410[e]	64.20	15.28	4.30	16.22	10
8420[e]	64.20	15.28	4.30	16.22	10
8610	36.64	35.07	4.36	22.92	10
8620	36.64	35.07	4.36	22.92	10
8630	36.64	35.07	4.36	22.92	10
8640	36.64	35.07	4.36	22.92	10
8650	36.64	35.07	4.36	22.92	10

[e]SICs 8410 and 8420 were assigned coefficients from SIC 8200.

Appendix R continued

SIC	Managers and Professionals	Clerical and Sales	Craftsmen and Operatives	Service, Laborers, Agricultural Workers	Industrial
8660	45.72	18.50	5.40	30.38	10
8670	45.72	18.50	5.40	30.38	10
8690 f	36.64	35.07	4.36	22.92	10
8810 f	0.00	0.00	0.00	100.00	14
8910	78.12	13.54	6.90	1.43	10
8920	66.15	21.33	9.33	3.17	10
8930	62.50	36.84	0.24	0.42	10
8990	66.15	21.33	9.33	3.17	10
9110	6.95	81.84	2.60	8.61	11
9120	36.29	38.37	19.21	6.12	11
9200	39.41	34.63	8.52	17.45	11
9300	24.22	22.06	8.94	44.78	11

f SIC 8810 is assumed to be comprised entirely of service and laborer occupations.

Source: U.S., Bureau of Labor Statistics, *Occupational Employment Patterns for 1960 and 1975*, Bulletin 1599, (Washington: Government Printing Office, 1968.)

Effect on Mean Income Estimates of Substituting 1975 U.S. Occupational Coefficients for Adjusted 1975 Philadelphia Occupational Coefficients

SIC	Occupational Group	1960 Coefficients			1975 Coefficients		1969 Mean Income, by Industry of SIC, U.S. (6)	1969 Mean Income		Philadelphia Employment		Weighted 1969 Mean Income	
		Philadelphia (1)	U.S. (2)	(1÷2) (3)	U.S. (4)	Philadelphia [Adjusted] (3×4) (5)		U.S. (4×6) (7)	Philadelphia (5×6) (8)	Number (9)	Percent (10)	U.S. (7×10) (11)	Philadelphia (8×10) (12)
20	1	0.081	0.114	0.71	0.123	0.087	15,772	1,940	1,372				
	2	0.179	0.167	1.07	0.176	0.188	12,811	2,255	2,408				
	3	0.662	0.598	1.11	0.622	0.690	10,022	6,234	6,915				
	4	0.078	0.121	0.64	0.080	0.051	8,310	665	424				
	All	1.000	1.000	1.00	1.001	1.006	a) $11,444	$11,094	$11,119 ÷ 1.006* = $11,053; $11,053 ÷ $11,094 = 0.996**	32,462	0.428	$4,748	$4,730
35	1	0.172	0.169	1.02	0.225	0.230	16,335	3,675	3,757				
	2	0.174	0.156	1.12	0.149	0.167	11,643	1,735	1,944				
	3	0.622	0.630	0.99	0.595	0.589	10,717	6,377	6,312				
	4	0.031	0.045	0.69	0.031	0.021	8,406	261	177				
	All	0.999	1.000	0.99	1.000	1.007	b) $11,852	$12,048	$12,190 ÷ 1.007* = $12,105; $12,105 ÷ $12,048 = 1.005**	11,520	0.152	$1,831	$1,840
53	1	0.140	0.215	0.65	0.166	0.108	13,070	2,170	1,412				
	2	0.684	0.629	1.09	0.672	0.732	9,680	6,505	7,086				
	3	0.088	0.077	1.14	0.085	0.097	9,071	771	880				
	4	0.088	0.079	1.11	0.078	0.087	6,486	506	564				
	All	1.000	1.000	1.00	1.001	1.024	c) $10,411	$ 9,952	$ 9,942 ÷ 1.024* = $9,709; $ 9,709 ÷ $9,952 = 0.975**	21,315	0.281	$2,797	$2,728
73	1	0.287	0.359	0.80	0.336	0.269	14,105	4,739	3,794				
	2	0.404	0.327	1.24	0.327	0.405	11,914	3,896	4,825				
	3	0.165	0.169	0.98	0.178	0.174	9,332	1,661	1,624				
	4	0.144	0.145	0.99	0.160	0.158	8,527	1,364	1,347				
	All	1.000	1.000	1.00	1.001	1.006	d) $11,313	$11,660	$11,590 ÷ 1.006* = $11,521; $11,521 ÷ $11,660 = 0.988**	10,632	0.140	$1,632	$1,613
Total										75,920	1.000	$11,008	$10,911

$10,911 ÷ $11,008 = 0.991**

Sources: 1. U.S., Bureau of the Census, *1960 Census of Population Detailed Characteristics, Pennsylvania* (Washington: Government Printing Office, 1963).

2. and 4. U.S. Department of Labor, Bureau of Labor Statistics, *Occupational Employment Patterns for 1960 and 1975*, Bulletin 1599: (Washington, Government Printing Office, 1968).

5. Column 3 × Column 4.

6. U.S., Bureau of the Census, *Current Population Reports*, "Income in 1969 of Families and Persons in the U.S.," Table 35, p. 75, (Washington, 1970).
  a). Nondurable Goods Mean Income
  b). Durable Goods Mean Income
  c). Retail Goods Mean Income
  d). Business Goods Mean Income

7. Column 4 × Column 6.

8. Column 5 × Column 6.

9. and 10. U.S. Department of Commerce, *County Business Patterns 1969*, (Washington, Government Printing Office, 1970).

11. Column 7 × Column 10.

12. Column 8 × Column 10.

*The Philadelphia mean income is overestimated by the difference between the sum of the occupational coefficients shown in column 5 and 1.00, e.g., 1.006–1.000 = .006; therefore the estimate 1.006 is adjusted for SIC 20 by dividing by 1.006. For SIC 35, we divide by 1.007, etc.

**The ratio of the estimated Philadelphia mean income in the industry to the average for the U.S. industry as a whole.

Appendix T

Percentage Distribution of All Worker Earnings by Industry and Occupation Group, U.S., 1969

	<$1,000 (1)	$1,000 <1,500 (2)	$1,500 <2,000 (3)	$2,000 <2,500 (4)	$2,500 <3,000 (5)	$3,000 <4,000 (6)	$4,000 <5,000 (7)
Industry 1 *Occupational Group*							
1.	0.03	0.02	0.01	0.02	0.01	0.03	0.04
2.	0.19	0.06	0.06	0.04	0.05	0.20	0.12
3.	0.07	0.03	0.03	0.03	0.03	0.06	0.08
4.	0.26	0.05	0.06	0.05	0.05	0.10	0.08
Industry 2 *Occupational Group*							
1.	0.01	0.00	0.01	0.01	0.01	0.01	0.02
2.	0.06	0.03	0.03	0.03	0.04	0.07	0.12
3.	0.06	0.03	0.02	0.03	0.02	0.08	0.08
4.	0.16	0.05	0.05	0.05	0.02	0.11	0.09
Industry 3 *Occupational Group*							
1	0.02	0.01	0.02	0.01	0.00	0.02	0.04
2.	0.20	0.04	0.03	0.04	0.03	0.09	0.12
3.	0.11	0.04	0.04	0.05	0.04	0.14	0.12
4.	0.21	0.06	0.05	0.06	0.04	0.13	0.10
Industry 4 *Occupational Group*							
1.	0.02	0.01	0.01	0.01	0.01	0.03	0.02
2.	0.08	0.03	0.04	0.04	0.05	0.08	0.11
3.	0.04	0.02	0.02	0.03	0.02	0.04	0.05
4.	0.10	0.08	0.04	0.04	0.02	0.09	0.08
Industry 5 *Occupational Group*							
1.	0.06	0.02	0.02	0.01	0.01	0.02	0.03
2.	0.10	0.04	0.03	0.03	0.03	0.09	0.09
3.	0.15	0.04	0.04	0.04	0.02	0.07	0.08
4.	0.30	0.04	0.05	0.04	0.04	0.11	0.10
Industry 6 *Occupational Group*							
1.	0.08	0.03	0.02	0.03	0.02	0.06	0.07
2.	0.34	0.10	0.08	0.06	0.05	0.11	0.08
3.	0.18	0.07	0.04	0.04	0.04	0.08	0.09
4.	0.47	0.12	0.08	0.06	0.05	0.09	0.04
Industry 7 *Occupationl Group*							
1.	0.05	0.02	0.02	0.01	0.01	0.03	0.04
2.	0.10	0.05	0.04	0.05	0.04	0.12	0.17

$5,000 <6,000 (8)	$6,000 <7,000 (9)	$7,000 <8,000 (10)	$8,000 <10,000 (11)	$10,000 <15,000 (12)	$15,000 <25,000 (13)	$25,000 or more (14)	Total
0.04	0.06	0.06	0.14	0.29	0.19	0.05	1.00
0.10	0.07	0.06	0.03	0.01	0.0	0.0	1.00
0.10	0.09	0.09	0.15	0.22	0.03	0.00	1.00
0.10	0.06	0.07	0.06	0.04	0.01	0.0	1.00
0.04	0.05	0.06	0.15	0.36	0.23	0.05	1.00
0.14	0.12	0.11	0.12	0.10	0.02	0.01	1.00
0.10	0.11	0.12	0.18	0.15	0.02	0.0	1.00
0.10	0.11	0.10	0.11	0.04	0.00	0.0	1.00
0.05	0.06	0.07	0.16	0.31	0.16	0.06	1.00
0.11	0.08	0.05	0.10	0.08	0.03	0.01	1.00
0.09	0.07	0.07	0.11	0.09	0.01	0.0	1.00
0.11	0.09	0.06	0.06	0.03	0.0	0.0	1.00
0.04	0.07	0.07	0.18	0.34	0.15	0.04	1.00
0.14	0.13	0.11	0.11	0.07	0.01	0.00	1.00
0.08	0.10	0.11	0.20	0.25	0.03	0.00	1.00
0.11	0.11	0.09	0.08	0.09	0.01	0.0	1.00
0.05	0.07	0.09	0.12	0.25	0.17	0.09	1.00
0.10	0.07	0.10	0.09	0.15	0.05	0.03	1.00
0.08	0.11	0.10	0.15	0.10	0.01	0.00	1.00
0.08	0.08	0.05	0.10	0.01	0.0	0.0	1.00
0.09	0.08	0.09	0.14	0.18	0.10	0.03	1.00
0.05	0.04	0.03	0.03	0.03	0.01	0.00	1.00
0.10	0.09	0.09	0.09	0.07	0.01	0.00	1.00
0.04	0.02	0.01	0.01	0.01	0.00	0.0	1.00
0.04	0.07	0.08	0.13	0.25	0.15	0.08	1.00
0.12	0.08	0.06	0.07	0.06	0.03	0.01	1.00

(continued)

	<$1,000 (1)	$1,000 <1,500 (2)	$1,500 <2,000 (3)	$2,000 <2,500 (4)	$2,500 <3,000 (5)	$3,000 <4,000 (6)	$4,000 <5,000 (7)
Occupational Group							
3.	0.11	0.09	0.05	0.03	0.04	0.11	0.06
4.	0.32	0.12	0.03	0.03	0.06	0.11	0.13
Industry 9 *Occupational Group*							
1.	0.09	0.03	0.02	0.02	0.02	0.03	0.05
2.	0.29	0.09	0.05	0.06	0.03	0.10	0.11
3.	0.13	0.04	0.03	0.04	0.03	0.08	0.08
4.	0.32	0.10	0.05	0.05	0.03	0.08	0.12
Industry 8 *Occupational Group*							
1.	0.28	0.05	0.03	0.04	0.03	0.05	0.05
2.	0.30	0.13	0.10	0.07	0.06	0.14	0.08
3.	0.27	0.08	0.09	0.08	0.09	0.12	0109
4.	0.64	0.09	0.05	0.04	0.03	0.05	0.03
Industry 10 *Occupational Group*							
1.	0.14	0.05	0.05	0.05	0.03	0.08	0.07
2.	0.24	0.08	0.08	0.06	0.04	0.13	0.13
3.	0.14	0.05	0.05	0.06	0.03	0.10	0.09
4.	0.28	0.10	0.09	0.08	0.06	0.14	0.10
Industry 11 *Occupational Group*							
1.	0.05	0.01	0.02	0.01	0.01	0.03	0.04
2.	0.11	0.04	0.02	0.03	0.02	0.06	0.10
3.	0.04	0.02	0.04	0.01	0.01	0.06	0.05
4.	0.13	0.05	0.02	0.03	0.02	0.04	0.05

$5,000 <6,000 (8)	$6,000 <7,000 (9)	$7,000 <8,000 (10)	$8,000 <10,000 (11)	$10,000 <15,000 (12)	$15,000 <25,000 (13)	$25,000 or more (14)	Total
0.11	0.13	0.08	0.10	0.10	0.01	0.0	1.00
0.07	0.04	0.04	0.04	0.02	0.0	0.0	1.00
0.05	0.06	0.07	0.13	0.20	0.18	0.04	1.00
0.07	0.05	0.05	0.03	0.04	0.02	0.01	1.00
0.14	0.10	0.10	0.11	0.10	0.02	0.00	1.00
0.09	0.051	0.04	0.05	0.02	0.0	0.00	1.00
0.10	0.06	0.07	0.06	0.10	0.05	0.02	1.00
0.07	0.02	0.00	0.01	0.00	0.0	0.0	1.00
0.04	0.05	0.03	0.04	0.02	0.00	0.0	1.00
0.02	0.01	0.01	0.01	0.00	0.00	0.0	1.00
0.07	0.07	0.06	0.09	0.13	0.07	0.04	1.00
0.11	0.06	0.04	0.02	0.01	0.00	0.0	1.00
0.08	0.07	0.11	0.12	0.09	0.00	0.0	1.00
0.07	0.05	0.02	0.01	0.01	0.00	0.0	1.00
0.04	0.07	0.08	0.16	0.30	0.15	0.02	1.00
0.11	0.13	0.14	0.16	0.06	0.01	0.00	1.00
0.08	0.12	0.15	0.27	0.15	0.00	0.0	1.00
0.08	0.11	0.10	0.18	0.18	0.02	0.0	1.00

Housing Demand Algorithm, Computer Program, and Data Inputs

U-1
Housing Demand Algorithm, Computer Program, and Data Inputs

```
1              REAL*8 TNAME
2              INTEGER*4 HHNO(10)
3              REAL*TOTHH,TOTU,PEPCEN(10,2),RENOWN(10,2),VALMAT
        1 (10,6),VALUM(10,6) ,RENMAT(10,4) ,RENTM(10,4) ,QUOT,
        2 VALUE(6)/6*0.0/ ,RENT(4)/4*0.0/
4      1000 DO 10 I=1,10
5        10 READ(5,2)(PERCEN(I,J),J=1,2)
6         2 FORMAT (6F5.3)
7           DO 20 I=1,10
8        20 READ(5,2)(VALMAT(I,J),J=1,6)
9           DO 30 I=1,10
10       30 READ(5,2)(R NMAT(I,J),J=1,4)
11       40 READ(5,1,END=9000) HHNO,TOTHH,TOTU,TNAME
12        1 FORMAT(10I6,2F6.0,A8(
13     2000 QUOT=TOTO/TOTHH
14           IF(QUOT.GT.10) QUOT=1.0
15     2500 DO 50 I=1,10
16           HHNO(I)-HHNO(I)*QUOT+.5
17           DO 50 J=1,2
18       50 RENOWN(1,J)=PERCEN(I,J)*HHNO(I)
19     3000 WRITE(6,3) TNAME
20        3 FORMAT('1',20X,A8,' TOWNSHIP'//' 2000 2000-2999
        1 3000-3999   4000-4999   5000-5999   6000-7999   8000-9999
        2 10-14,999   15-24,999   25,000+')
21           WRITE(6,4)HHNO
22        4 FORMAT('NO OF HH BY INCOME CLASS'//' ', 10I10///)
23           WRITE(6,5)(RENOWN(I,J),I=1,10),J=1,2)
24        5 FORMAT('-',' NO OF RENTERS BY INCOME CLASS' //10F10.2)
        1 2//' NO OF OWNERS BY INCOME CLASS'//10F10.2)
25     4000 DO 60 J-1,6
26           DO 60 I=1,10
27           VALUM(I,J)=VALMAT(I,J)*RENOWN(I,2)
28           VALUE(U)=VALUE(J)+VALUM(I,J)
```

(continued)

U−1 continued

```
29        60  CONTINUE
30      5000  DO 70 J=1,4
31            DO 70 1=1,10
32            RENTM(I,J)=RENMAT(I,J)*RENOWN(I,1)
33            RENT(J)=RENT(J)+RENTM(I,J)
34        70  CONTINUE
35            WRITE(6,6)
36         6  FORMAT('−'///' DEMAND OF OWNED HOUSING UNITS BY
              1 VALUE AND HOUSEHOLD INCOME'/)
37            DO 80 J=1,6
38            WRITE(6,7)(VALUM(I,J),I=1,10)
39         7  FORMAT('   ',10F10.2)
40        80  CONTINUE
41            WRITE(6,8)(VALUE(J),J=1,6)
42         8  FORMAT('ORESULTANT MATRIX: VALUE TOTALS: ',6F10.2)
43            WRITE(6,9)((RENTM(I,J),I=1,10),J=1,4)
44         9  FORMAT('−'/// 'DEMAND OF RENTAL HOUSING UNITS BY
              1 RENTS AND HOUSEHOLD INCOME '/(' ',10F10.2))
45            WRITE(6,8)(RENT(J),J=1,4)
46            DC 100 I=1,6
47       100  VALUE(I)=0.
48            DO 101 I=1,4
49       101  RENT(I)=0.0
50            GO TO 40
51      9000  STOP
52            END

          /GO
```

U–2
Household Income ($) by Township and Housing Units

	Aston	Birmingham	Concord	Edgmont	Middletown	Thornbury
Less than $2,000	445	244	624	90	457	239
$2,000–2,999	439	187	521	43	418	211
$3,000–3,999	675	259	744	49	614	329
$4,000–4,999	850	298	847	57	744	415
$5,000–5,999	1,144	354	1,006	61	972	559
$6,000–7,999	2,919	811	2,316	135	2,412	1,377
$8,000–9,999	3,361	812	2,359	119	2,737	1,682
$10,000–14,999	6,609	1,578	4,552	232	5,207	3,458
$15,000–24,999	3,992	994	2,831	146	3,019	2,276
$25,000+	717	252	697	41	545	422
All Households	21,151	5,789	16,497	973	17,125	10,968
All Housing Units	7,088	2,497	8,393	3,009	10,416	2,459

U–3
Income ($) by Tenure

	Rent	Own
Less than $2,000	0.237	0.763
$2,000–2,999	0.213	0.787
$3,000–3,999	0.231	0.769
$4,000–4,999	0.238	0.762
$5,000–4,999	0.242	0.758
$6,000–7,999	0.244	0.756
$8,000–9,999	0.138	0.862
$10,000–14,999	0.098	0.902
$15,000–24,999	0.062	0.938
$25,000+	0.037	0.963

U–4
Income by Value Matrix

Income	Less than $15,000	$15,000– 19,999	$20,000– 24,999	$25,000– 34,999	$35,000– 49,999	$50,000+
Less than $2,000	0.254	0.320	0.196	0.151	0.050	0.030
$2,000–2,999	0.316	0.368	0.140	0.098	0.050	0.029
$3,000–3,999	0.261	0.358	0.201	0.137	0.027	0.016
$4,000–4,999	0.250	0.328	0.209	0.157	0.038	0.018
$5,000–5,999	0.257	0.359	0.216	0.124	0.018	0.025
$6,000–7,999	0.200	0.398	0.239	0.120	0.032	0.011
$8,000–9,999	0.144	0.395	0.268	0.157	0.030	0.007
$10,000–14,999	0.105	0.317	0.268	0.242	0.054	0.014
$15,000–24,999	0.000	0.281	0.231	0.303	0.146	0.038
$25,000+	0.000	0.000	0.197	0.253	0.312	0.237

U–5
Income by Rent Matrix

	Less than $120	*$120-149*	*$150-199*	*$200+*
Less than $2,000	0.609	0.218	0.149	0.024
$2,000–2,999	0.606	0.248	0.131	0.014
$3,000–3,999	0.663	0.190	0.110	0.037
$4,000–4,999	0.540	0.300	0.134	0.026
$5,000–5,999	0.000	0.830	0.153	0.017
$6,000–7,999	0.000	0.811	0.174	0.015
$8,000–9,999	0.000	0.751	0.215	0.034
$10,000–14,999	0.000	0.000	0.250	0.750
$15,000–24,999	0.000	0.000	0.000	1.000
$25,000+	0.000	0.000	0.000	1.000

Bibliography

Advisory Commission on Intergovernmental Relations. *Unshackling Local Government: A Survey of Proposals by the Advisory Commission on Intergovernmental Relations.* Washington: Government Printing Office, 1968.

Advisory Committee to the Department of Housing and Urban Development. *Freedom of Choice in Housing: Opportunities and Constraints.* Washington: National Academy of Sciences, 1972.

Advisory Committee to the Department of Housing and Urban Development. *Urban Growth and Land Development: The Land Conversion Process.* Washington: National Academy of Sciences, 1972.

Advisory Committee to the Department of Housing and Urban Development. Subcommittee on the Planning Process and Urban Development, *Shifting the Locus of Responsibility for Domestic Problem Solving: Revenue Sharing and the Planning Process.* Washington: National Academy of Sciences, 1973.

American Society of Planning Officials. "Failure to Produce the Intended Results." *Problems of Zoning and Land Use Regulation.* Washington: National Commission on Urban Problems, 1968.

Anderson, R. Dennis. "Toward the Equalization of Numicipal Services: Variations on a Theme by Hawkins." *Journal of Urban Law* vol. 50: 2, Nov., 1972.

Babcock, Richard F. *The Zoning Game.* Madison: University of Wisconsin Press, 1966.

Babcock, Richard F. and David L. Callies. "Ecology and Housing: Virtues in Conflict." In Marion Clawson (ed.), *Modernizing Urban Land Policy.* Baltimore: Johns Hopkins, 1972.

Barr, MacDonald. *The Massachusetts Zoning Appeals Law: Lessons of the First Three Years.* Boston: Massachusetts Department of Community Affairs, n.d.

Baltimore (Md.) Regional Planning Council. *Industrial Land Development,* Technical Report 2, May 1959.

Berlin, G.L. and J.R. Lancaster. *Industrial Suburbanization: Exchange Bibliography 223.* Monticello, Ill.: Council of Planning Librarians, 1971.

Boley, R.E. *Industrial Districts, Principles and Practice,* Technical Bulletin 44. Washington: Urban Land Institute, 1962.

Bosselman, Fred and David Callies. "The Quiet Revolution in Land Use Control-Summary Report." In *State Planning Issues, 1972.* Lexington, Ky.: Council of State Planning Agencies and Council of State Governments, 1972.

Brooks, Mary. "Exclusionary Zoning." *Planning Advisory Service Report Z54.* Chicago: American Society of Planning Officials, 1970.

Brown, Peter G. "Cities and Suburbs: The Exploitation Hypothesis." *Maryland Law Forum,* II, 1972.

Brown, William H., Samuel C. Jackson, and John H. Powell, Jr. *Open or Closed Suburbs: Corporate Location and the Urban Crisis.* Tarrytown, N.Y.: Suburban Action Institute, 1970.

Bureau of Business and Economic Research. "Industry as a Local Tax Base." *Studies in Business and Economics* vol. 14: 1. College Park: University of Maryland, 1960.

Bureau of Statistics, Department of Internal Affairs, Commonwealth of Pennsylvania. *Pennsylvania Statistical Abstract, 1969.* Harrisburg, Pa., 1970.

Charkardian, Leon. "Innovations Affecting State Planning: Massachusetts Antisnob Zoning Law." In *State Planning Issues, 1972.* Lexington, Ky.: Council of State Planning Agencies and Council of State Governments, 1972.

Coke, James G. and John J. Gargan. *Fragmentation in Land Use Planning and Control,* Research Report 18, National Commission on Urban Problems. Washington: Government Printing Office, 1969.

Coke, James G. and Charles S. Liebman. "Political Values and Population Density Control." *Land Economics* 37, 1961.

Committee for Economic Development. *Reshaping Government in Metropolitan Areas.* New York: CED, 1970.

Committee on Banking and Currency, U.S. House of Representatives. *House and the Urban Environment.* Report and Recommendations of Three Study Panels of the Subcommittee on Housing. Washington: Government Printing Office, 1971.

Committee on Banking and Currency, U.S. House of Representatives, 92nd Cong. *HR9688.* Washington: Government Printing Office, 1971.

Committee on Interior and Insular Affairs, U.S. Senate. *National Land Use Policy.* Washington: Government Printing Office, 1972.

Crawford, Clan, Jr. *Strategies and Tactics in Municipal Zoning.* Englewood Cliffs, N.J.: Prentice-Hall, 1969.

Cullingworth, J.B. *Town and Country Planning In England and Wales.* London: George Allen and Unwin Ltd., 1970.

Davidoff, Paul, Linda Davidoff, and Neil Gold. "Suburban Action: Advocate Planning for an Open Society." *Journal of the American Institute of Planners* XXXVI: 1, 1970.

Davidoff, Linda, Paul Davidoff, and Neil N. Gold. "The Suburbs Have to Open
    Their Gates." *New York Times Magazine,* Nov. 7, 1971.
Davidoff, Paul and Neil N. Gold. "Exclusionary Zoning." *Yale Review of Law
    and Social Action* vol. 1: 2 and 3 (Winter 1970).
Delaware Valley Regional Planning Commission. *1985 Regional Projections
    for the Delaware Valley: Plan Report No. 1.* Philadelphia: Dela-
    ware Valley Regional Planning Commission, 1967.
Detroit City Planning Commission. *Population Capacity: A Study Determining
    the Number of Dwelling Units and the Population Detroit's Neigh-
    borhoods May Be Expected to Have When Major Proposals Ex-
    pected to Occur by 1980 are Completed.* City of Detroit, 1954.
Deutsch, Karl W. and Richard L. Meier. *The Confederation of Urban Govern-
    ments: How Self-Controls for the American Megalopolis Can
    Evolve.* Working paper 77. Berkeley: Institute of Urban and Region-
    al Development, University of California, 1968.
Downs, Anthony. *Urban Problems and Prospects.* Chicago: Markham, 1970.
Editors. "Suburban Snobbery." *The New Republic.* vol. 164: 26, June 26, 1971.
Franklin, Herbert. *Controlling Urban Growth—But For Whom: The Social
    Impact of Development Timing Controls As Illustrated By The
    Ordinance of Ramapo, New York.* Washington: Metropolitan Hous-
    ing Program, Potomac Institute, Inc., 1973.
Franklin, Herbert M. "Expounding on Impounding." *Metropolitan Clearing-
    house Memorandum 73-2.* Washington: Metropolitan Housing
    Program, Potomac Institute, 1973.
——. "Massachusetts Decision Upholds Zoning Appeals Law." *Metropolitan
    Clearinghouse Memorandum 73-6.* Washington: Metropolitan
    Housing Program, Potomac Institute, 1973.
Franklin, Herbert M. and Lois Craig (eds.). *Eighth Conference on Exclusionary
    Land Use Problems.* Panel discussion of American Law Institute
    Model Land Development Code. Washington: Exclusionary Land
    Use Clearinghouse [now the Metropolitan Housing Project], The
    Potomac Institute, 1971.
Freund, Eric C. "Zoning Ordinances and Pollution Control." In Clyde W.
    Forest (ed.), *Change: The Recurring Zoning Issue.* Urbana-Cham-
    paign: Bureau of Urban and Regional Planning Research, Univer-
    sity of Illinois, 1970.
Gans, Herbert J. *People and Plans.* New York: Basic Books, 1968.
——. "The Possibilities of Class and Racial Integration in American New
    Towns." In Harvey S. Perloff and Neil C. Sandberg (eds.), *New
    Towns: Why—And for Whom?* New York: Praeger, 1973.
Gilbert, Charles E. *Governing the Suburbs.* Bloomington, Indiana: Indiana
    University Press, 1967.
Grigsby, William G. "The Housing Effects of a Guaranteed Annual Income."
    In Michael Stegman (ed.), *Housing and Economics: The American
    Dilemma.* Cambridge: MIT, 1970.
Haar, Charles M. *Land Use Planning: A Casebook on the Use, Misuse, and Re-*

Use of Urban Land. Boston: Little, Brown and Co. (2nd ed.), 1971.

Hagevik, George (ed.). *The Relationship of Land Use and Transportation Planning to Air Quality Management*. New Brunswick: Center for Urban Policy Research, Rutgers University, 1972.

Hartsfield, Robert J. "The Houston Non-Zoning Experience." *Change: The Recurring Zoning Issue*. Urbana-Champaign: Bureau of Urban and Regional Planning Research, University of Illinois, 1970.

Heeter, David. "Toward a More Effective Land Use Guidance System: A Summary and Analysis of Five Major Reports." *Planning Advisory Service*. Chicago: American Society of Planning Officials, 1969.

Heeter, David G. "Toward a More Effective System for Guiding the Use of Land." In C.W. Forest and R.K. Joy (eds.), *Zoning Is Planning*. Urbana-Champaign, Ill.: Bureau of Community Planning, University of Illinois, 1969.

Heinberg, John D. *The Transfer Cost of A Housing Allowance: Conceptual Issues and Benefit Patterns*. Washington: Urban Institute, 1971.

Herbers, John. "Outlying Housing for Blacks in Columbia, S.C. Assailed: Program Said to Create Isolated Shanty Towns." *New York Times*, March 25, 1972.

Holmgren, Edward L. and Ernest Erber. "Fair Share Formulas." *HUD Challenge* (April 1973).

Ide, Edward and Associates. *Estimating Land and Floor Area Implicit in Employment Projections: How Land and Floor Area Usage Rates Vary by Industry and Site Variables* I, II. Washington: Federal Highway Administration, U.S. Department of Transportation, 1970.

Isard, Walter. *Location and Space Economy*. New York: John Wiley and Sons, 1966.

James, Franklin J. and James W. Hughes. *Economic Growth and Residential Patterns: A Methodological Investigation*. New Brunswick, N.J.: Center for Urban and Policy Research, 1972.

Johnson, Ralph J. "Housing Technology and Housing Costs." *The Report of the President's Committee on Urban Housing—Technical Studies* Vol. 2. Washington: Government Printing Office, 1968.

Kaiser, Edward J., Karl Elfers, Sidney Cohn, Peggy A. Reichert, Maynard M. Hufschmidt, and Raymond E. Stanland. *Promoting Environmental Quality Through Urban Planning and Controls*. Washington: Office of Research and Development, U.S. Environmental Protection Agency, 1973.

Kamm, Sylvan. "Land Availability for Housing and Urban Growth." *Papers Submitted to Subcommittee on Housing Panels*. Washington: Government Printing Office, 1971.

Klain, Ambrose. *Zoning in Suburbia: Keep it, Reject it, or Replace it?; Exchange Bibliography 180*. Monticello, Ill.: Council of Planning Librarians, 1971.

Kristensen, Chris, John Levy, and Tamar Savir. *The Suburban Lockout Effect.* Tarrytown, N.Y.: Suburban Action Institute, 1971.

Levitt and Sons, Inc. "Levitt's Comments." *Report of the President's Committee on Urban Housing—Technical Studies,* Vol. 2. Washington: Government Printing Office, 1968.

Little, Arthur D. *The Usefulness of Philadelphia's Industrial Plant: An Approach to Industrial Renewal.* Philadelphia: Philadelphia City Planning Commission, January, 1960.

Long, Norton E. "Creative Politics and Urban Citizenship." In David Popenoe (ed.), *The Urban-Industrial Frontier.* New Brunswick: Rutgers University Press, 1969.

Lustig, Morton, Janet R. Pack, Edward M. Bergman, Kent Eklund and Arnold Goldstein. *Standards for Housing in Urban Communities Based on Zoning for Work.* Philadelphia: Fels Center of Government, University of Pennsylvania, 1972.

Lustig, Morton, Janet R. Pack, Kent Eklund, Joseph Hayman, Glenn Neuks, Linda Pecaites, Bonnie Towles. *Standards for Suburban Housing Mix.* Philadelphia: Fels Center of Government, University of Pennsylvania, 1971.

Mace, Ruth R. and Warren J. Wicker. *Do Single Family Homes Pay their Own Way?* Washington: Urban Land Institute, 1968.

Mandelker, Daniel R. *The Zoning Dilemma.* New York: Bobbs-Merrill, 1971.

Mannino, Edward F. "Land Use Planning and The Political Process." *The Shingle.* Philadelphia: The Philadelphia Bar Association, April, 1971.

Marcus, Norman and Marlyn W. Gorves. *The New Zoning: Legal, Administrative, and Economic Concepts and Techniques.* New York: Praeger, 1970.

Margolis, Julius. *Metropolitan Fiscal Disparities: Problems and Policies, A Report to the Metropolitan Council of the Twin Cities Area.* Philadelphia: Fels Center of Government, University of Pennsylvania, 1971.

Martino, A.J.S.C. *Southern Burlington County NAACP v. Township of Mount Laurel* (summary), 117 N.J. Super 11 (Sup. Ct. 1971).

McGraw Hill Information Systems Company. "A Study of Comparative Time and Cost for Building Five Selected Types of Low-Cost Housing." *The Report of the President's Committee on Urban Housing—Technical Studies* Vol. 2. Washington: Government Printing Office, 1968.

Miami [Ohio] Regional Valley Planning Commission. *A Housing Plan for the Miami Valley Region—A Reprint.* Philadelphia: Housing Association of Delaware Valley, 1971.

Middlesex-Somerset-Mercer (N.J.), Regional Study Council. *Housing and Quality of our Environment.* Princeton, N.J., Dec., 1970.

Milgram, Grace. *The City Expands: A Study of the Conversion of Land from Urban Use, Philadelphia 1945-62.* Washington: Department of

Housing and Urban Development, Government Printing Office, 1968.

Miller, Herman, U.S. Department of Commerce, Bureau of the Census. *Income Distribution in the United States.* Washington: Government Printing Office, 1966.

Mattila, John M. "Metropolitan Income Estimation." *Urban Affairs Quarterly* vol. 6:2, Dec., 1970.

Mogulof, Melvin B. *Governing Urban Areas.* Washington: Urban Institute, 1971.

Moody, Eugene G. "Regional Implications of Local Land Use Changes." In C.W. Forest (ed.), *Change: The Recurring Zoning Issue.* Proceedings of Institute on Zoning. Urbana-Champaign: Bureau of Urban and Regional Planning Research, University of Ill., 1970.

Moynihan, Daniel P. *Toward A National Urban Policy.* New York: Basic Books, 1970.

Musgrave, Richard. *The Theory of Public Finance.* New York: McGraw Hill, 1959.

NARC Housing Reporter. Washington: National Association of Regional Councils.

National Advisory Commission on Civil Disorders. *Report of the National Advisory Commission on Civil Disorders.* New York: Bantam Books, 1968.

National Commission on Urban Problems. *Building the American City.* Washington: Government Printing Office, 1968.

New Jersey Division of State and Regional Planning. *Land Use Regulation: The Residential Land Supply.* Trenton, N.J., 1972.

Nixon, President Richard M. *Statement by the President on Federal Policies Relative to Equal Housing Opportunity.* Washington: Office of the White House Press Secretary, June 11, 1971.

Noble, Jack. "Zoning Limitations." *Regulatory Devices.* Chicago: American Society of Planning Officials, 1969.

Philadelphia City Planning Commission. *Comprehensive Plan for the City of Philadelphia,* 1960.

President's Committee on Urban Housing. *A Decent Home.* Washington: Government Printing Office, 1968.

Rapkin, Chester and William G. Grigsby. *The Demand for Housing in Eastwick.* Philadelphia: Institute for Urban Studies [now Institute for Environmental Studies], University of Pennsylvania, 1960.

Ratcliffe, Richard V. *Real Estate Analysis.* New York: McGraw Hill, 1961.

Rein, Martin. "Social Policy Analysis as the Interpretation of Beliefs." *Journal of the American Institute of Planners* vol. XXXVII: 5.

Reps, John W. "Requiem for Zoning." *Planning 1964.* Chicago: American Society of Planning Officials, 1964.

Rivkin, Malcolm D. "Diplomacy Planning: What It Is." *Urban Land* vol. 32: 4, April 1973.

Rose, Jerome G. "The Courts and the Balanced Community: Recent Trends in New Jersey Zoning Law." *Journal of the American Institute of Planners* vol. 39: 3, (July 1973).

Schiffman, Irving. *The Politics of Land Use Planning and Zoning: An Annotated Bibliography*. Davis, Calif.: Institute of Governmental Affairs, University of California, 1970.

Siegan, Bernard H. *Land Use Without Zoning*. Lexington, Mass.: Lexington Books, 1972.

Smith, Wallace F. "Filtering and Neighborhood Change." In Michael Stegman (ed.), *Economics and Housing*. Cambridge: MIT Press, 1970.

Stegman, Michael A. "Kaiser, Douglas, and Kerner on Low Income Housing Policy." *American Institute of Planners* vol. XXXV: 6, Nov., 1969.

Stinson, Thomas F. *The Effects of Taxes and Public Financing Programs on Local Industrial Development—A Survey of the Literature* Agricultural Economic Report 133. Washington: U.S. Dept. of Agriculture, Economic Research Source, 1968.

Sumichrast, Michael and Sarah A. Frankel. *Profile of the Builder and His Industry*. Washington: *National Association of Home Builders*, 1970.

Swan, Craig. "Labor and Material Requirements for Housing." *Brookings Papers on Economic Activity* 2. Washington: The Brookings Institution, 1971.

Szita, Ellen. "Exclusionary Zoning in the Suburbs: The Case of New Canaan, Connecticut." *Civil Rights Digest* vol. 5: 4 (Spring 1973).

Task Force on Land Use and Urban Growth. *The Use of Land: A Citizens' Policy Guide to Urban Growth*. New York: Thomas A. Crowell, 1973.

Toll, Seymour I. *Zoned American*. New York: Grossman, 1969.

U.S. Bureau of Census. *1970 Census of Housing* (print-out of housing variable 38 from second count data supplied by Delaware Valley Regional Planning Commission) Philadelphia: U.S. Census Summary Tape Processing Center, March 16, 1972.

——. *1960 Census of Population Detailed Characteristics, Pennsylvania*. Washington: Government Printing Office, 1963.

——. *Census Users' Guide I and II*. Washington: Government Printing Office, 1970.

——. *Compendium of Public Employment, 1967 Census of Governments*, vol. 3, Table 29, 1967.

——. "Income in 1969 of Families and Persons in the United States", *Current Population Reports*, Series P-60, No. 75. Washington: Government Printing Office, 1970.

——. *Journey to Work* PC(2)-6B Washington: Government Printing Office, 1960.

——. *Metropolitan Housing: Philadelphia, Pennsylvania, N.S. SMSA*. Washington: Government Printing Office, 1960.

U.S. Bureau of Labor Statistics. *Handbook of Labor Statistics*. Washington: Government Printing Office, 1970.

———. "The National Industry—Occupational Matrix and Other Manpower Data." Bulletin 1606. *Tomorrow's Manpower Needs* Vol. IV. Washington: Government Printing Office, Feb., 1969.

———. *Occupational Employment Patterns for 1960 and 1975.* Bulletin 1599. Washington: Government Printing Office, 1968.

———. *Special Labor Force Report: Employment and Unemployment in 1969.* No. 129. Washington: Government Printing Office, 1970.

U.S. Chamber of Commerce. *Modernizing Local Government.* Washington: Chamber of Commerce of the U.S., 1967.

U.S. Civil Service Commission, Annual Report of. *Federal Civilian Employment by Geographic Area* (pamphlet SM 68-04), Washington: Government Printing Office, 1969.

U.S. Department of Commerce. *County Report Text, Census of Agriculture, 1969.* Washington: Government Printing Office, 1971.

———. *1967 Enterprise Statistics: Central Administrative Offices and Auxiliaries.* Washington: Government Printing Office, 1971.

———. *Pennsylvania County Business Patterns.* Washington: Government Printing Office, 1959 and 1969.

———. *Standard Industrial Classification Manual.* Washington: Government Printing Office, 1967.

———. *The Standard City Planning Enabling Act.* Washington: Government Printing Office, 1928.

———. *The Standard State Zoning Enabling Act.* Washington: Government Printing Office, 1926.

U.S. Department of Housing and Urban Development. *Operation Breakthrough, Mass Produced and Industrialized Housing: A Bibliography.* Washington: Government Printing Office, 1970.

U.S. Department of Labor. *Employment and Earnings* vol. 17: 12. Washington: Government Printing Office, 1971.

———. Bureau of Labor Statistics. *Employment and Earnings, States and Areas 1939–69,* Bulletin 1370-7. Washington: Government Printing Office, 1970.

Urban Land Institute. "Rural Appearance Will Not Necessarily Follow Large-Lot Zoning." *The Effects of Large Lot Size on Residential Development* Technical Bulletin 32. Washington: Urban Land Institute, 1958.

Urban Institute. "Reconstituting Urban Area Governing Capacity: Balancing Overall Needs and Local Self Rule." *Search* vol. 3: 4 (July–August) Washington: Urban Institute, 1973.

von Furstenberg, George. "Improving the Feasibility of Homeownership for Lower Income Families Through Subsidized Mortgage Financing." *Report of the President's Committee on Urban Housing—Technical Studies* Vol. 2. Washington: Government Printing Office, 1968.

von Furstenberg, George and Howard R. Moskof. "Federally Assisted Rental Housing Programs: Which Income Groups Have They Served or Whom Can They Be Expected to Serve?" *The Report of The*

President's Committee on Urban Housing—Technical Studies,
Vol. 2. Washington: Government Printing Office, 1968.

Washington, Harold *et. al.* "Workers' Residential Rights Act," House Bill 4566.
1972 Final Legislative Synopsis and Digest. Springfield, Ill.: Legislative Reference Bureau, 1973.

Washington State Land Planning Commission. "Preliminary Analysis of Planning and Land Development Laws in Colorado, Hawaii, Maine,
Oregon and Vermont." *State Planning Issues '72.* Lexington, Ky.:
Council of State Planning Agencies and Council of State Governments, 1972.

Weiner, Peter H. "The Constitutionality of Local Zoning." *Land Use Controls
Quarterly* vol. 4: 4. Chicago: American Society of Planning Officials, 1970. Abstracted from the *Yale Law Journal* vol. 79, 1970.

Whitlatch, G.I. *Industrial Districts, Their Planning and Developments.* Industrial
Development Division, Georgia Institute of Technology, n.d.

Williams, Norman, Jr. "Planning Law and Democratic Living." *Law and Contemporary Problems* 20 (Spring 1955).

——. *The Structure of Urban Zoning.* New York: Buttenheim, 1966.

Williams, Norman, Jr. and Thomas Norman. "Exclusionary Land-use Controls: The Case of Northeastern New Jersey." *Land Use Controls
Quarterly* vol. 4: 4. Chicago: American Society of Planning Officials, 1970.

Wingo, Lowden. *Reform of Metropolitan Governments.* Baltimore: Resources
for the Future, 1972.

Index

American Industrial Development Corporation, 103
American Law Institute, 23
Anderson, R. Dennis, 57
Arrow, Kenneth J., 35

Babcock, Richard F., 13, 28, 57
Barr, MacDonald, 31
Bergman, Edward M., 49, 103
Berlin, G.L., 13
Boley, R.E., 103
Bosselman, Fred, 31
Brooks, Mary, 48
Brown, Peter G., 48
Brown, William H. III, 28
Burns, Leland S., 194
Business zoning districts, see commercial zoning districts

Callies, David L., 13, 31
CAO and A
  county employment in 1969, 232
  defined, 215
  employment by major industry group, 231
  employment in "equivalent" SICs, 233
Charkardian, Leon, 31
Citizen sovereignty, 6, 34, 35
Clawson, Marion, 13
Cohn, Sidney, 13
Commercial activity, maximum permitted intensity of, 91
Commercial zoning districts
  analysis of, 88
  allowed uses in, 90
  apartments in, 201
  customer and employee parking in, 97
Commonwealth of Pennsylvania, 109

Craig, Lois, 31, 32
Crawford, Clan, Jr., 58
Cullingworth, J.B., 57

Davidoff, Linda, 26, 28, 29, 48
Davidoff, Paul, 21, 26, 28, 29, 48
Deutsch, Karl W., 16, 27
Developing townships
  classification for, 198
Downs, Anthony, 57
Dwelling units, potential number, 101

Earnings
  distribution by industry, 132
  durable goods industries, 134
Earnings distribution
  by SIC, 130
  illustrative calculation, 130
  program for weighting two sets, 265
Earnings to income
  all industries, 137
  calculation of, 137
  for business and repair service industry, 137
  for SIC 7390, 137
Economic zoning districts
  See also industrial zoning districts and commercial zoning districts
Eklund, Kent, 49, 103, 164
Elfers, Karl, 13
Employment
  agricultural, 119
  federal civilian, 110
  federal postal, 116
  local distribution by SIC, 107
  local government, 114
  potential in industrial districts, 143

private household, 116
residential zoning districts, 114
state, 110
township totals, 120
Employment algorithm
coefficients, 241
computer program for, 253
an illustration, 106
corrected computer program, 259
sample estimate of employment for
district, 62, 253
Employment districts, 89
Employment patterns, derived from township zoning ordinances, 118
Employment rate, 114
by industries and SICs, 115
Environment, and land use, 5, 9, 23
Erber, Ernest, 32
Exclusion
and household income, 162
by median household income, 163
by township, 163
intercommunity, 5
interdistrict, 5
in township zoning ordinances, 160
measures of, 160
Exclusion principle, 43
Exclusion function, shift to other municipal
controls, 191
Exclusionary zoning, effects of, 9

FAR
definition of, 92
effect on worker household yield, 141
formula, 92–93
industrial district employment, 118, 120
maximum intensity of manufacturing
and commercial activity, 91–100
Fair Share Housing, 24
Fairfax County, Virginia, 24, 25
Fiscal imbalances, 34, 39–43
Fiscal resources, inequitable distribution
of, 39–43
Fiscal zoning, 6–8, 39, 40
Floor area per worker, 110
selected SICs, 111
Floor area ratios
deriving from township zoning ordi-
nances, 219
See also FAR
Forest, Clyde, W., 13, 26, 58
Franklin, Herbert, 29, 31, 32, 58
Freund, Eric C., 13
Freund, Ernest, 3

Gans, Herbert J., 48
Gilbert, Charles E., 103

Gold, Neil Newton, 21, 26, 28, 29, 48
Goldstein, Arnold, 49, 103
Grigsby, William G., 164, 179
Groves, Marlyn W., 28

Haar, Charles M., 10
Hagevik, George, 13
Hartsfield, Robert J., 27
Hayman, Joseph, 164
Heeter, David G., 31, 57
Height restriction
by district, 99
floors and feet of buildings, 99
Herbers, John, 194
Holmgren, Edward L., 32
House value
distributions by income, 152
and equivalent rents, 78
by gross residential density, 77
Household income
estimating housing requirements from,
155
and exclusion, 162
and housing demand, 150
Housing assistance, 45, 172, 173
Housing demand
and household income, 150
potential of Aston Township households, 157
Housing demand algorithm, computer
program and data inputs for, 287
Housing mix
and exclusionary zoning, 34
worker housing units and worker households, 187
Housing requirements, discontinuities and
the stock of housing, 156
Housing units
in Concord Township's zoning ordinance, 169
by median household income, 169
potential number of, 123, 169
potential requirements for, 158
by price, 67, 158, 169
by rent, 67, 158, 169
requirements for, 171
shortfall of, 158, 169
six developing townships, 66
stock of, 158
surplus of, 158, 169
by tenure, 158, 169
by township zoning ordinances, 158
Hufschmidt, Maynard M., 13
Hughes, James W., 58

Ide, Edward, 124, 125
Income distribution

four-county, 144
households, 143, 144
illustrative calculation, 132
six-township, 144
under alternative assumptions, 142
U.S. SMSA Fringe Areas, 142
worker households by township, 139
Income distributions
calculation of, 136
comparing township with other distributions, 143
similarities and differences by township, 140
Income estimates, effect of occupational coefficients, 277
Income of households, selected SICs, 136
Incomes, worker household, 143
Industrial activity, maximum permitted intensity of, 91
Industrial zoning districts, 95
allowed uses in, 90
analysis of, 88
employment in, 118
parking standards for, 95
Industry-occupational coefficients, 133
Isard, Walter, 49

Jackson, Henry M., 30
Jackson, Samuel C., 28
Jackson-Cross Associates, 83
James, Franklin J., 58
Jobs, total, 121, 252
Journey to work, 8, 9, 34, 37–39
Joy, R.K., 57

Kaiser, Edward J., 13
Kamm, Sylvan, 30
Klain, Ambrose, 10
Kristensen, Chris, 28

Labor force
agricultural, 123
district, 124
local government, 123
postal, 123
potential, 123
private household, 123
reference area, 252
township, 124
zoning districts, 121, 252
Lancaster, J.R., 13
Large-lot zoning, 6
environmental considerations, 5, 9
justified by sewage disposal requirements, 9
Lasker, Bruno, 3
Levy, John, 28

Little, Arthur D., 125
Long, Norton E., 8, 13
Lustig, Morton, 11, 48, 49, 103, 164

Mace, Ruth R., 11
Main shift jobs, 121, 252
Mandelker, Daniel R., 10, 19, 28, 57
Manufacturing zoning districts, see industrial zoning districts
Massachusetts Zoning Appeals Law, 23, 24
Marcus, Norman, 28
Margolis, Julius, 49
Martino, A.J.S.C., 194
Mattila, John M., 145
Meier, Richard L., 16, 27
Meister, Jack, 103
Milgram, Grace, 178
Miller, Herman, 146
Minimum lot size, categories by gross land area, number of housing units, and township, 64
Mittelback, Frank G., 194
Mogulof, Melvin B., 16–17, 27
Moody, Eugene G., 26
Moskof, Howard R., 178
Moynihan, Daniel P., 15–16, 26, 164
Multi-family structures, 79
estimating rents for, 205
rent distributions, 205
Multiple job holding rate, 12
Mumford, Lewis, 3
Musgrave, Richard, 49

National Association of Homebuilders, 70
National Committee Against Discrimination in Housing, 29
National Industrial Zoning Committee, 103
Neuks, Glenn, 164
New York Urban Development Corporation, 23
Nixon, Richard M., 30
Noble, Jack, 29
Norman, Thomas, 11, 29, 47
Nuisance, elimination by zoning, 4, 19, 20, 90

Occupational coefficients
effect on income estimation, 277
for income estimation, 129–136
1975 U.S., 267
Owner-occupied housing prices, 68

Parking standards
calculations of, 225–227
industrial districts, 94
selected enterprise, 98
Pecaites, Linda, 164

Pack, Janet, R., 49, 103, 164
Patman, Wright, 30
Performance standard
    and exclusionary zoning, 33–47
    workplace-residence, 45–47
    See also zoning, performance standard for
Perloff, Harvey S., 48
Philadelphia Bureau of Employment
    Security, 117
Popenoe, David, 13
Population, potential size, 101
Powell, John H., Jr., 28
Preston, Richard, 103
Prices
    by type of housing, 69
    minimum for new houses, 69
    of housing, by density, 69

Rapkin, Chester, 164
Ratio
    apartments to total use district areas, 202
    earnings to income, 137
    floor to land area, 121
    households to workers, 136, 137
    local government employment to popula-
      tion, 116
    main shift to total jobs, 111
    postal employees to population, 117
    worker households to housing units, 185
Reference areas
    definition, 106
    employment in, 252
    employment statistics for, 251
Reichert, Peggy A., 13
Rein, Martin, 49
Rent distributions, by income, 152
Renter-occupied housing, rents of, 76
Rents
    by residential density, 80
    by residential structure type, 80
    by township, 80
    mixed multi- and single-family units, 202
Reps, John W., 17–19, 27
Residential zoning districts
    analysis of, 100
    Concord Township, 171
    employment in, 114
    holding capacity of, 101
    six developing townships, 63
    minimum lot size and tenure, 1971, 66
    tenure in, 62
    type of structure in, 62
Restricted housing choice, 34
Rezoning
    commercial, 166, 184
    impact on commercial development,
      188–191

    impact on housing market, 190
    impact on industrial development,
      188–191
    industrial, 166, 184
    policy response, 190
    potential impact of, 188
    residential, 169, 184
    subversive strategies, 190
Rivkin, Malcolm D., 58
Rose, Jerome G., 29

Sandberg, Neil C., 48
Savir, Tamar, 28
Schiffman, Irving, 10–11
Siegan, Bernard H., 10, 18, 20, 27, 28, 48
Single-family housing, rents in, 78
Single job holding rate, 112
SICs and industries, 113
SIC
    CAO and A equivalents, 213, 216,
      231–233
    defined, 86
    essential link in analyzing commercial
      and industrial zoning ordinances, 86,
      88, 91, 92
    economic activities, 213
    light industry in townships, 214
    mean number of floors, 235, 237
    ratio of main shift to total workers, 237
Smith, Wallace F., 48
Stanland, Raymond E., 13
Statutory compliance
    and effective evasion, 191
    and internal isolation, 192
Stegman, Michael A., 29, 179
Stinson, Thomas F., 13
Structure type, in the six developing
    townships, 65
Suburban Action Institute, 21
Subversive strategies, and rezoning, 190
Szita, Ellen, 10

Tenure, in the six developing townships, 65
Tenure split, by household income level,
    154
Toll, Seymour I., 3, 10, 28
Towles, Bonnie, 164
Townships, selection criteria, 197

Unemployment rates, by industries and
    SICs, 115
U.S. Bureau of Budget, 90
U.S. Bureau of Labor Statistics, 112,
    128, 133
U.S. Bureau of Public Roads, 90
U.S. Bureau of Census, 64, 68, 70, 72, 76,
    79, 108, 109, 116, 128, 133

U.S. Civil Service Commission, 110
U.S. Department of Commerce, 107
U.S. Department of Housing and Urban
    Development, 22, 25, 91
U.S. Department of Labor, 112
U.S. Department of Transportation, 105
U.S. Federal Highway Administration, 112
U.S. Federal Housing Administration, 69
U.S. General Services Administration, 22

von Furstenberg, George, 178

Washington, Harold, 49
Weiner, Peter H., 48, 49
Westerhaver, David C., 3, 21
Whitlatch, G.I., 103
Wicker, Warren J., 11
Williams, Norman, Jr., 4, 10, 11, 21, 29,
    47, 49
Wingo, Lowden, 16, 26
Work trips
  and performance standard for zoning
    37–39

See also journey to work
Worker earnings, 128–140, 281–285
Worker household definition, 62, 82
Workers, total, 121, 252

Zoning
  elimination of, 17
  exclusionary use of, 4
  general strategy model, 173
  institutional incentives, 15–17, 21
  performance standard for, 25, 43
  reform of, 15, 21–25, 68
  repeal of, 15, 17–21, 35
  separation of uses, 4
  strategy map, 175
Zoning ordinances
  analysis of, 51–145
  major uses in townships, 55
  preclusive elements in, 47
Zoning use districts
  acreage in townships, 88
  township identification, 88

About the Author

Edward M. Bergman is Assistant Professor of Planning, Department of City and Regional Planning, University of North Carolina at Chapel Hill. His BS (Michigan State University: 1966), MCP and Ph.D. (University of Pennsylvania: 1968, 1972) degrees were all taken in the field of planning. Dr. Bergman's professional experience includes that of agency staff planner, planning consultant, research associate and professor of planning, experience which was gained in universities and at the city, township, regional and state levels of government. His current research and teaching interests in the areas of housing and employment are, in part, an outgrowth of interests begun in research on this volume. In addition to teaching courses on housing, he is currently the Principal Investigator of a National Science Foundation sponsored research project devoted to studying the effects of land use and other municipal controls on the costs of housing. Dr. Bergman's interest in employment expresses itself in teaching manpower planning coursework and in developing a manpower planning option within the Department of City and Regional Planning, University of North Carolina at Chapel Hill.